Legacies of Paul de Man

Legacies of Paul de Man

Edited by
MARC REDFIELD

FORDHAM UNIVERSITY PRESS
New York 2007

Copyright © 2007 Fordham University Press

All rights reserved. No part of this publication may be reproduced, stored in a retrieval system, or transmitted in any form or by any means—electronic, mechanical, photocopy, recording, or any other—except for brief quotations in printed reviews, without the prior permission of the publisher.

Library of Congress Cataloging-in-Publication Data
Legacies of Paul de Man / edited by Marc Redfield.—1st ed.
   p. cm.
Includes bibliographical references (p.) and index.
   ISBN-13: 978-0-8232-2760-0 (alk. paper)
   ISBN-10: 0-8232-2760-X (alk. paper)
   ISBN-13: 978-0-8232-2761-7 (pbk. : alk. paper)
   ISBN-10: 0-8232-2761-8 (pbk. : alk. paper)
 1. De Man, Paul. 2. Criticism. 3. Deconstruction.
   I. Redfield, Marc, 1958–
   PN75.D45L44 2007
   801'.95092—dc22
         2007004513

Printed in the United States of America
09 08 07   5 4 3 2 1
First edition

CONTENTS

Acknowledgments vii
Introduction: Legacies of Paul de Man
MARC REDFIELD 1

I. READING
Double-Take: Reading de Man and Derrida Writing on Tropes
CYNTHIA CHASE 17
Reading, Begging, Paul de Man
JAN MIESZKOWSKI 29

II. READING HISTORY
History against Historicism, Formal Matters, and the Event of the Text: de Man with Benjamin
IAN BALFOUR 49
Discontinuous Shifts: History Reading History
ANDRZEJ WARMINSKI 62

III. INSTITUTIONS OF PEDAGOGY
"At the Far End of This Ongoing Enterprise..."
SARA GUYER 77
Professing Literature: John Guillory's Misreading of Paul de Man
MARC REDFIELD 93

IV. THEORY, MATERIALITY, AND THE AESTHETIC
Thinking Singularity with Immanuel Kant and Paul de Man: Aesthetics, Epistemology, History, and Politics
ARKADY PLOTNITSKY 129
Seeing Is Reading
REI TERADA 162

Appendix 1
Courses Taught by Paul de Man during the Yale Era
    MARC REDFIELD   179

Appendix 2
Course Proposal: Literature Z
    PAUL DE MAN   185

Contributors   191

Notes   193

Index   223

ACKNOWLEDGMENTS

Early versions of these essays were published in *Romantic Circles'* Praxis Series (http://www.rc.umd.edu/praxis/deman/index.html). We thank the journal *Romantic Circles* and the editor of its Praxis Series, Orrin N. C. Wang. Special thanks to Kate Singer for her help with many technical matters, and to Mary Powell for the many hours she spent preparing the manuscript for submission.

The publication of Paul de Man's paper on Literature Z in Appendix 2 has been made possible with the help of Peter Brooks, David Quint, and the Yale Comparative Literature Department.

We thank Helen Tartar and Nicholas Frankovich, both of Fordham University Press, the former for her generous intellectual and administrative support for this project, and the latter for his care in seeing the manuscript through the production process.

Legacies of Paul de Man

Introduction: Legacies of Paul de Man
Marc Redfield

> An inheritance is never gathered together, it is never one with itself. Its presumed unity, if there is one, can consist only in the *injunction* to *reaffirm by choosing*. "One must" means *one must* filter, sift, criticize, one must sort out different possibles that inhabit the same injunction. And inhabit it in a contradictory fashion around a secret. If the readability of a legacy were given, natural, transparent, univocal, if it did not call for and at the same time defy interpretation, we would never have anything to inherit from it.
>
> —JACQUES DERRIDA, *Specters of Marx*

More than twenty years after his death, Paul de Man remains a haunting presence in the American academy. His name has retained its affective charge even as the context in which it first became nationally known has receded into the past, becoming as distant as disco music or the Ford or Carter administrations. The acrid debates about deconstruction and the "Yale School" and the bitter, high-profile purgings of junior faculty ranks at places like Yale and Princeton may now seem part of another world. And in certain ways it would no doubt be fair to say that the winds of controversy have calmed, and that de Man's legacy has become part of everyday academic life. His students, and the students of his students, hold teaching positions throughout the North American university system; they publish books and articles and contribute to volumes like the present one, and in the usual run of things they are rewarded in the usual minute ways for doing so: the c.v. grows a little longer; the annual report heftier. "Deconstruction" now figures in countless introductions-to-theory as an option on the menu (usually placed, in pseudochronological fashion, behind several fresher offerings—"New Historicism," "Cultural Studies," "Gender Studies," and so on). In these and other ways, the "university of excellence" (to recall Bill Readings's memorable phrase for our contemporary academic bureaucracy) may seem successfully to have absorbed and routinized the de Man phenomenon.[1]

Yet symptoms of a persistent malaise are not hard to find. The temperature of a discussion can still rise precipitately when de Man's name appears. Deserving scholars still sometimes suffer for being too closely linked to de Manian theory—particularly if they are young and untenured, and have the temerity to demonstrate interest in something that is supposed to have been consigned to the lumber-room of the past. At such moments we are reminded that deconstruction (and above all "de Manian deconstruction") is not really, or at least not entirely, an innocent subspecialty like any other. It is one thing to "do" narratology or reader-response criticism or even Marxist criticism, and another to "do" deconstruction: in this case, and arguably only in this case, the academy retains an interest in pronouncing a body of thought *dead*. De Man stands for a "theory" that again and again must be discovered to have died of natural causes, a victim of time, history, and its own internal inadequacies. Like the literal body of the theorist, it was once alive; now it is not; it should have the decency to rest quietly in its tomb.

Yet at the same time—and this is where things get complicated and interesting—even the most negative reactions to de Man often display a remarkable degree of fascination with the phobic object. At the 2003 MLA convention a special session titled "Is Now the Time for Paul de Man?" played to a packed auditorium: packed no doubt to some extent—but only to some extent—because Gayatri Chakravorty Spivak was one of the speakers. An uneasy charisma still radiates from the figure of "Paul de Man." Who else could possibly have inspired such a panel title? Of what other dead professor could it be implied that his "time" is in question; that his presence, if summoned, might be out of joint with our "now"? At once melodramatic and timid, cautious and reckless, the interrogative composing this panel title relays the half-confessed ambivalence felt by a profession toward a figure who seems at once irremediably part of, yet also somehow at odds with, ordinary institutional life.

That the "now" of de Man is a question, the question of a legacy somehow out of synch with its, or our, "time," is suggested by the strangely extended work of remembrance he has inspired. One might have expected the lavish outpourings of the *Yale French Studies* memorial issue in 1985 to have exhausted the personal testimonials, but there followed, of course, the discovery of the wartime journalism in 1987 and a second swell of passion, this one agonistic in mode and international in scope, with de Man rediscovered as the symbol of a "deconstruction" that many were by now desperately eager to pronounce dead—once again.[2] Once again (though this time with varying motives) professional literary critics called up memories of de Man and talked obsessively of his life and times. And now the years have flown by, but oddly delayed testimonials have kept coming, and not insignificant ones either: Avital Ronell, remembering and reflecting on de Man in her brilliant *Stupidity*;[3] most recently, Gayatri Chakravorty Spivak, at the 2003 MLA panel, noting that she was possibly de Man's first Ph.D. student, recalling his lack of sexism and racism at a time when such attitudes were suffocatingly common, and tracing the impact his thought had, and according to Spivak still has, on hers. Ronell, writing in her inimitable style, suggests that the wartime journalism affair made visible a rupture, lag, and repetition in de Man's reception that was in fact always there, composing the temporality of his legacy:

> One can say that, following the brief and violent return of Paul de Man after his death, thinking in America—or the quasi-mythical ambience that makes one sense the advent of thought—took a nosedive. I am not saying that everyone in the academic precincts suddenly became stupid (or that de Man was the opposite of stupid), but his ghost took something down with it and disrupted a type of mourning that should have produced considerable and worthy festschrifts, a festival of thought commemorating an unprecedented insistence on rigor and recollection.
>
> Instead we got the often brilliant, sometimes ridiculous, and altogether exceptional *Responses* volume [in 1989], which exhausted itself in the defensive feints that it was forced to perform. It was as if everyone was wiped out by the rescue mission demanded by the afterlife of Paul de Man. Nor was it clear that he had survived the crash, but he was bound to return again, in one or another of his forms, after the fog of a collective stupor had lifted. For some of us he had never really disappeared, no more so than when he was alive. In any case, a break had occurred, redoubling, perhaps, the rupture in his life when he tried to break away from Europe and the calamity he had cosigned in his youth. As with so many signs of rupture, the break was merely the repetition of prior, more sullen breaks and could not be limited to one moment.[4]

To be sure, the *nachträglich*, quasi-traumatic temporality of de Man's reception has hardly prevented people from writing about him: sometimes, as Ronell says, brilliantly. In addition to the personal testimonials (and I shall return in a moment to the question of why a memorializing, personifying imperative seems to be an inseparable part of de Man's reception), the critical studies have kept coming: Christopher Norris's *Paul de Man*

(1988); the collections *Reading de Man Reading* (1989) and *(Dis)continuities* (1989); a special issue of *Diacritics* (1990); Ortwin de Graef's *Serenity in Crisis* (1993) and *Titanic Light* (1995); the collection *Material Events* (2001); Martin McQuillan's *Paul de Man* (2001)—to mention only English-language books and collections focused exclusively on de Man. If one were to list even a representative sampling of the essays and book chapters on de Man that have appeared in other venues and languages over the last twenty years, the bibliography would go on for pages, and would display an impressive heterogeneity of perspective and focus.[5] Rodolphe Gasché's condemnation of the "general dreariness of the more recent de Man studies in North America" is one of the few weirdly wrong statements to be found in what is otherwise an exemplary contribution to a complex and by no means univocal reception.[6] For a thinker so often caricatured as a charismatic leader of "disciples," de Man has inspired a remarkably diverse body of work, even within the relatively narrow circle of critics who, in their varying ways or styles, regard themselves as his heirs.

And the specialized studies are only part of the story. Whatever de Man's legacy may be (and it is the task of this collection to try to keep in mind how opaque the figure of "legacy" may prove in this case), it is surely no simple or easily localized inheritance. Much has been said about this critic as a peculiarly powerful teacher, but de Man's influence on academic literary and cultural criticism far exceeds the limits of an identifiable school or clique, and often manifests itself in sketchy and unacknowledged fashion within scholarly work that may not desire (or even know that it has) a filiation to de Manian rhetorical reading. Sometimes other proper names possessing their own institutional force intervene (Butler, Derrida, Sedgwick, Spivak); at other times, in certain contexts, a concept or term turns out to carry, among its sedimented layers of meaning, stubbornly de Manian associations or concerns ("allegory," for instance, in romantic studies). The notion of "trauma" that has lately enjoyed considerable popularity among literary and cultural critics bears within itself, as a kind of metatrauma, residues of Cathy Caruth's and Shoshana Felman's powerful redeployment of a de Manian idiom.[7] One can make an even stronger claim. The reasonably widespread, if often vague, notion that super-close reading results in undecidability rather than organic unity; the not uncommon, if typically undisciplined, assertion that texts predict and choreograph the foibles of their interpreters—these tics of contemporary professional critical writing bear the faint but unmistakable trace of de Man's signature.

Yet it is not obvious what such a legacy means, when the donor is such a peculiarly fetishized and disavowed figure. All the signs suggest a pathology ultimately irreducible to the feelings of love, hatred, or ambivalence one can have for a particular human being. Elsewhere I have argued that de Man haunts the professoriat as a phantasmatic embodiment of "theory"—that when the chips are down and ideological pressures build, the much-inflated, much-circulated, and thoroughly vague signifier "theory" typically undergoes personification and becomes a specter that can be denounced (or defended) as "de Man."[8] Hence the scale and intensity of the wartime journalism debate, or the minor but persistent tradition in high–literary-theoretical writing according to which de Man performs a deviation from Derrida that must, over and over again, be condemned and expelled.[9] One might consider here too the peculiarly salient and symbolic role played by de Man in Walter Benn Michaels's recent *The Shape of the Signifier* (2004), in which a massively distorted account of de Man's notion of textual materiality (and of Derrida's notion of textuality) is held responsible for all the sins of fin de siècle cultural criticism.[10]

As the icon of theory—of a theory that theorizes theory as nothing more (or less) than the *resistance* to its own impossible, skewed "being"—de Man is an uneasily betwixt-and-between figure who refuses to go away and refuses to be pinned down.[11] Routinely taken to personify routinized academic "deconstruction," he becomes an irritant in excess of the obsessions he inspires. And though, on the one hand, the reasons for this must be sought in the theory itself, and ultimately have little to do with de Man as a person, on the other hand the work of personification, to which the "theory itself" teaches us to attend, constantly returns us to the name, figure, and institutional-pedagogical event of Paul de Man. De Man predicted this predicament, and to some extent every serious study of his work has to repeat it. The personifying figure, which makes de Man into theory and makes theory into a specter—something that should be dead, and always more dead, since it is never quite enough dead—persistently disrupts any sheerly formal approach to his texts, precisely because these texts so stubbornly reflect on the strange, vivifying, mortifying powers of figurative language.

* * *

The essays that follow offer a revealing cross-section of the kind of good work on de Man being done at the present time. Some are by well-known critics; some are by younger scholars. Some of these authors studied with de Man; some studied with his students; some have no straightforward pedagogical tie to de Man, but became interested in his work thanks to other intellectual and institutional mediations. The divisions under which, for the sake of expediency, I have organized these essays do not do justice to the complexity and subtlety of these texts, but may perhaps serve to draw attention to a few of the themes that have predominated in the reception of de Man's thought over the last two decades. And because the notion of legacy, particularly in de Man's case, raises questions about the institutional transmission of thought—about the relation between theory and pedagogy—this book concludes with two appendices containing relevant factual material: a list of courses de Man taught during his decade at Yale, and a previously unpublished document, almost certainly by de Man, proposing the undergraduate course that, in the spring of 1977, debuted at Yale as "Literature Z," team-taught by de Man and Geoffrey Hartman. Headnotes to the appendices discuss the importance of this course, both as a pedagogical effort and as an institutional base for the propagation of "de Manian" rhetorical reading.

What is reading? All of the contributions to this volume engage de Man's great theme, but our two opening essays focus with particular clarity on reading as a concept and praxis—on the ways in which, and reasons why, reading is never simply one theme among others, and indeed never entirely succeeds in becoming a "theme" at all. Weaving back and forth between de Man's "Anthropomorphism and Trope" and Jacques Derrida's "White Mythology," Cynthia Chase draws attention to moments in these essays in which "an abrupt slowing down of the reading" occurs, a slowing-down that exacts from us "a double-take, a surprise, or deepening uneasiness." In de Man's essay this moment occurs as he follows out Nietzsche's famous pseudodefinition of truth in "On Truth and Lie" ("What then is truth? A mobile army of metaphors, metonymies, and anthropomorphisms . . .") and encounters the word "anthropomorphism." Whereas metaphor or metonymy name substitutive patterns that underwrite an unthreateningly tautological and propositional definition of truth ("truth is a trope" in the sense of "truth is a proposition"), anthropomorphism disrupts the easy flow of this list of substitutable rhetorical terms for modes of substitution. Anthropomorphism may be a trope, but it is also an act of naming: it signals not just one more pattern of substitution, but also "an identification on the level of substance."[12] In anthropomorphism, one could say (though neither de Man nor Chase put it this way) that trope and the forgetting of trope intertwine. Chase finds a similar moment of slowdown and surprise punctuating Derrida's analysis of Aristotle's analysis of metaphor, at the point when Derrida, tracking a sequence of exemplary metaphors in several of Aristotle's texts, derives the possibility of tropological substitution from the catachresis "sun as sower." The sun is the grounding referent in the figural system—it is the figure of figuration and of generation—yet here the sun as sower retreats from visibility ("where has it ever been *seen*," Derrida asks, halting us in our tracks, "that there is the same relation between the sun and its rays as between sowing and seeds?"), because this sun-sower is functioning as something like a proper name and an anthropomorphism: as the blinding, impossible site of the positing of trope.[13] Noting that both de Man and Derrida explore the "possibility . . . that words might turn to names and names to unreadable inscriptions," Chase concludes with remarks that suggest the value of thinking about de Man's legacy in terms of a kind of impact or shock, transmitted by and as reading. "My own reading was prompted by my sense of a rhetorical effect," she affirms—the effect of a double-take, or (to invoke the legacy of an author about whom both Chase and de Man have had much to say) a shock of mild surprise. Read rhetorically, such shocks become the traces of "a kind of disconnecting" that, impossibly, makes sense-making possible.

The possibility that reading involves "a kind of disconnecting" also occupies Jan Mieszkowski in "Reading, Begging, Paul de Man," as he addresses himself to the problem of what "unreadability" is. Can unreadability be read? Taking as his initial example a sentence from Poe's "The Man of the Crowd," Mieszkowski shows us both how "even the most unassuming of prose paragraphs is rife with wild leaps of faith," and how we always make these leaps anyway, willy-nilly. As a theme, in other words, unreadability is thoroughly readable, and is thus, paradoxically, a comforting distraction from the actual puzzles and discontinuities that reading, as a praxis, endlessly encounters. Unreadability is an act that cannot coincide with its own knowledge of itself. The problem of unreadability is, of course, inseparable from whatever we seek to define as de Man's legacy; and Mieszkowski suggests that the epigrammatic power of de Man's writing repeats the problem of unreadability—that de Man's formulations, precisely because of their pithy acuteness, can divert us from the very difficulties they seek to describe and analyze. In his essay's final movement, Mieszkowski offers a reading of Heinrich von Kleist's short story "The Beggarwoman of Locarno" as "an example of the failure of language to exemplify either readability or unreadability." Pursuing the play of letters by which a beggarwoman (*Bettelweib*) comes begging (*bettelnd*) and is given a bed (*gebettet*)—before being rousted from it, slipping and dying, and coming back to haunt the castle—Mieszkowski suggests that "the whole story stands (or lies) under the shadow of a German proverb, *Wie man sich bettet, so liegt man*—You've made your bed, now lie in it." Mieszkowski (though he does not use this vocabulary) is identifying here what Michael Riffaterre would call the text's "hypogram"; and as he traces the text's slippages and uncertainties, showing us how, in Kleist's story, "the very acts of standing up and lying down . . . become ghostly fictions," he implicitly rewrites the Riffaterrean hypogram as a de Manian inscription: as, that is, as Mieszkowski puts it, the haunting pressure of "a randomness that could never be integrated into a story free of the specters of chance or accident."[14] Such, Mieszkowski suggests, is de Man's necessarily tenuous legacy and lesson: unreadability as the ongoing performance of its own undecidability.

Part II of this collection, "Reading History," turns to an issue that, as all careful readers of de Man know, was constantly at stake and under scrutiny in his work: the question of what history is, and what literary history is—a problem that often, for de Man, could be troped as the question of what "romanticism" is. In "History against Historicism," Ian Balfour sets out to unpack de Man's famous (in certain circles, infamous) closing sentence of "Literary History and Literary Modernity"—"the bases for historical knowledge are not empirical facts but written texts, even if these texts masquerade in the guise of wars and revolutions"—first by putting this sentence back into its rhetorical and historical contexts, and second, by reading it closely. Those two gestures—putting into context and close reading—are in fact, Balfour emphasizes, intertwined, even though since the Enlightenment they have often been represented as the binary opposition of "history" and "theory." Balfour draws our attention to the sentences in de Man's essay that precede and set up the closing sentence about the textuality of history: "To become good literary historians," de Man writes, "we must remember that what we usually call literary history has little or nothing to do with literature, and that what we call literary interpretation—provided only that it is good interpretation—is in fact literary history."[15] In what sense might (conventional) literary history have nothing to do with literature, and in what sense might (good) literary interpretation actually be literary history? Balfour's answer is both theoretical and historical: recalling de Man's critique of formalism in the 1950s, he sketches the differences between de Man's notion of rhetorical reading, on the one hand, and canonical forms of New Critical analysis, on the other, and proposes an evolution in de Man's understanding of the role of undecidability in reading, from the relatively "circumscribed undecidability" invoked in de Man's chapters on Yeats in his dissertation (1960), to the radical undecidability dramatized in "Semiology and Rhetoric" (1972) as an intratextual clash between mutually exclusive positions. That clash has a historical dimension to the extent that the text is a historical event: an event, in other words, that makes a difference that demands to be read. Literary interpretation is literary history not just because good reading requires philological knowledge, but because a literary text entails and demands its own critique. Drawing on Adorno's *Aesthetische Theorie*, Benjamin's *Begriff der Kunstkritik*, and the latter's invocation of Friedrich Schlegel's essay on *Wilhelm Meister*, Balfour emphasizes that the literary text demands criticism as its own supplement. The historicity of the artwork is the reading it generates: "the historical encounter is structured as a relation of one moment to another, and thus structured like reading or, more precisely, the precise form of reading and writing that is citation."

In "Discontinuous Shifts," Andrzej Warminski begins by emphasizing the centrality of the question of romanticism in de Man's work, as a way of framing the question of history. This last is a double question: it addresses the problem of what de Man's notion of "history" is, yet also that of the historical mode of the de Manian text itself. How are we to read the shift in de Man's work from the existentialist idiom he favored in the 1950s and 60s to the rhetorical approach he developed in the 1970s? Warminski's subtle meditation on de Man's famous *Kehre*, or "turn," asks us to think the shift from history to reading as a "failure" that in fact—in its own failing, shifting, or slipping—marks a shift from reading to history: to, that is, history as material occurrence, rather than history as theme. Warminski develops his reading by way of two of de Man's 1967 Gauss lectures. In "Patterns of Temporality in Hölderlin's 'Wie wenn am Feiertage,'" de Man reads Hölderlin both with and against Heidegger, suggesting that Heidegger's mischaracterization of Hölderlin as an apocalyptic poet stems from Heidegger's insufficiently nuanced understanding of the temporality of poetic form. Emphasizing the importance of form, language, and consciousness, de Man presses to conclusions that Warminski reads as double or split: "On the one hand, what de Man ends up with is a still more thorough 'ontologization' of language and of poetic form than Heidegger's.... On the other hand, the conclusions of de Man's reading of Heidegger nevertheless go in an entirely different direction and prohibit such a super-Heideggerian ontologization of poetic form." That is, on the one hand, de Man reontologizes the poem's discontinuous temporality by locating it "in the structure of being itself"; on the other, he insists on the irreducibility of the formal dimension of language, and, groping for ways to describe the poem's discontinuities, turns to a rhetorical terminology. This tension comes to fruition in the second Gauss lecture Warminski discusses, de Man's "Time and History in Wordsworth." Here again, a nominally Heideggerian reading strains at the seams to account for the temporality of poetic form; indeed, Warminski suggests, de Man was possibly pushed to rewrite this lecture in 1972 (substituting rhetorical for phenomenological terms at key moments) because of the deep instabilities already at work in the 1967 version. But Warminski's point is not that de Man thereby passes from an inadequate critical vocabulary to an adequate one: a rhetorical terminology is no less improper than any other—no less unequal to the task of capturing poetic discontinuity. "Already here," he insists, "at the very pivot of de Man's 'shift' to rhetoric and rhetorical terms, the move *to* rhetoric is already a move *past* rhetoric, to an awareness that tropological textual models will also not be able to account for what actually happens, what actually occurs, in and as the texts of Hölderlin and Wordsworth." It is precisely here that Warminski locates the irruption of material history: as "the passage, the passing, itself." The shift from history to rhetoric is already a shift to—or, better, a shifting that "is"—history as occurrence.

Any collection that seeks to deepen our understanding of the "legacy of Paul de Man" had better at some point turn, as we do in Part III, "Institutions of Pedagogy," to a consideration of de Man as a teacher and as an institutional presence. In the first essay in this section, Sara Guyer turns our attention to a rarely studied text in the de Manian corpus: de Man's introduction to the special issue of *Studies in Romanticism* that he guest-edited in 1979. The special issue was originally intended to be an outlet for work emerging from his 1977–78 NEH seminar at Yale, though it wound up showcasing the work of students in de Man's regular Yale seminars as well. Thus, de Man's brief introductory text, both in itself and in its relation to its occasion and context, offers rich resources for critics interested in "de Man" as an institutional and pedagogical event. Guyer attends to figures and fantasies of legacy, teaching, and reading legible both in David Wagenknecht's correspondence with de Man about the special issue, and in de Man's introduction: both texts bear witness to a violence constitutive not just of teaching but of discipleship. De Man's text, for all its brevity, turns out to be a highly complex performance: "While refusing to read the essays [in the special issue] as merely following in his own footsteps, and refusing to reduce their violence and their impact to an 'oedipal struggle,' de Man nevertheless frames their event as a betrayal." De Man represents his own generation as consciously burdened with failure and guilt, stemming from its inability either to synthesize the competing claims of close reading and history, or to ignore the synthesizing imperative. In contrast, the students, having learned their lessons all too well, commit their parricide without anxiety or guilt—oblivious, like Kleist's dancing marionettes, to the mutilations they perform. Guyer remarks the mutual violence of the exchange (the students' alternately explicit and unknowing acts of parricide; the teacher's canny, devastating act of infanticide), but she presses toward a subtler reading of de Man's text that discloses a paradox at the heart of the de Manian "legacy": the students' freedom from anxiety is both recuperative *and* disruptive, and the teacher's knowingness is also a submission to blindness. The students are not as free as they seem, since their unwitting betrayal of the teacher—a betrayal inseparable from following the teacher, learning his lesson, trying to be like him—reinscribes them within a legacy. This legacy is precisely what de Man calls parricide: a rupture that reaffirms a filiation. And the teacher, writing into his text the legacy that is his own death, ultimately writes blindly: "which is to say," Guyer concludes, "that this legacy bears the structure of an event."

My own contribution, "Professing Literature," offers a critique of John Guillory's influential chapter on de Man in *Cultural Capital* (1993). Guillory's powerful, though in my view deeply flawed, reduction of de Manian theory to sociological symptom occurs as a triple movement: he argues, first, that de Manian theory "objectif[ies] the charisma of the master teacher as a methodology";[16] second, that de Manian theory itself, in its equation of literature with rhetoric, constitutes an ideology that has as its rationale an institutional defense of literature; and, finally, that de Manian theory offers an "imaginary reduction of the social to an instance of the linguistic": the pathos of rigor functions as an unconscious recapitulation of contemporary "conditions of institutional life" (p. 245).[17] Guillory thus characterizes de Manian rhetorical reading as a symptom of, and a defense against, the increasing marginality of literary culture, and the increasing bureaucratization of the professoriat. My objection to this reading is at times straightforward—Guillory, I believe, at crucial points systematically misrepresents de Man—but my overall ambition is to argue that Guillory is both right and wrong: he is right that de Man's performance as a teacher and critic is inseparable from the professionalization of reading, but he is wrong to imagine that de Man's text fails to reflect on this aspect of its own coming-into-being. In laboring to characterize de Man's text as blind, Guillory's misreadings blind themselves to their own insight, which is that de Man was always—usually indirectly but often enough quite directly— writing about institutionalizations and illusions of aesthetic pedagogy. On the one hand, Guillory's text reads as a *summa* of anti–de Manian clichés that have circulated ever since de Man's work began to gain wide attention in the 1970s—and that, of course, is one reason why *Cultural Capital* has been so happily received by the professoriat; on the other hand, Guillory's forceful misreading opens up a truth beyond the reach of more timid interpretations. In the wake of Guillory's flawed but productive interpretation, it becomes possible to think of de Man's oeuvre as a fundamental reflection on institutionality and pedagogy precisely *because* it focuses so stubbornly on the problem of reading reading.

The title of this collection's final section, "Theory, Materiality, and the Aesthetic," invokes themes that have dominated much of the discussion of de Man's late work. But rather than offer further summaries of "theory as the resistance to theory" or of "aesthetic ideology" by way (say) of Schiller's reading of Kant, the two essays presented here reflect more broadly on what theory is, and how aesthetics remains both a resource and a trap for theoretical thought. More than any of the previous groupings in this collection, this one hints at possibilities of intellectual combat, for Arkady Plotnitsky's and Rei Terada's essays seem to pull at times in different directions. In his ambitious position paper "Thinking Singularity," Plotnitsky discloses the mutual inextricability of "aesthetics, epistemology, history, and politics," as his subtitle puts it, by focusing on the (non)concept of singularity that becomes thinkable in the wake of de Man's readings of Kant and Hegel. In his essay's first movement, Plotnitsky teases out ramifications of Kant's insistence, in the third *Critique*'s "Analytic of the Beautiful," that "all judgments of taste are *singular* judgments." Because judgments of taste must be radically singular and free, the *sensus communis* that underwrites aesthetic judgment is nothing less than the possibility of its own failure: "this essential possibility of failure of *sensus communis* . . . defines the universality of the judgment of taste." A certain "parliamentary model" of aesthetics and politics emerges from this structuring moment of possible failure. Plotnitsky then develops a contrast between what he calls "classical" and "nonclassical" theory: whereas classical theory posits its objects as knowable or at least thinkable, nonclassical theory understands its objects as irreducibly nonthinkable. Though a certain work of idealization is required to posit or conceive of an object as nonthinkable, nonclassical theory presses on to "an epistemological double rupture" whereby the idealization is identified as such. The unthinkable "is placed *inside* and is made, as the unthinkable, a consitutive part of this theory, rather than positioned beyond the purview of or otherwise *outside* the theory." Such thinking is materialist in its refusal of "any mystical agency, divine or human." Nonclassical thought, following lines of thought initiated by Kant, emphasizes the singularity—the "lawlessness of an object or event in relation to a given law"—of any judgment concerning the beautiful and the sublime. De Man's reading of Kant teaches us a "strong" form of nonclassical theory, under the terms of which the unrepresentable is "unrepresentable even as unrepresentable," and leads toward an understanding of history as discontinuous event. When de Man speaks of an irreversible movement from the tropological to the performative, he invokes the irreversibility of nonclassical processes: processes generative of effects that prohibit historical understanding from tracing them back to a cause. History—and like Balfour, Warminksi, and Guyer, Plotnitsky recalls that a privileged name for history, in de Man, is "romanticism"—history is thus, for de Man, at the furthest remove from cognitive-historical understanding. Plotnitsky sees a "gain in terms of knowledge that now becomes possible and was not possible classically"; he stresses, however, that "each nonclassical reading may itself be unique."

In "Seeing Is Reading," Rei Terada sets out to restore a proper degree of complexity to the relation between "seeing" and "reading"—a binary opposition that, like "phenomenality" versus "cognition" (or versus "materiality") has become something of a habitual tic in much de Man–influenced criticism. Reminding us that "the *word* 'seeing,' in all its ambiguity, does not necessarily belong to the conceptual apparatus of aesthetics," and (as a word) is itself "split between the perceptual and the cognitive," Terada warns against our tendency to retranscendentalize de Man's unredemptive materialism. She cautions in particular against what she sees as a "philosophically reactionary transcendentalism" influencing the techno-rhetoricism of the introduction written by Tom Cohen, Barbara Cohen, and J. Hillis Miller (henceforth "CCM") for their *Material Events* volume. We may say (though Terada does not put it this way) that she brings to this text a version of Heidegger's critique of technology: if, for Heidegger, technology represents the culmination of Western metaphysics in its objectification of the world in the service of a will to power, for Terada, CCM's transformation of de Manian materialism into "arche-engineering"—into a technology capable of envisioning a reprogramming of the human sesnsorium—amounts to nothing less than a thoroughgoing, if subtle, retranscendentalization. Despite the enormous differences in sophistication and political orientation separating CCM's de Manian arche-engineering from Elaine Scarry's anti–de Manian aesthetic ideology, Terada suggests that these disparate projects share a fundamental aestheticism: "The notion of the sensorium as film studio (in the head or in the world), replete with engineers, set designers, directors, and projectionists, is one of Western metaphysics' favorite motifs—the fantasy production lot of the aesthetic project." Scarry's humanism shares in this technoaestheticism: "Her version of mimesis is strong enough for virtual worldmaking: it is a specific, repeatable method for stimulating in the human body an image that responds to the content of a particular idea." Terada, for her part, emphasizes the skeptical thrust of de Man's writing. She offers a close reading of Kant's discussion of hypotyposis in section 59 of the *Critique of Judgment* as a meditation on the insoluble complexities of "seeing." Hypotyposis, like seeing, is "a figure whose effects are themselves described figuratively"; it is thus not only like seeing, but (therefore) like de Manian materiality. Materiality, according to Terada, serves as "de Man's X at the spot where aesthetics can go no farther": therefore, she suggests, we might best think of de Man's work as a kind of "radical empiricism."

No simple disagreement separates or links Terada and Plotnitsky; but the difference between the former's resolute skepticism and the latter's systematic weaving of discriminations suggests something of the thematic, stylistic, and methodological diversity of de Man's legacy. Since this legacy turns around the paradox—the endless self-fracturing or slippage—of a theory that "is" its own resistance to itself, we need hardly be surprised that arguments about de Man can be had even among knowledgeable readers of him. The present editor wonders, for instance—to remain a moment longer with the last two essays in the collection—whether de Man's thought would allow either Plotnitsky's opposition between "classical" and "nonclassical" theory or Terada's pragmatic rejoinder "so much for *that*" any more than provisional stability. Reading, as de Man endlessly affirms, cannot avoid falling into error any more than it can avoid pursuing truth; this skewed pseudodialectic cannot resolve itself as the truth *of* error, because, as all of our contributors emphasize in their own ways, the act of reading fails to coincide with its own knowledge of itself. Out of this dilemma spring the various but necessarily interwoven major themes of de Man's reception. In consequence, no attentive study of de Man can really be confined to the artificial rubrics under which, for pragmatic purposes, I have organized these essays. Explicitly or not, they all address questions of history, theory, materiality, and the aesthetic, and reflect on the institutions by way of which a legacy occurs. They all help us remember that a legacy calls to us from the past only to the extent that it remains "to come," *à venir*, speaking imperatively to us of work to be done.

I.
Reading

Double-Take: Reading de Man and Derrida Writing on Tropes

Cynthia Chase

De Man's late essay "Anthropomorphism and Trope in the Lyric," delivered in a series of lectures at Cornell University in the spring of 1983,[1] begins with an argument which proceeds as a reading of the first third of a sentence in "On Truth and Lie in an Extramoral Sense," the words affirming that truth is a mobile army of tropes.[2] It's a sentence famous or notorious enough so that, as one might say, "it hardly needs translation." Perhaps indeed it needs retranslation into a foreign tongue, or so one might be tempted to say given the disorienting usage of the word "translated" in the opening paragraph of de Man's essay. De Man quotes from Nietzsche in German and then alludes to his quotation as "translated" even though he hasn't translated it from German to English but left it in the original: "'Was ist also Wahrheit? Ein bewegliches Heer von Metaphern, Metonymien, Anthropomorphismen . . .' Even when thus translated before it has been allowed to run one third of its course, Nietzsche's sentence considerably complicates the assimilation of truth to trope which it proclaims."[3] I want to call attention to a way in which "Anthropomorphism and Trope in the Lyric" and two essays by Derrida frame what Nietzsche lists in his breakdown of "truth" into rhetorical terms, a "mobile army of metaphors, metonymies, anthropomorphisms" (Nietzsche 3:314). I'll be moving back and forth between the de Man and Derrida essays, drawing analogies, paying attention especially to a certain passage in "Anthropomorphism and Trope in the Lyric" and a comparable passage in Derrida's "White Mythology: Metaphor in the Text of Philosophy." In each essay there is an abrupt slowing down of the reading—or you could call it a drawn-out double-take.

There is an odd moment in the preceding essay in *Margins of Philosophy*, "The Supplement of Copula: Philosophy before Linguistics"—a stressed elision, which occurs in reference to a passage in "On Truth and Lie in an Extramoral Sense." Nietzsche's essay serves up an argument analogous to certain familiar arguments of and about philosophical language, but "with," Derrida writes, "an entirely other aim."[4] "White Mythology: Metaphor in the Text of Philosophy" can be read as elaborating on that elision. And the outcomes of Derrida's reading of Aristotle on metaphor can find a language, I would argue, in Nietzsche's essay's odd list of tropes as it is read by de Man.

In the text of Aristotle, as read in "White Mythology," thinking about metaphor takes place as a thinking through metaphor. Statements of truth come in the form of metaphor and in reflections about metaphor. Reading Aristotle, Derrida will almost not find anything but what can be thought of by means of analogies, the metaphorical linkage, by analogy, of one idea with another. But the reading brings us to a knot amid those woven-together threads, and something in the texture of Derrida's essay changes.

What had "White Mythology" and "Anthropomorphism and Trope in the Lyric" been saying?

Each essay has asserted or demonstrated that the tie between truth and metaphor is so close as to be a coinciding. "Anthropomorphism and Trope in the Lyric" sets out with a quotation from "On Truth and Lie in an Extramoral Sense." De Man has restated it blandly: "At this point, to say that truth is a trope is to say that truth is the possibility of stating a proposition. Truth is a trope, the trope truth is the possibility of stating a proposition."[5] A metaphor says A says B. "White Mythology" has been reading Aristotle and showing that statements of truth come in the form of metaphor and in reflections about metaphor, and that in these inaugural texts what one finds are metaphors that are philosophemes, which can be stated, and also offered in example, like truth, light. In "The Supplement of Copula: Philosophy before Linguistics," where Derrida is concerned particularly with Benveniste, Saussure, and again Nietzsche, "truth" is a "trope" means something a little different: the reversibility into each other of the two ostensibly opposing sides or phases of an argument or what Derrida calls a "philosophical scheme."[6] Here is an instance: someone challenges the authority of philosophical discourse by pointing to the fact that it's determined by linguistic constraints, such as abstract ideas consisting in metaphors or dead metaphors. But just that point is simultaneously a quintessential philosophical gesture—the determination to get to the true truth that metaphors ultimately cannot conceal; the meaning, always there, and essentially unaffected by its transportation from one sign, or analogy, to another. One or another version of that thesis, and its denial, or its reversal, form a "schema," or "philosophical scheme," and it's as if they formed a Moebius strip. "White Mythology" and "The Supplement of Copula" trace the contours of several such reversible philosophical arguments. One of the subjects explicit in the latter essay is "the truth" as "the possibility of stating a proposition,"[7] and how it may be related to the putting-into-question of the inevitability of "is" or "to be." Truth *is* a trope in these two different kinds of instance—the reversible schemas and the unavoidable metaphors—and these tropes are (although in two different ranges of reference) what "truth" is.

When Nietzsche resorts to the philosophical schema—or rather to that phase of the schema—whereby philosophy or truth is language or metaphor, he does so "with an entirely other aim," Derrida affirms, than those that accompany this schema in other texts (for instance, the aim to put philosophy in its place, "after" "linguistics"). In first undercutting the assumption that Nietzsche's sentence about tropes has a polemical thrust, de Man reads similarly. In the case of Nietzsche, for de Man as for Derrida, something else is going on. "The definition of truth as a collection . . . of tropes" is "a purely structural definition, devoid of any normative emphasis": a definition that "implies that truth is relational, that it is an articulation of a subject (for example, 'truth') and a predicate (for example 'an army of tropes') allowing for an answer to a definitional question (such as 'what is truth?') that is not purely tautological." Truth is a trope is a proposition. Nietzsche's sentence is "a statement with no critical thrust" when it is read as the assertion given in its first ten words.[8]

But Nietzsche's list has, by dint of its next item, "considerable critical power." It is power coming not first, as one might have anticipated, from the reference to "a mobile army." Rather—double-take—Nietzsche's sentence, Nietzsche's list, has critical power via the word *anthropomorphisms*. The sentence-fragment takes on critical power due to an anomaly in the list of rhetorical terms. De Man states this point with a gravity that slows us down and an abruptness that emphasizes the incongruity: "But 'anthropomorphism' is not just a trope but an identification on the level of substance. . . . The apparent enumeration is in fact a foreclosure which acquires, by the same token, considerable rhetorical power."[9] The presence of "anthropomorphism" in the list of tropes is an anomaly on which de Man's reading of the sentence turns, and the reading that had started starts again.

The double-take in "White Mythology" happens like this: We are moving along in the metaphors in many texts of Aristotle threaded together by Derrida, metaphors interwoven with Aristotle's pursuit of metaphors to say the truth about metaphor. Derrida has talked about the "tropic movement" of these figures, the mobility back and forth among such tropes as the eye, light, sources of light, gold, value, sources of value, generation, *re*generation, and truth. He has observed that the type of metaphor Aristotle's text brings out is analogy, metaphor as the comparison of two and hence four different elements: two similar meanings each of which has (or *is*) its own metaphor. The two meanings being compared are like each other, and they also are alike in their internal construction. Each meaning consists in its word and its word's meaning. The meaning's word essentially belongs to its meaning. They may even be impossible to detach from one another, which is the case with those metaphors in Aristotle's text. But, importantly, even where the concept and its signification merge, they do so in the context of a discussion or conceptualization *of metaphor*, that is, of two things and their comparison. Thus they are conceived (and conceived only) as essentially comparable yet distinguishable from one another. In other words, these are analogical structures—metaphors structured and stabilized as analogies. An analogy is a strong and suggestive unit. It is always implying, or could imply, another one, and it constitutes a possible proposition. An analogy forms connections with other possible propositions. That (we were seeing), in Derrida's Aristotle, is what truth is.

True metaphors generate other true ways of speaking. This would *naturally* be the case, since the single external and singular referent, and at the same time the generator of all these figures and analogies, is the sun—which produces rays, light, heat, life, true life, and so forth. The sun-figure's generativity is crucial to the integrity or wholeness of meaning. It's crucial to the system of truth and trope being one, to the spreading out from the basic philosophemes, or metaphors, of all the analogies, and all the truth statements, that it will be possible to find or to make.

"White Mythology" analyzes a "tropic movement" in and among several senses of value. Derrida argues that it is not possible, by using as a tool the concept "metaphor" or "analogy" or "value," to ground a science, or a conceptual structure able to house a knowledge of its own language—be it a metaphorology (a systematic knowledge of metaphors) or a science of linguistics (of language as a system of values). Theorizations on this order have their boundaries erased in advance. For the metaphor network, the concept of value, or the analogy theoretically deployed by any of these, drops into what Derrida calls "a wider discourse of figuration."[10]

Then far into the essay comes an odd moment. We seem to hear Derrida saying, "When has anyone ever seen the sun sowing?" Double-take. What Derrida has written is this: "Where has it ever been seen that there is the same relation between the sun and its rays as between sowing and seeds?"[11] Derrida's interrogative sentence doesn't just pose a rhetorical question. It mimes an incredulous query, a query that voices at the same time the presumption that somewhere it might have been possible to see that the sun sows.

There have been all those analogies, an extending and continuous fabric of light—figures all like or comparable to one or another quality of the sun; all those metaphor-philosophemes we couldn't do without (like "light" and like "like.") But here there's some trouble. Derrida has just quoted these sentences from Aristotle (*Poetics* 1457b25–30):

> "It may be that some of the terms thus related have no special name of their own, but for all that they will be metaphorically described in just the same way. Thus, to cast forth seed-corn is called 'sowing' [*speirein*]; but to cast forth its flame, as said of the sun, has no special name [*to de ten phloga apo tou heliou anonymon*]." How is this anonymity to be supplemented?
> "This nameless act, however, stands in just the same relation [*homoios ekhei*] to its object, sunlight, as sowing to the seed-corn. Hence the expression in the poet, 'sowing around a god-created flame' [*speiron theokistan phloga*]."[12]

That "'expression in the poet'" is a catachresis standing in for another figure.

It's more than an oddity: in there amid all those respectable figures (analogies) comes up their generator—a condition of possibility.

As Derrida has noted, Aristotle *needs* the figure of the ray-sowing sun, needs the true sun to be able to generate all those figures. The question arises whether the sun—the single unchallengeable and singular referent in this system of figures—ought to be able to be seen to do what it is said to do. If we cannot "see" the sun sow, it is because this generative "figure" and singular referent comes up like a proper name among all the figures (indeed an army of metaphors and metonymies) Derrida has been identifying in Aristotle's writings on metaphor. One can validly juxtapose here de

Man's conclusion about the occurrence of the word *anthropomorphism* in Nietzsche's list: "The apparent enumeration is in fact a foreclosure."[13]

As telling as the term *catachresis* would be the word *setzen*. *Setzen*, "to posit," is introduced in de Man's second Nietzsche essay "The Rhetoric of Persuasion."[14] The term *setzen* reappears in "Shelley Disfigured," an essay that, reading Shelley's broken-off poem "The Triumph of Life," concerns what is not quite lyric, like "Anthropomorphism and Trope" (which goes on to make that claim about Baudelaire's sonnet "Correspondances"). In borrowing from "the poet"—in settling on the assertion "the sun sows its rays"—Aristotle's text is positing something: "the metaphor of metaphor . . . an ellipsis of ellipsis."[15] It is positing what for the text's conditions of possibility to exist would have to be able to be—metaphorically, or without statement—would have to be able to be put in a comprehensible metaphor. That's why this one—a sowersun—isn't. It marks instead the positing of meaning. An anthropomorphism, writes de Man,

> takes one entity for another and thus implies the constitution of specific entities prior to their confusion, the taking of something for something else that can then be assumed to be *given*. Anthropomorphism freezes the infinite chain of tropological transformations and propositions into one single assertion or essence which, as such, excludes all others. It is no longer a proposition but a proper name, as when the metamorphosis in Ovid's stories culminates and halts in the singleness of a proper name, Narcissus or Daphne or whatever.[16]

Not a proposition and not a metaphor, "the sun sows its rays" is an anthropomorphism, that extra term in Nietzsche's hence impossible list. Instead of a simply comprehensible metaphor, we have what is in effect a proper name—Sowersun, for instance—one that entails not just light (all our analogies and metaphors), but the "freezing" of propositions. The metaphor of metaphor slides (writes Derrida) into having to be called an "ellipsis of ellipsis"; subjective and objective genitive (the two senses of "of") slide into each other. Metaphor disappears into "its bottomless overdeterminability."[17]

As de Man's essay calls our attention to the fact that "anthropomorphism is not just a trope but an identification at the level of substance," it acts out an intensified wariness.[18] Something similar has happened when "The Supplement of Copula: Philosophy Before Linguistics" alludes to Nietzsche on metaphor. Derrida quotes a passage that says: it could only be by "forgetfulness" that anyone could believe that it would be possible to say what is true by means of our words, for they represent the imposition by which "sensory excitations" are accorded the status of "objective judgments."[19] Derrida quotes from Nietzsche in order to show how inescapable the self-inverting scheme is whereby no matter how violent the reminder to the philosopher of the limits placed on him by his language, philosophy always reappropriates this critique (which consists in a version of the quintessential philosophical thesis).[20] But on every occasion on which he points to the fact that this "law of reappropriation by philosophy" comes into play in "On Truth and Lie," Derrida's text suggests that that is not all that is going on, and that what is going forward in the passages of that text is something yet to be explicitly understood. One such reference to Nietzsche occurs in Derrida's opening analysis in a reading that principally unravels the arguments of Benveniste's *Problems in General Linguistics* regarding philosophy's origination in empirically definable "facts of language." "The Supplement of Copula: Philosophy Before Linguistics" begins by talking about the line of thought that makes use of the notion of a "discourse," and in which the concept of a certain thing termed a "discourse" replaces other kinds of attention to texts that exist across an uneven, fractured history. "Philosophical discourse" is held to have become possible thanks to a specific linguistic situation and to be determined and constrained by features of the "language" in which it was framed. This thesis is a version, Derrida observes, of the recurrent philosophical move consisting in the pushing aside of the mere language of a text to get at its meaning or significance; even Nietzsche is drawn into the same collapsible construction, for instance in the paragraph in "On Truth and Lie" challenging the validity of existent words. It is in this context that Derrida writes that Nietzsche "must resort to an analogous argument [but] with an entirely other aim."[21]

It's again a text of Nietzsche that gives *Allegories of Reading* the word "posit," which as de Man begins quoting and reading the text in question loses its innocuous, inconspicuous character. I quote from the 1887 passage in *The Will to Power* (which is quoted in "The Rhetoric of Persuasion"):

> If, according to Aristotle, the *law of contradiction* is the most certain of all principles, if it is the ultimate ground upon which every demonstrative proof rests, if the principle of every axiom lies in it; then one should consider all the more rigorously what presuppositions [*Voraussetzungen*] already lie at the bottom of it. Either it asserts something about actual entities, as if one already knew this from some other source; namely that opposite

attributes *cannot* be ascribed to them [*können*]. Or the proposition means: opposite attributes *should* not be ascribed to them [*sollen*]. In that case, logic would be an imperative, *not* to know the true [*erkennen*] but to posit [*setzen*] and arrange a world that *should be true for us*.[22]

De Man comments, "What has and will be shown, within the confines of this particular fragment [the passage from which I quote above], is the possibility of unwarranted substitutions leading to ontological claims based on misinterpreted systems of relationship (such as, for instance, substituting identity for signification)."[23] In de Man's use of the term, "positing" has a peculiar impact on meaning. Again, from "Shelley Disfigured": "language posits, and language means (since it articulates), but language cannot posit meaning."[24] If meaning is posited, can it be "meaning" in the sense that it is possible to know—have words or alignments that say—what is true? To that question "On Truth and Lie" is saying no, in the paragraph Derrida refers to; but the necessity of positing is being introduced, is being inscribed. Inscribing positing is, so I'd put it, the "other aim" of Nietzsche alluded to in "The Supplement of Copula." A supplement of to be: Derrida signals that we should register the fact that what's being pressured, in this passage about words, is the value of the "is."

"On Truth and Lie" indeed "complicates the assimilation of truth to trope that it proclaims."[25] De Man next asserts the congruence of Nietzsche and Kant: Nietzsche's essay and the *Third Critique* are alike a denial or undoing of the certainty of meanings and of sensory objects, and the intent to recover a controlled discourse. Despite their considerable difference in tone, De Man writes, that tonal difference "cannot conceal the congruity of the two projects, their common stake in the recovery of controlled discourse on the far side of even the sharpest denials of sense-certainties."[26] Amid these lucid intents, however, in both texts there come into play patterns that cannot be assimilated to the main one. "What interests us primarily in the poetic and philosophical versions of this transaction," de Man writes, "is not, at this point, the critical schemes that deny certainty considered in themselves, but their disruption by patterns that cannot be assimilated to these schemes."[27] De Man's topic will not be the exploration of truth being trope, but rather a "disruption," one in the same area where a disruption is registered by "White Mythology." The disruption arrives as "anthropomorphism" is juxtaposed with "trope."

> Far from being the same, tropes such as metaphor (or metonymy) and anthropomorphisms are mutually exclusive. The apparent enumeration is in fact a foreclosure which acquires, by the same token, considerable critical

power. Truth is now defined by two incompatible assertions: either truth is a set of propositions or truth is a proper name. Yet, on the other hand, it is clear that the tendency to move from tropes to systems of interpretation such as anthropomorphisms is built into the very notion of trope. One reads Nietzsche's sentence without any sense of disruption, for although a trope is in no way the same as an anthropomorphism, it is nevertheless the case that an anthropomorphism is structured like a trope: it is easy enough to cross the barrier from trope to name, but impossible, once this barrier has been crossed, to return from it to the starting point in truth. Truth is a trope; a trope generates a norm or value: this value (or ideology) is no longer true. It is true that tropes are the producers of ideologies that are no longer true. Hence the army metaphor.[28]

Meaning is foreclosed for the statement "truth is tropes," the in itself undisturbing identification that "White Mythology" locates in "metaphor in the text of philosophy," as it is extended in the sentence of Nietzsche. The simultaneous assertion that truth is trope and truth is anthropomorphism implicitly disqualifies both assertions, since the first amounts to the statement that truth is a series of propositions (or metaphors), the second that it is an entirely different sort of list, that of names posited as the proper names of entities. "Anthropomorphisms" means the reference to entities the identity of which is fixed, whether through a metamorphosis over the course of a history, or through a definitional metaphor. Giving the name "anthropomorphisms" to what "truth is," Nietzsche's sentence refers to the taking as given of beings and things thereby being posited as existing in a certain way—posited in the mode of entities on the way to being named not by means of nouns and verbs, but by means of proper names. The figure of figuration and of generation is the sun, introduced in the nonfigure "the sun sows its rays." The "figure" of a sowing sun is the opaque proper name of a sower of figures such as light, value, exchange, gold; it is the name, say, "Sowing-sun" or "Sunsower." Derrida's listing of metaphors in the text of philosophy pulls up at a point at which it is true that in Aristotle's text "[t]ruth is now defined by two incompatible assertions: either truth is a set of propositions or truth is a proper name."[29]

The passage just quoted from "Anthropomorphism and Trope" should be set alongside "Rhetoric of Persuasion (Nietzsche)," the last of three chapters on Nietzsche in *Allegories of Reading*—in particular the section of the chapter that considers how the passage from a cognitive to a performative rhetoric is "irreversible," but is also interrupted, since there is no passage forward (or backward) to the possibility of knowing that language is in a particular instance *doing* something, that it is able to act or "perform." Language does not operate in the mode of knowing or constatation of truths, but in the mode of persuasion, of rhetoric as a type of power rather than a mode of knowing (the knowledge conveyed by metaphors, figures, or propositions). In the course of the breakdown that Nietzsche's text carries out, de Man is saying, we have arrived at a performative model of language, but by no means does this imply that we could revert, or proceed, to *knowing* what has occurred, or to knowing *whether* a performative came into play.[30]

The indispensable metaphor-philosophemes Derrida has tracked in Aristotle appear (in both Aristotle's text and in Derrida's) in the context of a conceptualization of metaphor or figure. That context affords them the structure of trope, of metaphor, of analogy, and, implicitly, of propositions. But suppose the conceptual distinction within the category "metaphor" were annulled, and those figures stayed around? Are such figures tropes? Or would "anthropomorphisms" be the appropriate term for all? The identification of metaphor with truth "in the text of philosophy"—inescapable—is what "Anthropomorphism and Trope in the Lyric" terms "an identification on the level of substance . . . the taking of something for something else that can then be assumed to be given." In short, it situates the "discourse of figuration" in a mythology. What seem to be our metaphor-philosophemes might as well be a *list* of "figures": a list of *names*. De Man's emphasis on Nietzsche's list of tropes—and its sudden incongruity at the word "anthropomorphism"—allows us to describe what happens with the sequence of exemplary, then incongruous, metaphors Derrida follows in Aristotle. Thus "White Mythology" jolts at the catachresis "*sowing* sun" and registers it as the proper name of the generative figure of generative figures in Aristotle. We are brought to a special kind of nonfigure: an ostensible proposition that consists in the "proper name" that is *only* an indicator, that indicates but does not communicate or express. And here, the referent of that indicating is only itself: indicating the necessity and the impossibility of it being a true name generating true figures. The list of tropes in Nietzsche's sentence and the list of figures in Aristotle would be, so the context of Derrida's and de Man's essays suggests, a list of proper names gone opaque, without a referent other than themselves.

The "figure" by which the action of a human being is ascribed to the single and only irreplaceable visible thing is an anthropomorphism of a peculiar kind, the source of visibility. The effect is to make the listed figures into the reiteration of one, like names of a god. Repeated enough times, the figure of a generative sun, in the words in which Derrida finds it in "White Mythology," becomes a stammered name (such as Sower-Sun). An idea we think we know about—the indistinguishability of an object and its inscription in a system of interpretation—would freeze or have frozen, in fact, thought.

That available illusion is being repulsed in some later sentences in de Man's argument. Some words of Baudelaire's "Correspondances" serve in these lines, which have an *unheimlich* atmosphere not dispelled by one's fitting them into a reading, or by referring them to Baudelaire's text. De Man writes:

> And if man (*l'homme*) is at home among "*regards familiers*" within that Nature, then his language of tropes and analogies is of little use to them [*sic*]. In this realm, transfer tickets are of no avail. Within the confines of a system of transportation—or of language as a system of communication—one can transfer from one vehicle to another, but one cannot transfer from being like a vehicle to being like a temple, or a ground.[31]

Proper names, like the verbal units that are proper names for things, recede. Explaining what is at stake in Derrida's readings in *Glas*, in "Hypogram and Inscription" de Man discusses Saussure's parenthetical and left-off work published by Starobinski under the title *Les mots sous les mots*. Saussure had been studying Latin inscriptions while seeking to determine whether certain patterns of letters were or were not anagrams. De Man describes Saussure as finally letting this line of thought trail away once it became sufficiently clear that there was going to be no way to decide the question one way or the other. The letters, across and among which Saussure could trace the names of certain Latin authors, were indubitably there: "randomly" or "by intention" of the inscribers? That alternative does not suffice to describe what Saussure was looking at, de Man writes. In the not-quite-for-sure anagrams, Saussure was seeing the indeterminably significant status of what had been supposed to be units of meaning or of legibility, the dismemberment of words.[32] The mobility of metaphor brings up, not at a central, or at a proper, name, but at an opaque figure such as that of the "cup without wine" that is the final trope in Derrida's list—a figure placed in the decontextualizing or overcontextualizing locale of a parenthesis.[33] A possibility being implied and analyzed by de Man and Derrida is that words might turn to names and names to unreadable inscriptions. Such would be the implication of drawing the two readings close, of that spooky slide from Aristotle to Nietzsche.

Yet the signature "Nietzsche," far from freezing up the sentences in Derrida's and de Man's essays, allowed for readings that undo the yoking of tropes to what would freeze them into "an identification on the level of substance," that of a god's substance or a Nature's substance or man's. My own reading was prompted by my sense of a rhetorical effect. De Man and Derrida exact from us a double-take, a surprise, or deepening uneasiness, at what appears as the added term in a list (of examples of true metaphors; of names of tropes). The readings in "Anthropomorphism and Trope in the Lyric" and "White Mythology" aim at a kind of disconnecting. Derrida drops philosophemes into "a wider discourse of figuration." "The Supplement of Copula" pulls to pieces Benveniste's conception of a determined and determining language of philosophy (namely Greek); it aims to pry apart the fused grammar and lexicon of the words akin to "be." De Man's readings of Nietzsche scatter a dismembered sentence. Their aim? To underdetermine the significance of tropes.

Reading, Begging, Paul de Man
Jan Mieszkowski

The opening sentence of Edgar Allan Poe's "The Man of the Crowd" cryptically informs us: "It was well said of a certain German book that *'es lässt sich nicht lesen'*—it does not permit itself to be read," a pronouncement that returns in the final sentence of the story when the narrator concludes his comments on the "worst heart" in the world with: "*Es lässt sich nicht lesen.*"[1] The reading pursued in the tale framed by these two lines certainly has its share of difficulties. The narrator sits in a London coffeehouse, contemplating the crowd on the street. At first able to classify the people he sees, subsuming each one under a type (clerk, gambler, beggar), he is eventually confronted with a unique countenance that "at once arrested and absorbed [his] whole attention on account of the absolute idiosyncrasy of its expression" (183). Almost immediately, he recasts this singular appearance as the external manifestation of an internal text: "'How wild a history,' I said to myself, 'is written within that bosom!'" (184). In an effort to read the physiognomy of this enigmatic man and the soul that lies within, the narrator gets up and follows his prey on a walk through the night and into the next morning. Perseverance, however, is not rewarded. No incident that might somehow clarify the inclinations or intentions of this extraordinary personage ever takes place, and ultimately, the project has to be abandoned. It is from the standpoint of this explanatory-event-that-wasn't that "The Man of the Crowd" begins with the narrator's declaration that there are "secrets which do not permit themselves to be told," "mysteries which will not *suffer themselves* to be revealed" (179; emphasis in the original).

As the narrator and his object of inquiry travel in tandem through the crowded streets of London, it gradually dawns on us that either one of them may rightly lay claim to the title "man of the crowd." In trying (and failing) to read the stranger, the narrator has to come to terms with what it means to read, or not to be able to read, his own bosom. In a story that begins and ends with a reflexive construction about a book that does not permit itself to be read, the possibility that the Other may turn out to be oneself neither confirms nor denies the authority of self-consciousness as much as it forces us to ask whether the inability to read—either one's own bosom or the countenance of a stranger on the street—is itself legible. In other words, does this allegory of unreadability permit itself to be read, and if so, in what respect, if any, is something genuinely unreadable in play?

The problem is already evident in the first sentence of the story, in which the citation of a remark in German—"*es lässt sich nicht lesen*"—is followed by a dash that evidently introduces a translation of the preceding words: "It does not permit itself to be read." Superficially, the construction inspires confidence, providing us with an English version of the original so that we can understand the sentence about a book that will not permit itself to be read even if we are not acquainted with the German language and the nuances of the reflexive *sich lassen*. But is it clear what it means to say that Poe's own sentence does or does not permit itself to be read? If one cannot in some minimal sense decode the German, then one does not actually read the first part of the sentence; rather, one glosses the proposition as an undecipherable clause, the meaning of which may never be clarified. At the same time, this obscurity does not constitute an insurmountable obstacle. Just as one need not know precisely which "certain German book" Poe is referring to in order to proceed to the second paragraph and beyond—again, we do not learn the identity of this book until the story's last sentence—so one does not need to be able to decipher every word or phrase to make headway with the tale. If absolute lucidity were the standard for progress, then many readers would presumably never make it past the epigraph in French from La Bruyère (for which no translation is provided). In this respect, we could say that the sentence about a book that does not permit itself to be read permits itself to be read, but only in a very particular way, only insofar as its unreadably German dimension is revealed to be its most transparent part.

Yet what convinces a stranger to the German language that the words following the dash are a translation, much less an "accurate" translation, of what comes before them, particularly since what is under discussion is something that does not allow itself to be read? Do we have any reason to be confident that this German phrase is more accommodating of our investigations than the "certain German book"? Irrespective of one's mastery of English or German, what one needs to read at the beginning of "The Man of the Crowd" is the dash, but if this means rendering the punctuation mark coherent, this happens only by blindly trusting that it can be treated as an expression of equivalence between two statements—rather than, for example, as a sign of contrast or opposition. The result is that even a native speaker of English may omit to unpack the English "translation" on the most basic level. Instead of pursuing the elementary hermeneutic gesture of asking what it means for something not to permit itself to be read (much less inquiring what this "certain book" might be), we are inclined to accept Poe's first sentence passively, following the presentation of obscurity and its subsequent clarification to a speedy conclusion as the foreign jargon is resolved into a more familiar vernacular. Along the way, concerns about the "deeper" meaning of these statements fall to the wayside.

Taking our cue from the motif of the unreadable, we might generalize from this passage and argue that Poe's text hints that we always read in this fashion, that is, that every foray into even the most unassuming of prose paragraphs is rife with wild leaps of faith across both literal and figurative "dashes," dashes that may or may not coordinate words and sentences in the ways we suppose—or at least in the ways we have to suppose if we are going to impose any semblance of sense on them. In these terms, reading is as much a violent series of positings as a judicious process of decoding. The opening sentence of "The Man of the Crowd" can thus be regarded as a miniature allegory of the unstable relationship between syntactic and semantic paradigms that plagues all literary works. To read the beginning of Poe's story is to confront both the impossibility of knowing how one reads the dash and the impossibility of not doing so. There is, after all, no alternative: "—" *is* "="; the German *is* the English, or at least, we are forced to proceed as if the one says the same thing as the other, even if we truly do not know what we are talking about where one or both of the languages is concerned. In this way, the "unreadability" of the opening sentence ("it does not permit itself to be read") turns out to be entirely commonplace. Any sentence in "The Man of the Crowd" may present similar problems, irrespective of how many references it contains to rare books, and yet it is precisely our ability to identify a particular element of a sentence as (at least provisionally) unreadable that makes our progress through it so easy.

Our discussion of the opening line of Poe's story has identified a potentially disruptive feature in its logic, but it may be that all we have done is to repeat the song-and-dance of obscurity and clarification that the sentence itself stages with its German and English versions of an unattributed quotation. Moreover, the interpretive procedure by which we have arrived at an account of the unreadable dimension of any reading potentially contradicts its own conclusion, since we were able to show that the sentence confounds our ability to articulate a clear difference between the readable and unreadable dimensions of the text only by tacitly presupposing such a difference from the start. In this context, it is important to recall that the main part of Poe's tale, elegantly framed by the two instances of "*es lässt sich nicht lesen*," speaks straightforwardly about secrets of the human heart that *cannot* be revealed. Such mysteries are more extreme than a book of prayers whose title needs to be looked up in a reference manual. They point toward something that must by its very nature remain hidden, a secret that is truly secret because to expose it is necessarily to transform it into something else.

The negativity of this self-eliding figure suggests that Poe's story cannot simply be read as a metastory about the permanent disjunction that obtains between an object and the modality of its representation. The inability to read the secrets of the human heart could be described as an allegory of unreadability, but such a gesture would serve only to dissimulate the fact that we do not know what these secrets are. It is also far from clear whether such a classificatory move would advance our interpretation of "The Man of the Crowd." Confirming the reflexivity of the text with respect to its representational structure leaves us, as it were, on the surface, for the meaning of the story is established with no consideration for its parts. The result is that our allegory of unreadability remains hyperlegible. It is all but independent of the narrative of which it is ostensibly comprised, and this is the case whether this unreadability is characterized with reference to the first sentence of the story, the relationship between the first sentence and its repetition in the story's final sentence, or the mystery of the man the narrator follows through the night. In identifying the allegorical nature of the text, we unexpectedly neutralize our attempts to understand it, and irrespective of how elaborately we construe the dialectical relationship between the readable and the unreadable, we by no means confirm our ability to take seriously the straightforward conclusion of Poe's narrator that there are some things that do not permit themselves to be read. In "reading ourselves reading," we may have done no better than Poe's narrator, who in the end can read neither himself nor the singular figure he stalks.

Among late-twentieth-century critics, Paul de Man offers a unique perspective on the complex demands encountered by even the most elementary investigation into the theory of reading. Wreaking havoc with the traditional paradigms of exegesis and interpretation, his work unsettles the models of causation and development organizing our ideas about history, questions the assumptions about knowledge and representation structuring our aesthetics, and denounces the woefully incomplete understanding of the performative power of language that informs our moral philosophy. Perhaps most remarkably, de Man consistently reveals the degree to which the putative "themes" of a text are at once constituted and undermined by a figural logic in which the authority of linguistic reference is both vital and irreducibly aberrant. In the final analysis, it is scarcely an exaggeration to say that his œuvre forces us to confront nothing less than the "impossibility of reading," an impossibility that no hermeneutics or poetics, no science of semiotics or taxonomy of rhetoric, no historical research or speculative logic, can dispel.

De Man possessed an uncanny ability to craft lapidary conclusions for his arguments, pronouncements that with memorable eloquence describe—some would say, prescribe—fundamental disjunctions between grammar and rhetoric or between the phenomenal and the material. If it is rarely so easy to refer to the gist of such difficult demonstrations by citing the author's pithy summaries, the comprehensive quality of these maxim-like utterances can give the impression that there is nothing left for the literary critic to do but reconfirm the relevance of de Man's findings for everything he did not get around to discussing explicitly. The question is whether in striving to honor his achievements by reproducing them we unwittingly contravene them.

If both de Man's allies and his detractors tend to evaluate his corpus through expositions of his most memorable synoptic formulations, his work is a testimony to the impossibility of reading becoming a purely synthetic praxis. Writing about Rousseau, de Man argues: "A text such as the *Profession de foi* can literally be called 'unreadable' in that it leads to a set of assertions that radically exclude each other. Nor are these assertions mere neutral constations; they are exhortative performatives that require the passage from sheer enunciation to action. They compel us to choose while destroying the foundation of any choice."[2] If the *Profession de foi* compels "us to choose while destroying the foundation of any choice," understanding it cannot merely be a question of identifying the elements of the text that do not fit in perfectly with the rest, as deconstruction is frequently said to do. The unreadability of Rousseau's work is not a factor of obscurity, inconsistency, or the nonsensical; nor is it an effect of the "free play" of the signifier. De Man calls our attention here to a clash—a clear and direct clash—between two demands, a discord that undermines the very coordination of reference and signification that the text presents as its own distinguishing mode.

In these terms, reading is an engagement with a strife that never assumes the form of a determinate negation that could be subordinated to a logical hierarchy and subsequently recuperated through further negations. As with Poe's dash, our conclusions about how to evaluate the legibility or illegibility of a particular punctuation mark, sentence, or even an entire work never align with the procedure through which we can and must ascribe meaning to a text. "Reading," writes de Man with characteristic flair, "is a praxis that thematizes its own thesis about the impossibility of thematization."[3] Reading never culminates in a coherent set of mutually informing syntheses and analyses. It relates to itself not as a self-determining or self-realizing operation, not as a self-confirming process of trial and error or the testing of hypotheses, but as a dynamic in which readability and unreadability threaten to be at once mutually informing and entirely irrelevant for one another.[4] This is why de Man is adamant that no account of the complexities of the allegorical nature of language will ever form the basis for a procedure of metareading that could facilitate a stable set of judgments or a reliable system of knowledge. For him, the choice to read is always the choice to undertake the destruction of the grounds for precisely such a choice; hence, it is always the choice to undertake an impossible choice, to undertake the making-impossible of the choice called "reading." It is with good reason that many literary critics have been openly hostile to de Man's work and its implications for the status of literary interpretation as a feasible, not to mention teachable, enterprise.

In following de Man in his efforts to contend with the problems we inevitably face when we use language to talk about language, it will be helpful to consider in greater detail how his work does or does not "assist" us with the practical exegesis of a text. To this end, we will now turn to Heinrich von Kleist's "The Beggarwoman of Locarno." Written in 1810, this twenty-sentence prose piece is often referred to as the shortest *Novelle* in the German canon. The plot, such as it is, is simple: A Marquis is rude to a beggarwoman who ends up dying in the corner of one of his castle's rooms; some years later, she appears to return in the form of a ghost who rehearses the unfortunate woman's last steps at midnight; this paranormal phenomenon is investigated on successive days, and when it seems to be genuine, the Marquis goes berserk and burns down his castle, dying in the process. Although E. T. A. Hoffmann praised the tale for its unique treatment of the experiences of horror and shock (*Schreck*), it is quite unlike Hoffmann's own work, lacking an uncanny dimension or a feeling that intrigue or evil lurks just out of sight. Indeed, the tone of Kleist's text has often been compared to that of a legal brief. The couple of details it provides about its characters' emotions come across as functional premises rather than glimpses into individual psyches. The Marquise is said to assist the beggarwoman out of pity; the Marquis is described as oddly horrified when he hears the story about a ghost, although he does not understand why—but rather than rounding out the representation of a situation, these points serve to give us the impression that we are being provided with just enough information to facilitate the most formal of links between sentences.

As in all his prose works, Kleist creates dramatic tension in "The Beggarwoman" with extraordinary brevity. As is also typical for his writing, however, it is difficult to attribute the effects that the various scenes create to the relations between the characters or between the characters and their actions. Kleist begins:

> At the foot of the Alps near Locarno in Upper Italy, there was an old castle, the property of a Marquis; as you go southward from St. Gotthard, you see it lying now in ruins. In one of its tall and spacious rooms, on a bundle of straw that had been thrown down for her, a sick old woman who had come begging (*bettelnd*) to the door was once given a bed (*gebettet*) by the mistress of the house out of pity.[5]

If the study of literature is concerned, as de Man once noted, with letters rather than with people, these first sentences provide considerable food for thought. As the story begins, the beggar has been put to bed—in German, the *Bettelweib* has been *gebettet*. From an etymological perspective, the Grimms' Dictionary confirms that the letters (b-e-t-t) these words share are significant: the two have a common root in the Gothic *bidjan* ("to ask for") with its sense of "supplication."[6] On some level, the connection should be obvious: in begging, one metaphorically throws oneself before a potential benefactor just as one might lie down to go to sleep. Of course, we have been told that the castle now *lies* in ruins, so the fact that the beggarwoman was lying on a bed of straw on the floor may not be altogether a good thing. As we further pursue the collusion between the content of the sentences and the lexical properties of the words, it may turn out that connecting things that share letters is not an entirely risk-free undertaking, either. Kleist continues:

> Returning from the hunt, the Marquis happened to enter the room (*zufällig in das Zimmer trat*) where he customarily kept his guns, and he angrily ordered the woman to get up from the corner where she was lying and move behind the stove. As/Because (*Da*) she rose, the old woman slipped on the polished floor with her crutch and severely injured her back; as a consequence of which she did stand up, though with unspeakable difficulty, and went across the room as she had been told, but behind the stove, with groans and sighs of pain, she sank down and died.

Virtually every aspect of this story is structured as a series of movements and postures that take place in relation to horizontal and vertical axes. One rises, one sinks, one lies—ruined. In this strange pose-prose, every sentence is riddled with words that reinforce the emphasis on spatial coordinates and vectors.[7] Ultimately, even time itself comes to be subordinated to the layout of the haunted room—things happen in the middle of this space in the middle of the night, and so on.

Parallel to this language of lying down and standing up is a logic of orders and entreaties; for instance, the Marquis enters the room and commands the beggar to move. In this manner, he attempts to confirm both that one can get up and lie down when and where one pleases and that people will get up and lie down when and where they are so instructed. In the shift from one *Bett* to another, the *Bettelweib*, or at least her ghost, somehow goes astray, which is to say that the Marquis fails in his effort to get begging permanently bedded in a bed behind the stove (that is, to get *Betteln gebettet* in a *Bett*). Like the beggarwoman, the Marquis' command slips as he tries to keep her begging out of sight. Ironically, this means that begging will not be seen but will be heard as the ghost repeats the beggarwoman's efforts to do as she was told and become invisible.

The sense that the effort to dismiss begging and its accompanying postures may be futile is heightened in the story's next section, where it is explained that some years later poor financial *standing* forced the Marquis and Marquise to try to sell their castle. A prospective buyer, a knight, is invited to spend the night in the very room where years before the beggarwoman had fallen, although nobody seems to recall anything about the incident. Just after midnight, the guest appears and announces "that his room was haunted, for something invisible to the eye had risen up from the corner with a sound as if it had been lying on straw, and slowly and feebly, but with distinct steps, crossed the room and sank down moaning and groaning behind the stove." Having tried to lie down in the room in which the beggarwoman was once to be tucked away, the would-be buyer pleads to be allowed to spend the night elsewhere. Kleist's word for pleading is *bitten*, which is etymologically related to both *betteln* and *Bett*.

Lest there be any doubt about the semantic authority of these b-t-t associations, it should be observed that the Marquis' first step upon being confronted with this report about the specter is to place a bed in the room in question and to spend the night there himself. In this regard, it might be said that the whole story stands (or lies) under the shadow of a German proverb, *Wie man sich bettet, so liegt man*—You've made your bed, now lie in it. If the point, however, is that nobody in this story can stay in bed, this may be because the Marquis' initial order to the beggarwoman was only made because he happened to walk into the room by "chance" (*Zufall*). The beggarwoman happens to fall because he happens to drop by. One happenstance leads to another, or rather, to a "missed stance."

For even the casual reader of Kleist, this question of *Zufall* will sound decisive. Virtually every text Kleist wrote seems to stand (or fall) by the German word *Fall*—whether the crucial connotation is a physical event, the biblical fall, or the standing of words or conditions themselves, since *Fall* also means "case" in the sense of grammatical case as well as "event" or "instance." In the case (*Fall*) of this tale, a *Fall* occasioned by "accident" (*Zufall*) leads to an unhappy "incident" (*Vorfall*) with a prospective buyer and so ultimately to the entire castle falling down.

Yet falling is only part of the story, for Kleist's narrative proves to be curiously inconsistent in its statements concerning accidents. At the outset, we are informed that the Marquis just happened to walk in on the beggarwoman, but the detail is immediately mitigated by the further qualification that this was the room in which he usually kept his guns, as if it was only "somewhat" accidental that he went there after having been hunting. In the broader context of the story, the notion that things take place by accident is belied by the insistent return of particular words and expressions. Just as the ghost echoes the demise of the beggarwoman, retracing her journey across the room, so almost every other detail turns out to have a prior verbal analogue, as if even a text this short could do little more than requote itself. The beggarwoman slips when she *rises up*, and the same phrase describes the way in which a rumor *rises up* among the servants that there is something strange afoot in the bedroom. No matter how much falling may be going on, there is always another form of language to rise to the occasion, the *Vorfall*, which is of course also a word for what the Marquis is trying to do, namely, to return things to the way they were before the beggarwoman's fall, *vor dem Fall*.

Of course, not everything permits of repetition. Although the beggarwoman's slip is potentially the most ordinary event in the tale—the floor is slick; she falls—it is also the paradigmatically singular event. Night after night, the ghost rehearses her movements after she takes her spill, but it never repeats her initial tumble. Unlike the story's other literal and figurative falls, the beggarwoman's blunder occurs only once, a point reinforced by the phrase that characterizes the incident. Kleist writes that the beggarwoman slipped *"da sie sich erhob"*—meaning either *"as* she rose up" or *"because* she rose up"—heightening our sense that even the most precise exposition of the text's language cannot provide us with a clear causal chain. The beggarwoman slides—*sie glitscht*—but the fall never becomes the kind of glitch in a system that could be corrected or expelled as something foreign.[8]

It is precisely this aspect of the beggarwoman's fall that has prompted some critics to view the story as a moral parable in which the Marquis is punished for a crime. From this angle, the plot takes on an almost tragicomic quality, as if one casual act of rudeness could lead, through a series of freakish steps, to total devastation. In fact, a sense that the various elements of the story are almost preposterously difficult to coordinate with one another pervades the entire narrative. Immediately following the statement that the beggarwoman sank down and died, the narrative jumps forward several years. No reader of the tale has any trouble associating the second section with the first; it never occurs to us that it is merely coincidental that the ghost should appear in this room and haunt it in this way. Yet almost as if to cast doubt on this assumption, neither the Marquis nor any of the other characters ever makes reference to the connection between the specter and the uninvited guest of a few years earlier, and when the ghost makes a direct appearance as an agent in the narrative, it is as an impersonal "he" rather than a "she." Lamenting the failure of Kleist's characters to connect the past with the present or the visible woman with the invisible ghost, one commentator has argued that it is as if Kleist's imagination was paralyzed the day he wrote the story.[9] The result is a text in which nothing can be put together with anything else, a sort of nightmare of the Kantian mind in which synthesis, in particular the synthesizing power of time, is no longer possible and experience has become a chaotic pastiche of discrete elements.

Further scrutiny of the story's syntax bears this out. As Emil Staiger has observed, the tale's first fourteen sentences are organized by a hypotactic grammar in which the responsibilities of the comma, the semicolon, and the colon are pushed to the limits of what the German language will allow.[10] Far from creating a clear hierarchy of cause and effect, this peculiar prose contributes to the sense of a shaky edifice held together by very little. The more precise the articulations become, the less evident it is that they facilitate meaningful juxtapositions between agents or events, as if the conjunctions and punctuation marks joining the clauses are more important than what they connect.[11]

In this space in which neither what is prone nor what is standing holds sway, the Marquis remains vigilant. Three nights in a row, he tries to bed down in the haunted room in order to put the rumors to bed. Unfortunately, the more determined he and his wife become to make a thorough evaluation of the situation, the more it appears as if the very acts of standing up and lying down have themselves become ghostly fictions—less physical phenomena than something one assumes must be happening because it sounds as if it were the case. It may be that the Marquis and Marquise fail because they are determined to attribute this phantom incident, this *Vorfall*, to some "unimportant and accidental (*zufällig*) cause." In never really trying to escape the logic of *falling*, they unwittingly remain within the space of standing and slipping inaugurated by the beggarwoman's initial actions. It comes as no surprise, then, that *Zufall* again has a role to play as the Marquis and Marquise lie down for the last time in the haunted room. For better or worse, on this occasion their dog happens to be present to serve as another witness—we are told that he finds himself before the door of the haunted room exactly as the old woman found herself before the castle door several years earlier. At this point, the story switches from the past to the present tense, as if to indicate that we are now at a decisive juncture and that everything prior has only been a set-up for what is about to happen. Finally, it would seem, the beggarwoman's singular slip is to be followed by another *unique* event. If the syntax of the story has to this point been hypotactic to an almost absurd degree (even for German), the sentences suddenly become simpler, even paratactic. The grammar now mimics the "tap tap" of the ghost's crutch rather than the elaborate weaving of premises and conclusions that distinguished the first part.

In this final encounter with the ghost, the specter is for the first time described not simply by association—that is, in the thrice-repeated "it sounded *as if* someone lying on the floor got up . . ."—but with the facticity of agency: "Someone human eyes cannot see rises on crutches in the corner of the room." The emphasis on what *human* eyes cannot see necessarily turns our attention to the canine witness, inviting us to regard him as the substantial link that had previously been missing between the visible and the invisible, the natural and the supernatural. Once again, however, we have been baited into a conclusion for which the necessary details are not available. Nothing in the scene makes it clear that the dog is reacting to something he sees rather than hears. We moved easily from *Bett* to *betten* and from *betteln* to *bitten*, but dog—in German, *Hund*—never resolves itself into the *Grund*, the ground or explanation, for the peculiar noises sought by the Marquis and Marquise. Like the other sleepers in the haunted room before him, the *Hund* wakes up at the witching hour, the *Geisterstunde*, but his behavior remains just another confirmation of something that cannot be confirmed, a gesture toward a connection that joins nothing. In this sense, the true significance of *Hund* may lie in its last three letters, u-n-d, *und*, the most ordinary of German conjunctions and, as it so happens, the most ubiquitous word in Kleist's story.[12]

"The Beggarwoman of Locarno" begins with a castle *lying* in ruins and ends with the Marquis' bones *lying* there, too. In this triumph of the horizontal over the vertical in which whatever gets upright and walks is at some point doomed to take a spill, even the language of orders—Stand up! Go to bed!—is confronted with a *circum-stance* in which no one, including the person who gives the orders, is able to maintain his or her stance. As elaborate as the hypotactic constructions they facilitate may be, Kleist's conjunctions never turn into substantives, and *und* in particular never assumes a coherent form—as, for example, a *Hund*. Like every other conjunction in this story, *und* remains in a haunted space in which one is never quite sure of its purpose. Does it link events in causal relations, or does it simply juxtapose statements with one another, setting them disjointedly side by side? In these terms, the hypotactic grammar of the first section of the story is eventually brought low by the *tap tap* of a paratactic specter that reduces everything to ruinous confusion. The story's ghost is the phantom of sentence constructions that are never substantial enough to build a hierarchy that could get, or perhaps stay, off the ground.

From this perspective, we could invoke de Man's conclusion to his reading of Percy Shelley's "The Triumph of Life" in which he argues that the poem "warns us that nothing, whether deed, word, thought, or text, ever happens in relation, positive or negative, to anything that precedes, follows, or exists elsewhere, but only as a random event whose power, like the power of death, is due to the randomness of its occurrence."[13] Kleist's twenty-sentence novella would therefore be an allegory of events, a tale in which no occurrence—the slip of the beggarwoman, the death of the Marquis—can be understood by situating it within a deterministic logic that would purport to explain what it means by referring it to something else. The point is not that an event generates its own narrative or that the narrative creates an event as a retrospective excuse for the act of storytelling. Nor is it sufficient simply to speak of a tension between what occurs and the act of representing what occurs. The ghost plagues the castle not by demonstrating that the original fall of the visiting beggar had consequences for the future, but by revealing that the initial tumble was already haunted by a randomness that could never fully be integrated into a story cleansed of the specters of chance or accident. The event of Kleist's ghost is the event of events because it at once sets up and brings down the stances and circumstances of time and place in virtue of which we would customarily locate something and identify it as meaningful by describing when and how it takes place. From this standpoint—although it is precisely not a *stand*point—all events are spectral because all events call into question their own capacity to happen.

In what sense, then, are we to speak of language "taking place"? Or, to put it another way, would it be correct to conclude on the basis of our reading of Kleist that all words are irremediably fallen? In the final sentence of the story, the Marquis' bones are said to lie "in that corner of the room from which he once ordered the beggarwoman of Locarno to stand up" ("... *von welchem, er das Bettelweib von Locarno hatte aufstehen heißen*"). These last phrases present the command to stand with a German expression based on the verb *heißen*, "to be called" or "to mean." In this manner, the story concludes with a demand that language addresses to itself—perhaps with authority, perhaps only as an act of supplication. This is language's plea to itself that it stand up and make a name (*heißen*) for itself, or at least in some respect establish itself as meaningful. Following Poe's "The Man of the Crowd," the question is whether Kleist's story permits itself to stand or fall, or even to try. The irony of "The Beggarwoman of Locarno" may be that language is never certain to answer its own entreaty, which is to say that the word *Fall* can never be as good as its name and become one case of falling, one *Fall des Falls*, among others. All language, we might say, is ghost-speak, although it is we, not ghosts, who speak it.

As a consequence, our interpretation of Kleist's story cannot take refuge in any particular figure of falling—whether it be the shape of a moral allegory ("the Marquis got what he deserved") or a constellation of lexically related words ("u-n-d binds the collapse of the *Grund* via the presence of the *Hund*").[14] The language of begging happens, or rather "happen-stances," in the space opened up by the beggarwoman's singular slip, hovering between the horizontal and the vertical, between a logic of commands and a logic of pleas, between cause and accident. This is a language that places a demand upon itself for a standing that it can never realize because it is a language that will stand for no demands whatsoever. Neither synthesis nor analysis, this discourse confronts us not with the positing or negating power of the word, but with a linguistic force that will no longer permit us to characterize it in terms of what it does or does not allow to take place.

The term for such a language can only be Locarno. In a story in which there are no proper nouns following the opening sentence, it is striking how precisely the castle's location is mapped out, "near Locarno." Etymologically, the name is Celtic, Loc-ar-on, meaning a town situated beside a river or a lake. Of course, it is an Italian town, so we can also read it as Loc-Arno, the Arno being the river running through Florence. Arno itself has a Celtic or Ligurian, that is, pre-Latin, etymology meaning "river," as a result of which we might also imagine it as the Locus-Arno, a (Latin) place by a (Celtic) river. On the other hand, Loc- may come from the Celtic (Gaelic) *Loch*, water, in which case the story would be called "The Beggarwoman of Water by Water"—the locative designation of "a city by a river" now replaced by the paratactic parallelism of the ghostly crutch: water, water / tap, tap. The spectral Locarno is the place where the belief that nothing can *take place* without a reason (*Grund*) is qualified by the curious detail that everything takes place, again and again, without ever thereby acquiring a place, a *Grund*, of its own. In this sense, the story's title names the effort—the inherently untenable effort—by which language attempts to stop begging and stand up.

Poe's "The Man of the Crowd" is distinguished by a phantom event, an act on the part of the man with a singular countenance that will explain his mysterious nature but that never happens. Paradoxically, it is this very absence of a clarifying incident that confirms Poe's narrator's decision to judge a book by its cover and conclude that the man he is following is intrinsically unreadable. In Kleist's story, it is in the very process of effecting numerous aftershocks that events destroy their own standing as meaningful occurrences to the point of severing their links to the incidents they bring about. In this regard, "The Beggarwoman of Locarno" must be read as an example of the failure of language to exemplify either readability or unreadability—the failure, if you like, of language to do our begging, much less our bidding.

To his credit, Paul de Man was one of the few literary critics who never expected any more or less. If his legacy remains, like that of the beggarwoman, tenuous, it is because he offers us a lesson about the inability of our allegories of intellectual history to account for the linguistic structure of the events they strive to depict. De Man bequeaths us not a stance from which to pontificate about the ineluctable tensions between grammar and rhetoric or performance and constation, but a challenge to the reflexivity of analysis, a challenge, that is, to the belief that being able to describe the dynamic interaction of form and content or subject and object is tantamount to being able to identify what does and does not permit itself to be read.

The Beggarwoman of Locarno by Heinrich von Kleist

At the foot of the Alps near Locarno in Upper Italy, there was an old castle, the property of a Marquis; as you go southward from St. Gotthard, you see it lying now in ruins. In one of its tall and spacious rooms, on a bundle of straw that had been thrown down for her, a sick old woman who had come begging (*bettelnd*) to the door was once given a bed (*gebettet*) by the mistress of the house out of pity. Returning from the hunt, the Marquis happened to enter the room (*zufällig in das Zimmer trat*) where he customarily kept his guns, and he angrily ordered the woman to get up from the corner where she was lying and move behind the stove. As/ Because (*Da*) she rose, the old woman slipped on the polished floor with her crutch and severely injured her back; as a consequence of which she did stand up, though with unspeakable difficulty, and went across the room as she had been told, but behind the stove, moaning and groaning, she sank down and died.

Some years later, finding himself in difficult financial circumstances (*bedenkliche Vermögensumstände*) owing to war and bad harvests, the Marquis was visited by a Florentine knight who wanted to buy the castle on account of its fine position. Extremely anxious to bring the business to a successful conclusion, the Marquis gave instructions to his wife to prepare the abovementioned room, now beautifully furnished, for their guest. But imagine their surprise when the knight came into their room pale and distracted in the middle of the night, solemnly assuring them that his room was haunted (*daß es in dem Zimmer spuke*), for something invisible to the eye had risen up from the corner with a sound as if it had been lying on straw, and slowly and feebly, but with distinct steps, crossed the room and sank down moaning and groaning behind the stove.

Horrified, although not knowing why, the Marquis laughed at the nobleman with forced merriment and said he would immediately get up and keep him company in the haunted room for the rest of the night to calm him down. But the knight pleaded (*bat*) to be allowed to spend the rest of the night in another room, and when morning came, he ordered his horses to be brought around, bade farewell, and departed.

Unfortunately for the Marquis, this incident (*Vorfall*) created a great sensation, frightening away several would-be buyers; and when the rumor strangely and mysteriously arose among his own servants that queer things were happening in the room at the midnight hour, he determined to dispel the matter by investigating it himself that same night. So he had his bed (*Bett*) moved into the room at twilight and sleeplessly waited for the middle of the night to come. To his horror, as the clock chimed the witching hour (*mit dem Schlage der Geisterstunde*) he became aware of the mysterious noise; it sounded as if a person (*Mensch*) rose up from rustling straw, crossed the room, and sank down sighing and groaning behind the stove. The next morning when he came downstairs, his wife asked what he had learned; he looked around with a nervous and troubled glance, and after locking the door, assured her that the rumor was true. The Marquise was more terrified than ever before in her life, and begged him to make a levelheaded investigation with her before the rumor grew. Accompanied by a loyal servant, they spent the following night in the room and heard the same ghostly noises; and only the pressing need to get rid of the castle at any cost enabled the Marquise to smother the terror which she felt and in the presence of the servant put the noise down to some unimportant and accidental (*gleichgültige und zufällige*) cause that could easily be discovered. On the evening of the third day, both of them went upstairs to the guestroom with beating hearts, anxious to get at the cause of the disturbance (*um der Sache auf den Grund zu kommen*). There they found the watchdog, who happened (*fand sich zufällig der Haushund*) to have been let off his leash, standing at the door of the room. They took him with them into the room without giving any particular reason, both perhaps unconsciously wishing to have another living being in the room besides themselves. About eleven o'clock, the two of them sit down, one on each bed—two candles on the table, the Marquise fully dressed, the Marquis with the dagger and pistol he had taken from the cupboard beside him; and while they entertain one another as best as they can by carrying on a conversation, the dog lies down in the middle of the room, his head on his paws, and falls asleep. At the instant of midnight, the horrible sound can be heard again; someone (*jemand*) human eyes cannot see rises up in the corner of the room on crutches; one hears the straw rustling beneath him; and at the first step—tap, tap—the dog wakes up, pricks up his ears, rises growling and barking from the floor, and moves backwards toward the stove, exactly as if somebody were making straight for him. At this sight, the Marquise, her hair rising, rushes from the room. The Marquis, who had snatched up his dagger, calls "Who's there?" but receives no reply, while like a madwoman, she orders the coach to be brought out, determined to drive off to town at once. But before she can gather a few things together and get them out the door, she notices the castle going up in flames all around her. Overcome with horror and tired of life, the Marquis had taken a candle and set fire to the wooden paneling all around him. In vain, she sent people in to rescue the wretched man; he had already found his end in the most dreadful manner possible; and his white bones, gathered together by his people, still lie in that corner of the room from which he once ordered the beggarwoman of Locarno to stand up.

II.
Reading History

History against Historicism, Formal Matters, and the Event of the Text: de Man with Benjamin

Ian Balfour

In the dynamics of the past four or five decades of literary theory and criticism, one could witness an often palpable struggle between the competing claims—and the partisans—of "theory" and "history." The structuralism born in Saussure and reaching its methodological acme, say, in the writings and teachings of Lévi-Strauss was thought—in its freezing, if only momentarily, of cultural history—to be relatively indifferent to what counted as history, if by history, one understood change, contingency, and temporal heterogeneity or difference that had to be registered if any given moment or sequence of moments were to be understood at all. This charge may well be unfair and certainly does not apply equally well to all those commonly called structuralists, certainly not the early Barthes, for one. No doubt, the sort of theory that came, as we are told, immediately in the wake of structuralism, the so-called poststructuralism, understood difference—or in Derrida's case, *différance*—to include, if not quite to foreground, historical difference. But the critics of poststructuralism, and especially those who yoke it with postmodernism, still find that mode of thought to be "soft" on history, not least on the grounds of poststructuralism's putative relativism. But it is hard to generalize about the precise status of history in the varieties of thought in the loose, baggy monster called "poststructuralism." The sweeping charges made against poststructuralism in the name of history tend themselves to be weakly historical.

At least since Hegel—and one might have said since Vico, had that almost solitary figure been more widely read and influential—it has been pervasively on the agenda of philosophy and of the human sciences to try to reconcile and do justice to the double demands of history and theory, to treat the subjects and objects under scrutiny historically ("in their contexts") and theoretically, for their conceptual import, at one and the same time. It was in the Enlightenment broadly understood, the canonical and largely persuasive story goes, that historical consciousness dawned on European philosophy in a profound way, well beyond even the polar oppositions of "us" and "them" codified in the various "quarrels" of the Ancients and the Moderns.[1] The item remains on the agenda of the humanities today and shows few signs of fading away.

How are we to understand Paul de Man's works in the light of this conjunction of—or tension between—history and theory? One reason de Man's work fell out of favor in the last two decades surely has to do with the rise of the New Historicism and related historicisms and materialisms: the swing of Foucault's pendulum, as it were. A widespread sense prevailed that de Man's thinking posed, in unduly formalist fashion, the literary text against or outside of history rather than embedded in it, or perhaps that de Man reduced history to a matter of textuality, narrowly construed. Routinely cited as proof of this reduction is one of de Man's most notorious dicta, namely the provocative conclusion of the essay "Literary History and Literary Modernity," where he claimed that "the bases for historical knowledge are not empirical facts but written texts, even if these texts masquerade in the guise of wars or revolutions."[2] Even though very different theorists, Jameson for one, make essentially the same claim for the necessarily textual character of history—that is, "the bases for historical knowledge"—de Man's formulation rankled people a lot more, presumably because we know from elsewhere that Jameson treats at length a good deal of what normally passes for history ("what hurts"), not least the brutal determinations of class. And about de Man we tend to be not at all certain and perhaps downright suspicious, all the more so in light of the posthumously revealed collaborationist writings. It's safe to say that de Man's position was widely held to be promoting textuality—such was Edward Said's fairly representative view—at the expense of history.[3]

Yet the axiom that the bases for historical knowledge are written texts comes only as the climax, if that is the word for it, of a long and dense passage that conveys a somewhat different and fuller picture of de Man's stance toward history, especially literary history. Immediately preceding the famous pronouncement on the textuality of history, de Man claims: "To become good literary historians, we must remember that what we usually call literary history has little or nothing to do with literature and that what we call literary interpretation—provided only that it is good interpretation—is in fact literary history."[4] None of this is so self-evident and it seems to run counter to the standard genealogies of deconstruction, especially in its de Manian mode, often traced partly to the once New Criticism. And so we might step back for a moment and consider New Criticism as a mode with and against which de Man worked out his early positions and postures about the critical project.

The New Criticism was associated in America, especially in its academic contexts (i.e., apart from, say, the institution that was T. S. Eliot), with Cleanth Brooks, William Wimsatt, and the transplanted (from England) I. A. Richards but also, in de Man's case, particularly with Reuben Brower. Its paradigmatic object was the lyric poem, mined for its verbal ironies, paradoxes, and ambiguities: most typically, the poem's complexities were all chalked up to aesthetic richness. Donne might well stand at the pinnacle of the New Critical canon, with his densely intellectual poems constituting a congenial aesthetic counterpart to the prose of the New Critics themselves, who prided themselves on or aspired to many of the same virtues embodied in Donne.

And it's no small matter that the focus on the lyric poem was so well suited to the scene of pedagogy. Not only were the great professors of New Criticism authors of scholarly books and essays, many of them wrote textbooks widely used in high schools. Their influence, direct and indirect, was massive. Almost all of a sudden, in the heyday of New Criticism—in the forties, fifties, and sixties—the exemplary scene of teaching in an American high school would not be one more installment in a sequence of classes on Huckleberry Finn but a close reading of a poem by Robert Frost.

De Man describes the parameters of teaching and learning with Reuben Brower in the famous Hum. 6 course at Harvard as follows:

> Students, as they began to write on the writings of others, were not to say anything that was not derived from the text they were considering. They were not to make any statements that they could not support by a specific use of language that actually occurred in the text. They were asked, in other words, to begin by reading texts closely as texts and not to move at once into the general context of human experience or history. Much more hum-

bly or modestly, they were to start out from the bafflement that such singular turns of tone, phrase, and figure were bound to produce in readers attentive enough to notice them and honest enough not to hide their nonunderstanding behind the screen of received ideas that often passes, in literary instruction, for humanistic knowledge.[5]

In this same mode, Brower also advocated what he called "reading in slow motion," rather in the spirit of Nietzsche, who claimed that whatever shortcoming classical philologists had, at least they read slowly.[6] This discipline, more often called "close reading," was thought—misleadingly, I think—to be antithetical to historical understanding, as if close reading meant pressing one's eyes too near to the page and so losing sight of the world beyond the text. Even a cursory glance at the works of New Critics suggests how much they knew about history and how they were concerned to articulate it—one need only consult Cleanth Brooks on Faulkner or Wimsatt on Pope—even if their sense of history was certainly pre-Foucauldean and non-Marxist, to say the least. Rarely do any of the trinity of race, class, and gender surface in a significant way in their analyses, though some questions of power and hierarchy do. In *The Well-Wrought Urn* Brooks had tried to assuage some critical readers of his earlier *Modern Poetry and the Tradition* (1939), not least by including a long appendix on "Criticism, History, and Critical Relativism," in which he pointed out how the various readings of *The Well-Wrought Urn* looked forward to a "new history of English poetry," agreed that to understand Shakespeare we need "to know what Shakespeare's words mean" (thus entailing at least some historical or philological work), and so on.[7] One can, in Brooks's view as well as de Man's, be doing literary history without providing a thick description of the historical moment of the text's production. But programmatic statements about history—even appeals to history—are one thing and the texture of historical understanding evidenced throughout a sustained analysis of a literary text is another. Some of this same divergence might be pertinent within the writings of Paul de Man.

Within the uneasy alliance of all those called New Critics, William Empson cuts a singular figure in numerous respects and, as it happens, Empson was the New Critic who fascinated de Man the most. Empson was perhaps the most complex and seemingly contradictory of the New Critics, for he was author of, on the one hand, a veritable blueprint of "formalist" close reading in *Seven Types of Ambiguity* (as well as the related, more "linguistic" project, *The Structure of Complex Words*) and, on the other, far more historically, sociologically, and politically oriented studies such as *Some Version of Pastoral*, which offered a sustained meditation on "proletarian literature," among other things. And this is to say nothing of his vividly cranky style of polemics, which demonstrated time and again that the act of criticism was thoroughly enmeshed in the "real world." It is instructive to reread de Man's old essays on the New Criticism, such as the one on "The Dead-End of Formalist Criticism" (originally in French as "L'impasse de la critique formaliste") to find him critiquing the very thing—namely the limits of a certain formalism—of which he would later be so roundly accused. Thus, at least fairly early on in his career, and perhaps spurred on by his understanding of historicity and temporality in Heidegger and his understanding of allegory in relation to temporality and history in Benjamin, de Man argued for a kind of criticism that attempted, among other things, to account for the claims of history. But not at the expense of—and indeed any accounting for history, literary or otherwise, was to be informed by—what was commonly called "close reading."

For de Man, close—or as he preferred to call it—"rhetorical" reading radicalized and transvaluated the categories of New Criticism, with the epistemological and ontological stakes raised and rendered problematic as, for example, in the shift from ambiguity to undecidability. One can glimpse something of the texture and the stakes involved in such a shift by juxtaposing de Man's reading of the famous ending of Yeats's "Among School Children" with the readings of critics in the orbit of New Criticism, such as Frank Kermode's or Cleanth Brooks's, the latter contained in *The Well-Wrought Urn*. In the long section on Yeats in de Man's dissertation, reprinted as a chapter in *The Rhetoric of Romanticism*, de Man rehearses Kermode's reading of Yeats where the poet is "presented as the successful seeker for 'the reconciling image.'"[8] For Kermode, in de Man's gloss, "the image of the dancer is said to be the supreme instance of the reconciliation (a reconciliation which presupposes, of course, an initial severance) because it contains the ideal attributes of both body and imagination" (188). In this nexus of concerns, the poem "Among School Children" is "singled out" as "heralding the triumph of the reconciliatory image" (197), crystallized in the famous final lines of the poem:

O chestnut-tree, great-rooted blossomer,
Are you the leaf, the blossom or the bole?
O body swayed to music, O brightening glance,
How can we know the dancer from the dance?

Immediately following this citation, de Man comments: "It might seem far-fetched or even perverse to find here anything but a splendid statement glorifying organic, natural form, its sensuous experience and fundamental unity. Tracing back the images of the dancer and the tree in romantic and symbolist poetry, Mr. Kermode adds the testimony of history to the instinctive delight with which one welcomes a climax for which everything in the poem . . . seems to be a perfect preparation" (198). Yet de Man provides an alternative "tracing," an alternative history within Yeats's oeuvre, reading the passage in question as, in Yeatsian terms, an emblem rather than an image (corresponding roughly to the distinction between allegory and symbol in the vocabulary of romantic theory and in general). In this light, de Man claims the famous closing lines can acquire "very different connotations." He goes on to say: "Assuming . . . that a difference exists between what is represented by the dancer and what is represented by the dance, by the leaf, and by the blossom, the question could just as well express the bewilderment of someone who, faced with two different possibilities, does not know what choice to make. In that case, the question [How can we know the dancer from the dance?] would not be rhetorical at all, but urgently addressed to the 'presences' in the hope of receiving an answer" (200). Whereas here, as later in "Semiology and Rhetoric," de Man opposes two different possibilities—rhetorical question or real question—considered to be mutually exclusive (the line can't be mean both at the same time), at a late moment in the dissertation chapter, de Man comments: "The ways of the image and the emblem are opposed; the final line is not a rhetorical statement of reconciliation but an anguished question; it is our perilous fate not to know if the glimpses of unity which we perceive at times can be made more permanent by natural ways or by the ascesis of renunciation, by images or emblem" (202). It seems unambiguous here that the true reading of the line is the "negative" one, the one that stresses the difficulty of knowing rather than celebrates the inseparability of dancer and dance. By (partial) contrast, the later, official reading proposed in "Semiology and Rhetoric" leaves the matter suspended in properly undecidable fashion, with the two mutually exclusive readings existing side by side, thus constituting a decisive difference from the New Critical norm, a difference that underscores difference.[9] Even Brooks, in the ringing conclusion of his essay, which so often stressed the priority of form, returns to the thesis of organic inseparability:

> But we cannot question her as a dancer without stopping the dance or waiting until the dance has been completed. And in so far as our interest is in poetry, the dance must be primary for us. We cannot afford to neglect it: no amount of notes on the personal history of the dancer will prove to

be a substitute for it, and even our knowledge of the dancer qua dancer will depend in some measure upon it. How else can we know her? "How can we know the dancer from the dance?" (Brooks, *The Well-Wrought Urn*, 191)

Brooks's end was in his beginning, for despite the significant attention to literary or textual ambiguity (which can have no very precise counterpart in nature) the very title of Brooks's chapter on the poem is "Yeats' Great Rooted Blossomer," thus enlisting the organic, natural image from the poem to describe the poem itself.

This juxtaposition of readings shows something of what is at stake in thinking though formal matters and their relations to the thematic. In the context of de Man's chapter from the dissertation, this attention to form, rhetoric, grammar, image and emblem, and so on, is enlisted in a properly literary historical problematic. To determine with precision what exactly Yeats's poems are saying will allow one to gauge more accurately Yeats's relation to the tradition, distinguishing the specificity of his work (and the phases of his work) from various romantic and symbolist precursors. Such work is literary-historical but not exactly in a way that we would now generally recognize as "historicist." There is little in de Man's long chapter that would situate Yeats's poetry in the world of Irish politics, say. For example, when de Man treats Yeats's "Meditations in Time of Civil War," there is little sense of the war itself. Nor is there any discussion of a poem such an "Easter, 1916," surely now one of the most canonical of Yeats's poems.

The undecidability that de Man discerns in "Among School Children" remains primarily an epistemological affair, not—or not yet—the undecidability of the later Derrida, where it becomes the very site of, and a provocation to, responsibility. (For Derrida, an easily decided decision is no decision at all. Such decisions can more or less be programmed and as such are not properly decisions in the first place.) Still, even this more modest or circumscribed sort of undecidability seems linked to difference and even, most particularly in Yeats, to the "controlled violence" so characteristic of his later work, and thus by no means simply nonhistorical.[10]

At the outset of the early essay, "Form and Intent in the American New Criticism," de Man had charted, in retrospect, an opposition between the highest and most characteristic achievements of the major European and American critics and found the latter lacking in one respect: "In evaluating what American criticism had to gain from a closer contact with Europe, one would have stressed the historical knowledge and a genuine feeling for literary form." De Man went on to contend that the New Criticism "was never able to overcome the anti-historical bias that presided over its beginnings." This inability was one of the reasons that prevented it from making major contributions in spite of "considerable methodological originality and refinement."[11] European literary criticism, in de Man's characterizations, tends to stand for a historically informed study of literature or, even better, a synthesis of attention to both history and form. That is the standard against which the New Critics fall somewhat short. Empson, once again, is the exception or near-exception. On the one hand, there is the attention to what counts as history noted above, to say nothing of his politically antinomian positions. On the other hand, sometimes what Empson conceives of as historical, such as the tension between nature and society in the pastoral tradition, turns out to be, in de Man's view, primarily a version of a more purely structural, in the sense of nonhistorical, division between nature and mind in general. Thus in the latter respect, Empsonian criticism would be somewhat blind to its status as pseudohistorical.

In his most searching—at least in methodological terms—work, *Seven Types of Ambiguity*, Empson explores the complexities of language in one local analysis after another, such that the analyses of the various types of ambiguity reach a point where the author comes to confront what would later be christened, in deconstructive writing, "undecidability." In this, the seventh and last type, we are no longer, according to de Man's account, dealing with ambiguities whose richness can be easily admired but rather with mutually exclusive significations whose uneasy coexistence defies reconciliation. This for de Man is more than a matter of a local difficulty in interpretation but has, instead, full-blown ontological implications, insofar as the division in signification points to and is a version of nothing less than a division within being itself. To the extent that the literary text is shown to expose in a profound way the ontological status of poetic language, as a heightened version of language as such, it is not simply historical, though it is also always emphatically that.

But let us return now to the passage from de Man with which we began and inquire further into why it might be for de Man that what we usually call "literary history" has "little or nothing to do with literature"? In de Man's view, what counts as literary history seems normally to operate at one or more removes from the literary text and what passes for history is often a rather clumsy application of period concepts, producing analyses that confirm what one thinks one knows in advance, that a poem generally thought to be romantic will turn out to be—quelle surprise!—romantic. Or, in related fashion, literary history will tend to read through what de

Man terms "the screen of received ideas," as noted in the passage about Brower's course quoted above. The garden variety of literary history constitutes a sort of nonreading that is, in effect, not even open to what a text might actually, in its specificity, be saying. Such literary history is thus non- or, worse, pseudohistorical.

But why would literary interpretation, provided only that it is "good interpretation" be, of necessity, literary history? To begin with: because the text is, of itself, already historical—indeed a kind of event—and a certain historical, philological knowledge is a necessary basis for even beginning to read it. Figuring out what a text is saying—and de Man will often ask in the "most naïve," "most literal" fashion what a text is saying—will produce historical understanding or knowledge. And the very historical being of a work of art cannot be separated from what might appear merely posthumous to it. Consider this passage from Adorno's *Aesthetic Theory*, which seems to me close to the spirit of de Man's thinking on history:

> [I]f finished works only become what they are because their being is in a process of becoming, they are in turn dependent on forms in which their process crystallizes: interpretation, commentary, critique. These are not simply brought to bear on works by those who concern themselves with them: rather they are the arena of the historical development of artworks in themselves, and thus they are forms in their own right. They serve the truth content of works as something that goes beyond them, which separates this truth content—the task of critique—from elements of its untruth. If the unfolding of the work in these forms is not to miscarry, they must be honed to the point where they become philosophical. It is from within, in the movement of the immanent form of artworks and the dynamic of their relation to the concept of art, that it ultimately becomes manifest how much art—in spite of, and because of its monadological essence—is an element in the movement of spirit and of social reality. The relation to the art of the past, as well as the barriers to its apperception, have their locus in the contemporary condition of consciousness as positively or negatively transcended; the rest is nothing more than empty erudition. . . . The opposite of a genuine relation to the historical substance of artworks—their essential content—is their rash subsumption to history, their assignment to a historical moment.[12]

Adorno's claims are derived in no small measure from Walter Benjamin, whose mark on de Man's thinking is profound. Both these thinkers are generally, and not without reason, thought to do more justice to the demands of history than is de Man. In the long passage quoted above Adorno is drawing on Benjamin's notion of "critique," formulated in the most elaborate fashion in Benjamin's dissertation, *Der Begriff der Kunstkritik in der deutschen Romantik* (*The Concept of Criticism in German Romanticism*). There Benjamin himself drew on Friedrich Schlegel's exemplary reading of Goethe's *Wilhelm Meisters Wanderjahre* to formulate a far-reaching theory of the work of art as both entailing its own critique (in advance, so to speak) and necessitating a critique "external" to the work, a strangely "necessary" supplement to what seems like the autonomous work of art. Benjamin extended Schlegel's notion of critique by conceiving of the work of art as that which gazes at the reader or spectator and in turn demands its gaze be met. This already means that it makes little or no sense to consign a work of art simply to the moment of its production. The reflection that is critique is required of and by the work, in principle, again and again and simply is not able to be limited to one and only one historical moment. Critique, then, is nothing if not historical, insofar as repetition and difference are built into the notion of the (critical) work of art, but it perhaps is not historical in the conceptual framework that prevails in "historicism."

This structure of critique bears an affinity with translation, as theorized in Benjamin's landmark essay "The Task of the Translator" and as commented on by de Man. Here, too, the translation emerges as an oddly necessary supplement. ("Il faut tout traduire," Derrida once said.) And it is a structure than brings us close to Benjamin's concept of history (*Geschichte*), insofar as the paradigm for historical knowing—and even of historical action—is the relation of one moment to another, the moment known and the moment of knowing (*Erkennen*). Translation stresses the finitude and even, provisionally, the finality of the relation between original and translation, given the fact that one tends not to translate a translation, such that the historical dynamic set in motion by the original is brought to an end (*Ende*) by the critical reading that is translation. But the translation had already set the original in motion—destabilized it, decanonized it, according to de Man—which is another way in which critical reading or translation is something like a historical act in relation to the already historical act that is the literary text.[13]

To consign a work of art to its past, to the moment of its production, for Adorno and de Man is also, in effect, not to read it. And what, in any event, is the moment of its production? Is it the moment or moments of its conception, its first or final inscription, its publication, its being read? Derrida raises some of these questions in his long essay on Paul Celan by asking what is the "date" of a poem and suggesting that the singular "date" of a poem is traversed by the iterative structure of dating and its complex histories. The problem of the date would be one version of the more general problematic of the difficulty of consigning a work of art to a discrete past and would be related to what de Man calls variously, in his essay "Shelley Disfigured," "burying" or "monumentalization." "Einmal ist keinmal," Benjamin ventriloquizes, "One time is no time." The dictum is the traditional opening for the fairy tale, translated, usually and aptly, as "once upon a time." It is this fairy-tale tag that Benjamin finds emblematic of "historicism." In Benjaminian—and Derridean and de Manian—history there is no pure "once upon a time," even if a text also always demands to be read in its singularity. It is just that the singularity of the text is partly constituted by its citational character: the text always cites, but it does not cite just anything and it cites in a certain way, never being just of the order of sheer citation, as even in Borges's mind-experiment of the *Don Quixote* written by Pierre Menard, repeating the original word for word and yet still somehow with a (historical) difference.

Benjamin claims in the drafts to the theses that "the true historical method is a philological one." By this he did not mean to reduce history to textuality but to foreground, once again, how the historical encounter is structured as a relation of one moment to another, and thus structured like reading or, more precisely, the precise form of reading and writing that is citation. Like the violence of quotation, this negatively dialectical model of text and reading wrenches the text, momentarily, from the homogenizing, totalizing, containing narratives within which literary history likes to enfold it. This is not to say that the quotation is not somehow historical. Indeed, citation, in Benjamin's theses, is the very model for revolutionary action, following the lead of the spectacular opening pages of Marx's *The Eighteenth Brumaire of Napoleon Bonaparte*.

It is in the theses "On the Concept of History" that Benjamin most resolutely takes what he calls "historicism" to task for the naiveté and insidiousness of its "once-upon-a-time" view of history. Benjamin links such historicism with the politically and epistemologically suspect phenomena of no less than fascism and vulgar Marxism. Benjamin argues for a revised mode of historical materialism that would do justice to the structure of history as an antinarrative relation of moments, for a history against historicism. Close to the end of "Shelley Disfigured," de Man contends that "[r]eading as disfiguration, to the very extent that it resists historicism, turns out to be historically more reliable than the products of historical archeology."[14]

De Man's insistence on the event of the text no doubt owes a good deal to Austin's foregrounding of the speech act and especially the performative character of crucial and unacknowledged dynamics of language. All texts are events, even when largely constative. And then within this general class, some texts for de Man—his chief examples are from Rousseau, such as the organizing excuse of *The Confessions*—are more of the order of "textual events" than others. De Man explicitly admitted that his notion of "textual event" was rather obscure.[15] Derrida agrees about the obscurity but registers a proximity to de Man on just this obscure matter in his essay "Typewriter Ribbon: Limited Ink (2)," where he draws attention to the conjunction of the categories of the event and the machine in de Man, which have to be thought together.[16] The de Manian "textual event" seems to occur in situations where the stakes are higher than usual, as in the politics of the social contract, but the problematic is that which besets the text in general, of which de Man says, "A text is defined by the necessity of considering a statement, at the same time, as performative and constative, and the logical tension between figure and grammar is repeated in the impossibility of distinguishing between two linguistic functions which are not necessarily compatible."[17] This general problematic of the textual event requires reading in each and every instance, and unlike the discourse of the natural sciences, literary theory, like political theory, always has to confront the singularity of the example—which is not only or not fully an "example"—in question. The grandeur and the misery of the example is that it pretends to be fully exemplary of the whole of which it is meant to be an example and yet it is never quite. Not all examples—as anyone who has ever tried to teach or even just to persuade anyone else knows full well—are equally good. It is out of conceptual rigour—and against the grain of a potential popularity and perhaps even efficaciousness—that Kant in *The Critique of Pure Reason* steers clear of example.

It may well be that in de Man's work the programmatic appeals to history, somewhat in the manner of Cleanth Brooks, are not or do not seem to be borne out in the texture of history elaborated in the readings proper. And indeed, even the programmatic appeals to history tend to be made in rather negative fashion, that is, outlining rather more what sort of history de Man is not doing. Thus, the resonant, provocative conclusion of "Anthropomorphism and Trope in the Lyric":

> Generic terms such as "lyric" (or its various sub-species, "ode," "idyll," or "elegy") as well as pseudo-historical period terms such as "romanticism" or "classicism" are always terms of resistance and nostalgia, at the furthest

remove from the materiality of actual history. If mourning is called a "chamber d'éternel deuil où vibrant de vieux râles," then this pathos of terror states in fact the desired consciousness of eternity and of temporal harmony as voice and as song. True "mourning" is less deluded. The most it can do is to allow for non-comprehension and enumerate non-anthropomorphic, non-elegiac, non-celebratory, non-lyrical, non-poetic, that is to say, prosaic, or, better, *historical* modes of language power.[18]

The italicized word "historical" no doubt would strike many as un–de Manian, but I hope now it should be somewhat clear, given how de Man conceives of the literary text, that the word should come as no surprise.

I do not mean to suggest that de Man has somehow surreptitiously answered everyone's possible concerns about history and historicity, but I would contend that the dismissal of de Man on the grounds of his thinking being anti- or nonhistorical has been altogether too precipitous and largely off the mark. At the risk of appealing to ex post facto proof of the historical power and claims of de Manian reading, I would simply invoke some of the numerous examples of close reading of texts, events, and textual events partially enabled by de Man's thinking. I think of the work of Gayatri Chakravorty Spivak in any number of domains, especially on the postcolonial; of Samuel Weber on technology and the media; of Tom Keenan on human rights (and the media); Cathy Caruth on trauma; Shoshana Felman on testimony and the holocaust; Lee Edelman on queer textuality; Deborah Esch on the AIDS pandemic; or Marc Redfield on terrorism and war. Perhaps not all of this work would have received de Man's blessing, though I suspect he would have admired it all. While none of it can be reduced to being "de Manian" (though that, as reductions go, would say a lot), it has been partly enabled by his thinking, and the profession at large would do well to work through this body of post–de Manian thinking and acting and one of its sources, as we still continue to come to terms with the untimely thinking and writing of Paul de Man.

Discontinuous Shifts: History Reading History

Andrzej Warminski

Surely one of the most valuable "legacies of Paul de Man" is the genuinely critical conception of history he draws out of the texts of the romantics. As is well known, romantic literature was, for de Man, a privileged locus for asking the question of history (in particular, the question of *our* history). Indeed, one could say that de Man's thinking of history—in fact, what he in his last essays calls "material history" or "the materiality of actual history" (and what no doubt constitutes one of the most valuable and enduring legacies he has bequeathed to us)—gets produced by his reflection on, and reading of, the romantics. But to say this may seem a bit odd, for de Man's own verdict on this work sounds rather like the confession of a failure, in particular the failure to arrive at a "historical definition" of romanticism. Looking back with some misgivings upon the essays collected in *The Rhetoric of Romanticism*—for him a "somewhat melancholy spectacle" in that it offers "such massive evidence of the failure to make the various individual readings coalesce"—de Man writes that these readings seem always to "start again from scratch and that their conclusions fail to add up to anything."[1] He continues: "If some secret principle of summation is at work here, I do not feel qualified to articulate it and, as far as the general question of romanticism is concerned, I must leave the task of its historical definition to others. I have myself taken refuge in more theoretical inquiries into the problems of figural language."[2] De Man makes the same gesture in the opening sentences of the preface to *Allegories of Reading*, and this time formulates the "failure" explicitly as a "shift" *from* history *to* reading (and thus to a "rhetoric of reading"): "*Allegories of Reading* started out as a historical study and ended up as a theory of reading. I began to read Rousseau seriously in preparation for a historical reflection on Romanticism and found myself unable to progress beyond local difficulties of interpretation. In trying to cope with this, I had to shift from historical definition to the problematics of reading."[3] That this shift is once again a move from historical definition to the problems of figural language, that is, to *rhetoric*, is clear enough in the following sentences of the preface and their account of a "rhetoric of reading" where "rhetoric is a disruptive intertwining of trope and persuasion." So: de Man's own account of his work on the romantics and romanticism would seem to indicate, if anything, a turn *away from* history and *to* the theoretical problematics of reading, rhetoric, and figural language. Nevertheless, it might be prudent not to take de Man's own remarks about his alleged "failure" too literally. It might be better to take a page from de Man's own book, as it were, and actually *read* what it is that happens, what takes place, in this alleged "shift"—and its necessity ("I had to shift")—from history to reading and rhetoric. If we do so, it turns out that this shift is in fact already (always already) a shift *past* the rhetoric of reading and *to* ... history, indeed, to the material history of de Man's last essays. Ironically (and *un*dialectically) enough, the "failed" attempt at a historical definition of romanticism turns into a certain "success" for de Man's thinking of history.

The mechanism and the necessity of de Man's apparent shift from historical definition to the problematics of reading and rhetoric are best legible in his 1967 Gauss lectures, *Romanticism and Contemporary Criticism* (and *not* so much in the essays on Rousseau collected in *Allegories of Reading*, in which the shift has, in a sense, already been completed), in particular the lecture on Heidegger's interpretation of Hölderlin ("Patterns of Temporality in Hölderlin's 'Wie wenn am Feiertage'") and the lecture on Wordsworth (and on Geoffrey Hartman's interpretation of Wordsworth in his 1964 *Wordsworth's Poetry*) called "Time and History in Wordsworth." The latter is particularly helpful for understanding the shift because it consists of two "layers"—an original "preshift" lecture written in 1967 and some "postshift" passages interpolated into the lecture around 1972 that reformulate the lecture's thematic concerns (death, time, and history) in explicitly rhetorical terms. Nevertheless, the actual push toward rhetorical terms and rhetorical reading occurs already in the lecture on Heidegger's interpretation of Hölderlin's "Wie wenn am Feiertage," and it occurs on account of the lack of other terms and the failure of any other reading to do justice to Hölderlin's text. In short, the turn to rhetoric occurs on account of the lack in *Heidegger's* terms and *Heidegger's* failure to think the "temporality of poetic form," as de Man puts it, when he comes to interpret Hölderlin's poetry. How so?

De Man begins his critical reading of Heidegger in a hopeful vein: Heidegger's "ontological understanding of Hölderlin's key concepts as they are seen to operate within the limits of particular poems" is a promising development that could lead to a "reorientation of literary interpretation toward an ontological understanding."[4] Such an understanding is promising because it "does allow, in principle, for the combination of a sense of form (or of totality) with an awareness that poetic language appears as the correlative of a constitutive consciousness, that it results from the activity of an autonomous subject. Neither American formalist criticism nor European phenomenological criticism has been able to give a satisfactory account of this synthesis: the former had to give up the concept of a constitutive subject, the latter that of a constituted form" (57). De Man's statement of the advantage of such an ontological orientation is pithy, as it calls to mind his critiques of the American New Criticism, its misunderstanding of the concept of intention, and its consequent reification of poetic form, and his critiques of a phenomenological criticism like that of the Geneva School, which ignores questions of form and, in a sense, simply does not read.[5] Now Heidegger, de Man's argument continues, seems particularly qualified to undertake "this renewal of critical method" even though literary interpretation was not his own academic field. Although *Sein und Zeit* nowhere deals with literature, except for some passing references, "it does contain insights that can give a more concrete direction to an ontological interpretation of texts" (57). De Man's statement of these insights amounts to an extremely compact summary of *Sein und Zeit*. Because it contains in germ everything to come in de Man—including the impetus for the shift from history to reading—it is worth quoting in full:

> *Sein und Zeit*, indeed, stresses not only the privileged, determining importance of language as the main entity by means of which we determine our way of being in the world, but specifies that it is not the instrumental but the interpretative use of language that characterizes human existence, as distinct from the existence of natural entities. And this interpretative language possesses a structure that can be made explicit. This structure is in

essence temporal—a particular way of structuring the three dimensions of
time that is constitutive for all acts of consciousness. The main task of any
ontology thus becomes the description of this temporal structurization,
which will necessarily be a phenomenology of temporality (since it is the
description of consciousness) as well as a phenomenology of language
(since the manner in which temporality exists for our consciousness is
through the mediation of language). One understands that, as the "purest"
form of interpretative language, the one least contaminated by empirical
instrumentality and reification, poetic language is a privileged place from
which to start such a description. And conversely, one sees that an approach
to poetic language that would, by a description of its temporal structure,
bring out its interpretative intent, would come closest to the essence of this
language, closest to accounting for what Heidegger calls "das Wesen der
Dichtung." We could thus legitimately expect from the Heideggerian
premises a clarifying analysis of poetic temporality, as it is seen to act within
the poetic form. (57–58)

Although the terms de Man uses to summarize Heidegger may be a bit
too phenomenological, too *Hegelian* phenomenological (e.g., "consciousness"), his account is precise and rigorous. And in its very precision and
rigor it presents Heidegger's fundamental ontology with a redoubtable
task: namely, to be not only a "phenomenology of temporality"—something Heidegger manages quite well, thank you—but also a "phenomenology of language." This latter half of the task is more difficult and has far-reaching consequences because it necessarily entails, sooner or later, some
account of "the *manner* [my emphasis] in which temporality exists for our
consciousness," and that "manner," that is, the way that language "mediates" consciousness and temporality, may include factors and functions of
language irreducible to a hermeneutics of self-understanding, no matter
how fundamental the ontology it bases itself on: in short, that "manner"
may include the rhetorical dimension of language. Although de Man does
not yet put it that way, one could already say that the reason Heidegger's
interpretations of Hölderlin's poetry are so disappointing—indeed, so
downright *wrong*, according to de Man—is on account of his inability to
read the *manner* (i.e., ultimately the *rhetoric*) in which temporality exists
for the "consciousness" of Hölderlin's poetic language.

In any event, ironically (but, as always, rigorously and consistently)
enough, the result is that the great thinker of temporality cannot think,
cannot read, the temporality of the poetic form of Hölderlin's poem. In
his interpretation of "Wie wenn am Feiertage," Heidegger's misreading
consists of his flattening out, levelling, the temporal articulations and ten-

sions of the poem in the service of an apocalyptic pattern. De Man summarizes: "By its gradual widening out from particular physical nature to history, to the gods, and finally to being itself, the poem dramatizes a process of all-encompassing totalization that stretches from the beginning to the end of the text. The progression takes place without discontinuity and moves in one single direction, toward the full disclosure of being. The pattern is apocalyptic, a temporal movement that culminates in a transcendence of time" (64). The poet, in Heidegger's interpretation, is "someone who stands in the presence of being in the past (when he is waiting for the disclosure), in the present (when it takes place in the heroic acts of history), and the future (when, like the countryman caring for his land, the concern of his work will maintain, for others, a mediate form of contact with being)" (65). In short, Hölderlin would be an apocalyptic poet, "an eschatological figure, the precursor who, during a period of temporary alienation from being (*Seinsvergessenheit*), announces the end of this barren time and prepares a renewal" (65).

Now, according to de Man, this interpretation of Hölderlin as an apocalyptic poet is wrong in general and, in the particular case of Heidegger's interpretation of "Wie wenn am Feiertage," it is wrong in specific ways for specific reasons. It is wrong in general because Hölderlin, rather than being an apocalyptic poet, is precisely he who warns *against* the danger of believing that the poet can accomplish the kind of proximity to being Heidegger sees in the poem. Indeed, the poem instead "cautions against the belief that the kind of enthusiasm that animates a heroic act is identical with the predominant mood of a poetic consciousness" (67). But more important than the erroneous results of Heidegger's interpretation is the specific *way* in which Heidegger manages to get things so wrong in his resolute misreading of "Wie wenn am Feiertage" in terms of an apocalyptic pattern. Heidegger is able to flatten out the temporal tensions of Hölderlin's poem in two ways. First, Heidegger ignores and treats as unproblematic a certain "ambiguity of metaphorical reference" (62) in the poem's opening simile that makes it impossible to decide whether "they," the poets, are like the countryman who goes out to look at his field *after* the lightning storm or whether they are like the trees that stand exposed *during* the storm and get blasted by the lightning. The ambiguity is important because its temporal tension is what gets unfolded in the rest of the poem—indeed, it is what constitutes the temporality of this poem's poetic form. And it gets unfolded in terms of the triadic tonal pattern of Hölderlin's theory of the alternation of tones (*Wechsel der Töne*), as the poem modulates from the "naive" tone of its opening scene, to the "heroic" tone of the heroic acts of history it describes later, to end in the reflective, meditative tonality that Hölderlin calls "ideal." Heidegger cannot read the alternating tones of Hölderlin's hymn because he ignores the poem's Pindaric triadic structure and simply cuts off the fragmentary lines that would have constituted the strophes of the poem's end—that is, makes the poem "whole" by truncating it. So: by glossing over the ambiguity of metaphorical reference in the poem's opening simile and by ignoring the poem's tonal structure and truncating its ending, Heidegger completely disregards its poetic form. And since its poetic form is the temporal structure of the poem's self-understanding, disregarding it means also disregarding the poem's temporal structure. Again, it is a case of Heidegger—*the* thinker of temporality—not being "Heideggerian" enough! The consequences for Heidegger are clear: in short, there is a flaw in Heidegger's method, as de Man puts it, "that leads to a misinterpretation of Hölderlin as an apocalyptic poet, when Hölderlin's main theme is precisely the nonapocalyptic structure of poetic temporality" (71). This flaw, de Man concludes vigorously, is "the substitution of ontological for what could well be called formal dimensions of language. The ontologization of literary interpretation, which seemed so promising in the Heidegger of *Sein und Zeit*, does not mean that literature can be read, so to speak, from the standpoint of being, or from that of a poet who is said to act as a direct spokesman for being. The standpoint can only be that of a consciousness that is ontologically (and not empirically) oriented but that nevertheless remains a consciousness, rooted in the language of a subject and not in being" (71).

But if the results for Heidegger's "method" of his having substituted "ontological for what could well be called formal dimensions of language" are clear, the results for de Man's own developing "method" are more complicated because they are double. On the one hand, what de Man ends up with is a still more thoroughgoing "ontologization" of language and of poetic form than Heidegger's. The main difference would be that whereas for Heidegger the poem's temporal movement takes place "without discontinuity" and moves "in one single direction"—again, according to an apocalyptic pattern whose temporal movement culminates in a transcendence of time—for de Man the poem's temporal structure is one in which "beginning and end come together within the tension of the radical discontinuity that seemed to keep them apart" (70). In connecting the beginning of the poem with its end, the radically discontinuous temporality of the poem's poetic form nevertheless remains a principle of totalization. Indeed, de Man goes so far as to call it a "hermeneutic circularity" (71) and to deposit its discontinuous temporality in the structure of being itself.

"The principle of totalization is indeed ontological," he writes, "in that it has to be sought in the discontinuous structure of being itself" (72). So, on the one hand, in his ability to read the discontinuous temporality of Hölderlin's poem—and in his depositing of this discontinuity in the discontinuous structure of being itself—de Man would seem to be more "Heideggerian" than Heidegger. On the other hand, the conclusions of de Man's reading of Heidegger nevertheless go in an entirely different direction and prohibit such a "super-Heideggerian" ontologization of poetic form. Indeed, what can de Man mean by charging Heidegger with having substituted "ontological for what could well be called formal dimensions of language"—and by saying that the poetic consciousness is rooted in the language of a subject and *not* in being—and then going on to deposit the discontinuous temporality of poetic form in the discontinuous structure of being itself? The tension—in fact, a certain discontinuity—between "ontological and what could well be called formal dimensions of language," between a poetic consciousness rooted in being and a poetic consciousness rooted in "the language of a subject," is legible throughout de Man's attempt at an ending for his essay. For what de Man has come up with in his more-Heideggerian-than-Heidegger, thoroughgoing ontologization of language and poetic form are "formal structures"—the reversals and discontinuities of which they are capable—that work according to laws different from those of "the structure of being itself." That these "formal" structures are specifically linguistic, indeed already *rhetorical*, structures is evident, as de Man tries out various names for the "discontinuous element" that constitutes the temporal structure of Hölderlin's poetic form. Adorno's "parataxis" is one possibility, which (parataxis) is linked by Auerbach to what he calls a "figural style." Hölderlin's own term for this discontinuous element is "the caesura referred to in the commentaries on the Oedipus tragedies, which marks a reversal of tone as well as a reversal of time and in which the end reestablishes with the beginning a contact which it seemed to have lost" (72). De Man's ending needs to introduce these explicitly rhetorical terms—parataxis, caesura, figural style, and others—because the discontinuous temporality his reading of Hölderlin has disclosed is one whose reversals can no longer be accounted for in ontological terms. That de Man's reading of Hölderlin has pushed Heidegger's fundamental ontological terms to their breaking point is especially legible in an almost stuttering formulation de Man uses in trying to distinguish the totalizing yet discontinuous temporality proper to Hölderlin's poetry from an organic unity (like that of Schelling's philosophy of identity) and from a purely dialectical one (like that of Hegel): "Nor is it purely dialectical, in the Hegelian sense," writes de Man, "for time itself, which remains unproblematically forward-directed in Hegel, here becomes itself a discontinuous element of a structure that consists of a series of temporal reversals" (72). The tortuousness of the formulation becomes apparent if we try to paraphrase it: if *time* itself becomes *itself* a discontinuous element of a structure that consists of a series of temporal reversals, then time becomes a discontinuous element of a structure that consists of a series of discontinuous reversals that will never allow us to say how time itself could ever become, or be, itself! In short, de Man's reading of the temporality of poetic form proper to Hölderlin's poetic language has disclosed a discontinuous temporality and structures of reversal and substitution that cannot be accounted for in the terms of Heidegger's fundamental ontology—or even in the rhetorical terms of Adorno and Auerbach insofar as these are still compatible with their fundamentally hermeneutic orientation.

The tension or discontinuity in the double ending of "Patterns of Temporality" comes to full fruition in "Time and History in Wordsworth," de Man's veritably "Hölderlinian" reading of Wordsworth. In fact, one could say that the double ending of "Patterns" produces the two layers of "Time and History." De Man's readings of "The Boy of Winander" and the Duddon sonnet can be called Hölderlinian because they consist of a certain "application" of Hölderlin's "caesura" for an understanding of the reversals and substitutions that lie at the basis of both poems and that de Man, in a sense, "re-reverses." In the case of "The Boy of Winander," the poem substitutes the death of a third person (the Boy) in the past for the death of the first person ("I") that lies in the future. "Wordsworth is thus anticipating a future event as if it existed in the past. Seeming to be remembering, to be moving to a past, he is in fact anticipating a future. The objectification of the past self, as that of a consciousness that unwittingly experiences an anticipation of its own death, allows him to reflect on an event that is, in fact, unimaginable" (81). In the case of the Duddon sonnet, the poem substitutes one temporality—a movement that goes from nature to history—for another, more authentic, temporality—a movement that goes from nature to the dissolution of self and the loss of the name. In doing so it reverses middle and end (of the poem) and makes it seem as though the derived, secondary temporality (in shorthand, empirical "history") could *contain* the more original, authentic temporality of dissolution, mutability, and ceaseless deathward progressing, when, in fact, it is the other way around: the authentic temporality (one clearly based on Heidegger's analytic of *Dasein* and the finitude proper to it on account of its being fundamentally a being-unto-death) *contains* "history." In other words, both poems perform a reversal and a substitution that makes the impossible—reflecting on one's own death, history-as-progress overcoming mutability—possible. But already in the first, thematic layer of the lecture, de Man recognizes that the impossibility is made possible only thanks to a certain sleight-of-hand that, already, is clearly a linguistic, indeed rhetorical, sleight-of-hand. In "The Boy of Winander," conquering time, the surmise that would allow one to reflect on one's own death is possible only as a "fiction" that "since it is a fiction . . . can only exist in the form of a language" (82). That this language is necessarily a figural language is legible in de Man's formulations of how it is that this "fiction" can allow one to look back upon, as it were, one's own death: "The poem is, in a curious sense, autobiographical, but it is the autobiography of someone who no longer lives written by someone who is speaking, in a sense, from beyond the grave" (81) and "it is the epitaph written by the poet for himself, from a perspective that stems, so to speak, from beyond the grave" (82). It is clear that speaking or writing from beyond the grave is "possible" only thanks to the rhetorical shifts of "in a sense" and "so to speak." Although in the first-layer reading of the Duddon sonnet the rhetorical shift is not as marked, the fact that the substitution and reversal—of history and temporality, of the poem's end and middle—are in fact a rhetorical structure is, in a sense, still more explicit, since its reversal and substitution of container and contained, *enveloppant* and *enveloppé*, amounts to the very definition of a particular trope, namely metonymy. Indeed, it is no doubt the rhetorical shifts and rhetorical structures of his own language that push de Man to perform a self-reading that forces the thematic readings of "The Boy of Winander" and the Duddon sonnet to turn into readings "properly speaking"—that is, rhetorical readings in explicitly rhetorical terms—in the second layer of the lecture. In "The Boy of Winander," the substitution of a first-person subject by a third-person subject, the "Boy" for "I," is now said to be based on a "metaphorical substitution," just as in the Duddon sonnet the reversal of "history" (contained) and authentic temporality (container) is said to be based on a "metonymic figure." But this passage, this shift, from a thematic reading and its terms (death, finitude, history, temporality, and mutability) to a rhetorical reading and its terms (metaphor, metonymy, metalepsis) should not mislead us into thinking that the thematic has simply been left behind, surpassed, as though de Man had succeeded in reducing temporality and history to a question of merely tropological substitutions and transformations. If we read his second-layer interpolations with any attention at all, we cannot make this mistake. For it is clear that in "The Boy of Winander" the "metaphorical substitution" of the first by a third person, of a living self by a dead self, "is, of all substitutions, the one that is, thematically speaking, a radical impossibility: between the living and the dead self, no analogical resemblance or memory allows for any substitution whatever" (201). In fact, as de Man goes on to say, "the metaphor is not a metaphor since it has no proper meaning, no *sens propre*" (201) and could more properly be called "the metonymic reversal of past and present that rhetoricians call metalepsis" (201). But even to call this reversal a metaleptic metonymy would be claiming to know more than one can about the radically discontinuous nature of this reversal. Just as there can be no analogical resemblance between the living self and the dead self, so there can be no contiguity or juxtaposition, no "next-to-ness," between a dead past and a living present that would allow for a "properly" metonymic substitution. In time the dead self may be "near to" the living self—just as the child, according to a sentence de Man crossed out, "being the father of man . . . stands *closer* [my emphasis] to death than we do" (202)—but this proximity has no empirical, phenomenal, thematic existence, and therefore the "metonymy" is a blind, mutilated metonymy—in fact, more of a catachresis than a metonymy. In short, the "metaphorical substitution" is in fact a self-undoing trope that self-deconstructs into the catachrestic imposition of a name. "The poem does not reflect on death," de Man concludes, "but on the rhetorical *power* [my emphasis] of language that can make it seem as if we could anticipate the unimaginable" (201).

In the same way, the metonymic reversal of the Duddon sonnet, because it "is a rhetorical device that does not correspond to a thematic, literal reality" (202), also gets undone in what de Man is already able to call (after his reading of *Of Grammatology*) a "de-constructive rhetoricity" (203). This is thematically, literally, understandable: if the poem performs a reversal and a substitution of contained (empirical history) for container (the authentic temporality of dissolution), then its rhetorical device amounts to the equivalent of saying that the water or the wine can contain the glass. And if the "glass" here is the authentic temporality of ceaseless dissolution, then even "properly speaking," as it were, it was not much of a "container" to begin with! In any event, the point is not to dwell on the mechanics and the details of this "de-constructive rhetoricity"—we can read all about it in *Allegories of Reading* and elsewhere—but rather to insist that already here, at the very pivot of de Man's "shift" to rhetoric and rhetorical terms, the move *to* rhetoric is already a move *past* rhetoric, to an awareness that tropological textual models will also not be able to account for what actually happens, what actually occurs, in and as the texts of Hölderlin and of Wordsworth. And, as we can read in *Aesthetic Ideology*, what actually occurs—that which is truly, materially, historical—is not the textual linguistic model into which the tropological model empties out and passes (for example, of language as performative) but rather the passage, the passing, itself: a break, gap, or discontinuity like the one that cleaves Kant's Third Critique (between the tropological "model" of the mathematical sublime and the performative "model" of the dynamic sublime).[6] In "Kant and Schiller," de Man does not hesitate to say directly what thinking history as event, as occurrence, ultimately means, and he does it in terms particularly resonant for our discussions of "Patterns of Temporality" and "Time and History": "History is therefore not a temporal notion, it has nothing to do with temporality, but it is the emergence of a language of power out of a language of cognition."[7] In saying starkly that history is not a temporal notion, that it has nothing to do with temporality, de Man draws out the full implications of his 1967 readings of Hölderlin and Wordsworth and their disclosure of reversals and substitutions whose discontinuity is not temporal but rhetorical. What this also means is that de Man's alleged "shift" from history to reading and rhetoric—*as* one that is also a shift *past* rhetoric—is in fact a shift *from* history *to* history, a shift whose own discontinuous "passage" or passing "from" and "to" is what happens, what actually occurs, materially and historically, in and *as* "de Man."[8]

* * *

For a coda it would be good to offer an example or an emblem of de Man's discontinuous shift from history to history. If we are right to call this shift material and historical, then what would be the equivalent of this moment "in the order of language"?[9] In de Man's last essays, this equivalent always turns out to be what he calls the materiality of inscription, the prosaic materiality of the letter. And the double-layered lecture on Wordsworth in fact provides a material inscription that renders the discontinuous shift—from history to reading, from rhetoric past rhetoric, from history to history—vividly legible. In passing from his reading of the "complex temporal structurizations" in "The Boy of Winander" to the Duddon sonnet in order to take one further step in an understanding of "his [Wordsworth's] temporality," de Man, in the second layer of the lecture, simply inscribes the word "rhetorical" above the word "temporal" (in "temporal structurizations") and the phrase "rhetorical movement" above the phrase "his temporality" (202), in both cases without crossing out what he had originally written in the first version of the lecture. However legible this shift or passage "from" temporal "to" rhetorical may be, it also remains singularly unreadable and incomprehensible in terms of any narrative that would tell stories of "from" and "to," "before" and "after," or even "first layer" and "second layer." What happens happens "between" the two inscriptions and, as such (that is, as something that happens), is genuinely, materially, historical—de Man's history and our legacy.

III.
Institutions of Pedagogy

"At the Far End of This Ongoing Enterprise . . ."

Sara Guyer

> The master is destined, then, not to smooth out the field of relations but to upset it, not to facilitate the paths of knowledge, but above all to render them not only more difficult, but truly impracticable.
>
> —MAURICE BLANCHOT, *The Infinite Conversation*

Paul de Man's brief introduction to the 1979 issue of *Studies in Romanticism* devoted to "The Rhetoric of Romanticism" might be understood as his most explicit treatment of the question of legacy. The introduction is a strange and often contradictory text in which de Man provides an historico-fictional account of his own "generation"—understood synchronically *and* diachronically, both as a group of individuals *and* as an act of genesis. At the same time, by editing a volume of work by his students, de Man here introduces a new "generation," one that already in 1979 is understood to be his issue.

De Man initially intended this special issue on "The Rhetoric of Romanticism"—which shares its title (in advance) with his own posthumous collection of essays on Wordsworth, Kleist, Shelley, Hölderlin, and Yeats—to be an outlet for work emerging from his 1977–78 NEH seminar. Yet, the issue's final table of contents includes only two essays—Stephen J. Spector's "Thomas de Quincey: Self-Effacing Autobiographer" and William Ray's "Suspended in the Mirror: Language and the Self in Kleist's 'Über das Marionettentheater'"—that originated in the NEH seminar.[1] The remaining essays—by Cynthia Chase, Barbara Johnson, Timothy Bahti, and E. S. Burt—grew out of de Man's regular graduate courses at Yale. In some obvious sense, then, de Man's introduction responds to the question of the relation between the work introduced and his instruction of its authors. In other words, the essay responds to the implicit question—phrased in the idiom of Kleist's "Marionettentheater," the occasion of de Man's most sustained discussion of pedagogy—of whether or not, in pulling a few strings to gather these essays and get them published, he also "pulls their strings."[2] At the same time, the introduction raises other questions—about the relation between scholarship and pedagogy more generally, about literary history, inheritance, and freedom. Do de Man's voice and authority alone give these essays their motion and their force? Are these essays, like an automaton, moved by an external generator, rather than by their own spontaneous or automotive energy? And, if so, is this external generation also the source of their extraordinary elegance? Is it the authoritative teacher himself who allows for their "light touch," that is, for the very grace that he will claim distinguishes their work from his and exposes the "awkward" and "lopsided" efforts of his generation, the very grace that he goes so far as to suggest also means his death?[3] What is de Man's relation to his students' virtuosic displays of rigorous reading, that is, what is his relation to this putative legacy? What is his relation to it *as* legacy, and what, if anything, does de Man's introduction have to do with this legacy's production—or for that matter, its foreclosure?

From the outset, David Wagenknecht, the editor of *Studies in Romanticism*, questioned the essays' capacity to stand on their own. On April 10, 1978, upon having read Timothy Bahti's "Figures of Interpretation, The Interpretation of Figures: A Reading of Wordsworth's 'Dream of the Arab,'" Wagenknecht wrote to de Man to say that the essay could appear in the journal only if de Man took responsibility for it and for the issue as a whole:

> Was it Huckleberry Finn who said of *Pilgrim's Progress* the statement was interesting but tough? In my case I have to confess the toughness finally overcame my interest: my erasures in the margins reflect an original annoyance which I found more difficult to overcome than to erase. The style, which simultaneously maximizes fussiness and vagueness—verbal operatives tend to be so abstract that almost anything can be related to, equilibrated with, adequated to anything else—caused me at last to mourn for Wordsworth. But I made up my mind to be more manly, to overcome prejudice, and to press on. Having done so, my attitude remained fundamentally the same.[4]

Wagenknecht confesses here that despite his best efforts at engagement, Bahti's essay left his energies "overcome." Yet beyond his distress with

Bahti's style, the difficulty seems due, at least in part, to a notion of reading as a dialectical practice. Admittedly paralyzed by the essay—and its relentless verbal chain—Wagenknecht calls upon his "manliness" to help him overcome his paralysis. But to no avail. The failed labor of attempted negation (the negation of a predisposition and weakness) leads only to further frustration, and to the recovery of a dialectical practice not in reading, but in mourning. Yet, rather than lament the apparent failure of dialectical reading, Wagenknecht instead laments the loss of the subject of Bahti's essay: Wordsworth himself. For unlike Wordsworth's poetry, which puts the reader "in the company of flesh and blood," Bahti's essay threatens the reader's manliness and power of mind. Rather than fulfill the romantic project through its contemporary criticism, Bahti's essay, in Wagenknecht's account, leaves its subject dead.[5]

In aligning the possibility of reading Bahti's essay with the necessary admission of Wordsworth's death, Wagenknecht implies that Bahti is responsible for this death—or at least for its actualization. Moreover, Bahti is held responsible not only for sacrificing Wordsworth (a dead man), but for a sacrificial "assault" against "the man Harold Bloom has called 'the most defiantly Wordsworthian of modern critics,'" Geoffrey Hartman, Bahti's living teacher, who has most rigorously accounted for the dialectical, which is also to say, *sacrificial*, structure (*Akedah*) at work in Wordsworth's poetry.[6] It is Bahti's treatment of Hartman that leads Wagenknecht to consider the essay in the context of a scene of instruction—and raises the question, which will recur in de Man's introduction, of the violence that constitutes that scene.

In his letter to de Man, Wagenknecht praises—and also dismisses—Bahti's piece as "a brilliant graduate student 'performance.'" He calls "honest" the fact that Bahti devotes the first nine pages of his essay to Hartman, but then admits that "the consequent impression that this is a very parochial, intra-Yale performance is very *unpleasant*."[7] He explains that "it is sometimes difficult for the reader less obsessed with [Hartman's] texts than the author is even to derive a clear sense of what Hartman was talking about," and he proceeds to worry that an essay caught between "obsequiousness" and "assault" against one's teacher "begins to suggest *unpleasant* things about life in graduate school."[8] Indeed, for Wagenknecht the "unpleasant" performance—this performance of unpleasantness—seems to be an Oedipal performance, a performance, he insists, that has less to do with the reading of texts than it does with the relations between students and their teachers. Yet, if it is the essay's violent "obsession" with Hartman that Wagenknecht finds suspect, and if it is Bahti's claim that mediation in Hartman is not a work of mind but of trope that he finds interesting, if not completely convincing, he responds *not* by holding Bahti finally accountable for the assault, but rather by inviting de Man to account for the work of his student and to become the issue's guest editor.[9] In other words, Wagenknecht agrees to publish Bahti's paper in *Studies in Romanticism* only on the condition that de Man will accept responsibility for its violence. As he tells de Man: "I think that there should be clear indication that the editorial choices were finally yours, that the *issue* in the last analysis, has a guest editor. To me—should this be your inclination—this would all the more imply the necessity of an introductory preface by yourself discussing the seminar and explaining *your* attitude toward the various essays."[10]

After several months of silence, de Man finally responds to Wagenknecht: he submits a table of contents for the volume, defends the publication record of the various authors (Johnson, Chase, and Burt), and agrees "to write a brief introduction about the methodological *assumptions* that stand behind the choice and the treatment of the topic."[11] As an essay on the scene of instruction as well as a key moment in it, this introduction—like Wagenknecht's letter—bears witness to the essays' violence. It registers not only the carefully articulated assault against Hartman or the thoroughgoing disarticulation of Wordsworth, but also the violence disguised by loyalty and discipleship.

At first glance, the introduction seems a complex, even defensive, response to Wagenknecht's double request. In it, de Man offers both an argument about the event of these papers (one that resonates with his introduction to Carol Jacobs's *The Dissimulating Harmony*) and an exemplary autobiographical account of the study of romanticism from the 1950s to the 1970s. The introduction opens with an apparent rejoinder to Wagenknecht's dismissal of Bahti's essay as the acting out of an infantile drama performed in a local idiom. De Man begins:

> The essays collected in this issue come as close as one can come, in this country, to the format of what is referred to, in Germany, as an *Arbeitsgruppe*, an ongoing seminar oriented towards open research rather than directed by a single authoritative voice. Some of the papers originated in a year-long seminar sponsored by the National Endowment for the Humanities conducted at Yale during the year of 1977–78. It was entitled "The Rhetoric of Romanticism," and the title seemed suitable enough to be retained in this expanded version of the initial group. The additional papers were often written in connection with various graduate seminars, but it

would be an injustice to see in them only the products of a single "school" or orthodoxy, thus reducing their challenge to mere anecdote.[12]

The essay initially describes not the success of these works, but their limitation: "They come as close as one can come" to an *Arbeitsgruppe*—to this truly democratic possibility of free inquiry and "open research," a possibility that remains for de Man paradoxically unrealizable within an American (rather than a German) institution—and in a seminar organized through and funded by the National Endowment for the Humanities.[13] Yet whether this lingering authoritarianism is attributed to national or personal identity, it indicates that the essays, whose freedom and innovation he will recognize, also fail to constitute a truly open seminar. Rather, gathered under the title of the NEH seminar that de Man organized, they appear to be indistinguishable, at least in name, from the work of Paul de Man.[14] However, as soon as he states the essays' limited freedom, he also claims that it would be an "injustice" to understand them as "products of a single 'school' or orthodoxy" or as the echo of "a single authoritative voice." It would be an injustice, because this attribution would coincide with the avoidance of reading—the substitution of a history of the works' formation for the difficulty of their reading, and thus the assumption that one knows in advance what these essays say and do. Indeed the substitution not only would be fallacious and limited, but it also would rely upon an inaccurate and ideological version of history. More than merely claim this, de Man claims that the papers demonstrate it—which is precisely the reason why they must be read. While they may have emerged in connection with a seminar that did not fully eschew the authoritative voice of its teacher, these essays—despite their ambitions—ultimately break with, rather than sustain, his lesson. They inherit not a methodology (despite de Man's acknowledgment of the remarkable closeness of their reading), but a textual object (the romantic canon).[15]

Nevertheless, the event of these essays proves to be indissociable from the question of de Man's legacy, and this becomes especially clear when de Man registers the opposition between their event and a historical (or psychoanalytic) account of their emergence:

> Both in what these papers have in common and in what sets them apart from each other, something is happening that is by no means confined to the idiosyncrasies of a particular configuration of individuals. It has to do with a larger question which can be considered as a generational process—although this perspective, too, is misleading; one can as little wish away the innovative and subversive impact of these essays by attributing it to Oedipal

struggles as to academic provincialism. The validity of a genetic or generation model for literary history is one of the received ideas that the papers leave behind. It is a matter of chance that the contributors turn out to belong by and large to the same generation, thus providing at least a conveniently fallacious point of view from which to attempt a collective characterization of their achievement.[16]

To insist that "something is happening" here is to acknowledge this work as an event. In happening and so in differing (indeed in differing from itself)—despite every aim and intention—this work involves a rupture, one that de Man cautions against domesticating through a fiction of generation (whether construed as a narrative of cultural mythology or intellectual history).

De Man sets out by looking beyond the obvious "idiosyncrasies of a particular configuration of individuals" (e.g., the *generation* of students who studied literature with de Man at Yale in the 70s) in order to recognize their evocation of "a larger question which can be considered as a generational process." If "generational process" names the event of this work—generation understood as temporalization rather than as a stable configuration of individuals—it does so as a question, the question of generation itself, and the mark of generation's constitutive incompletion ("Is something happening?" And further: "If something is happening, what is happening?" "Is nothing happening?" "Can nothing happen?").[17] Generation—as a generational process—comes to signal a truly temporal predicament: it signals the impossibility of a birth just the same as a death.[18]

And so, it is in calling for a reading of this work rather than for an account of its emergence that Paul de Man's own life—his history, his survival, his legacy—comes into question. While de Man claims that the pieces themselves invalidate a historical account that would position them as his legacy or as a Yale production, it is not only their abandonment of "a genetic or generational model for literary history" that challenges the charge of "academic provincialism." Rather, what de Man calls their "innovative and subversive impact" already indicates the displacement of and difference from their teacher that their mimesis enacts. While refusing to read the essays merely as following in his own footsteps, and refusing to reduce their violence and their impact to an "Oedipal struggle," de Man nevertheless frames their event as a betrayal. In stating the radicality of the work collected here, de Man disavows responsibility for it (a gesture that is indistinguishably generous and dismissive), and goes so far as to call the work that would appear to be the legacy of his seminar the instrument of his own death.[19] To say (as de Man does) that "something is happening," and that what is happening "is by no means confined to a configuration of individuals," is also to say that what occurs is a generation that exceeds generation.[20] There is a generational process beyond generational models, a generation that withholds grasping and maintains itself in the form of a question of generation, a generation as the event of generation, that is also, and indistinguishably, a generation without generation. Yet, the claim to this work's importance and its event beyond narrative, the claim to its generation beyond generation, remains a devastating accusation.

In order to elaborate his accusation, de Man offers a lengthy (and surprising) parable of *his* generation and its emergence. The narrative of his generation—a generation whose attachment to the study of romanticism he attributes to guilt, anxiety, and failure—calls into question the enduring status of genetic models of literary history supposedly eschewed by *this* generation.[21] Like the narratives that would account for the emergence of the work introduced here, this narrative only can be a literary example. However, it opens in an uncomfortably avuncular tone and a clichéd or mechanical idiom. De Man recalls that when "people of my generation" began to write, *they* suffered. *They* actually had to confront romanticism as a question of history; *they* actually had to face up to betraying their elders:

> People of my generation (now roughly speaking in their fifties) interested in Romanticism began to write in the shadow of historical works that considerably refined on preconceived notions of periodization but without losing the sense of historical order to which these works owed their learning and aesthetic discrimination. The answer to such questions as: What is (or was) Romanticism and did such a thing ever occur? became increasingly difficult to formulate but the question itself continued to make sense.[22]

De Man's description of his generation suggests the extent to which he is its *product*, not despite, but because of, his abandonment of history for theory. The fact that, as he explains in its preface, *The Rhetoric of Romanticism*—his only book on romanticism—is a fragmentary collection of essays "establish[ed]" by his editor, rather than the historical reflection that he intended *Allegories of Reading* to be, indicates not the abandonment of history for theory, but the resistance of history and the so-called historical outlook.[23] This claim, on the one hand, relies upon the fiction of generation that domesticates the difficulty of reading and situates de Man's failure to effect a historical study as a historical or generational effect. But it also recognizes de Man's enduring attachment to romanticism (despite his "more theoretical inquiries into the problems of figural language") as sustaining "the sense of historical order" that dominated the work of his elders.[24] De Man explains that although his teachers' work led many of the more *faithful* students of *his* generation to "start out with the ambition to write their own syntheses or *summae* of Romanticism" (on the model of their teachers), no volumes of this sort ever were produced. "For all I know," de Man continues, "some may still be about to succeed, yet the fact remains, looking back over the production of the last twenty years, that no general works on Romanticism were produced comparable in scope and serenity to those of the previous decades. More important perhaps, the reasons for this apparent failure became themselves part of the problem."[25] *Allegories of Reading*, which appeared in the same year as the *Studies in Romanticism* issue, is one of these failures. In its preface, de Man explicitly aligns his work—his desire for and failure to execute a historical project, the interruption of narrative by reading, and the remainder of history as a canon—with that of his generation:

> *Allegories of Reading* started out as a historical study and ended up as a theory of reading. I began to read Rousseau seriously in preparation for a historical reflection on Romanticism and found myself unable to progress beyond local difficulties of interpretation. In trying to cope with this, I had to shift from historical definition to the problematics of reading. *This shift, which is typical of my generation*, is of more interest in its results than in its causes. It could, in principle, lead to a rhetoric of reading reaching beyond the canonical principles of literary history which still serve, in this book, as the starting point of their own displacement.[26]

If *Allegories of Reading* is not a "historical reflection on Romanticism," if it is the failure or the interruption of that work, this may not be exactly the same as saying—as de Man will say—that it is "in no way a book about romanticism or its heritage."[27] At stake in this description is the very interruption of cognitive and performative language that de Man explains will emerge in the book itself—that is, the interruption of the difference between a book *about* romanticism (cognitive, constative) and a book *of* romanticism and its disruption (performative).[28] In each of these cases, the introductory apparatus raises the question of history and generation—the question of romanticism and the trace of its enduring order on the work of Paul de Man. And, in the introduction to the volume of *Studies in Romanticism* (as, in the foreword to the second edition of *Blindness and Insight*), the constellation of historical and generational questions emerges as inextricable from guilt and betrayal.[29]

Scholars of his generation, de Man claims, discovered the impossibility of carrying out the work of *their* teachers. Their desire to write "syntheses or *summae* of Romanticism" left them—like the Jena romantics in Blanchot's description—without work in the unproductive discovery "that the writing of literary history and the reading of literary texts are not easily compatible." They discovered that "distinctions become so diversified that no discussion of generations, movements, or specific experiences of consciousness is any longer conceivable."[30] Yet, de Man's account of this discovery, the discovery of his generation, emerges in a narrative of his generation, the very mode that here is rendered impossible.

At the zero-point of his reflection—the point at which the inconceivability of a discussion "of generations, movements, or specific experiences of consciousness" (in the case of romanticism) occurs within a narrative "of generations, movements [and] specific experiences of consciousness," de Man not only describes, but also dramatizes, the double bind of his generation. Indeed, the account he provides is indissociable from the predicament whose discovery he reports in it. In other words, his narrative is an example of the trap that it presents. It is an allegory, or what de Man calls his "invention," the invention of a "generation," and at the same time it indicates invention's impossibility:

> Caught between historical norms inherited from their predecessors and their own reading practice, the "generation" which, for the sake of convenience, I have chosen to invent (and to which no individual will exactly correspond), finds itself in an awkward double bind, reflected in writings that are lopsided in their emphasis on textual analysis as compared to the paucity of the historical results to which they continue to aspire. The tension produced frustrating books and teachers, skillful at best in the techniques of reading but inconclusive with regard to the problems which the readings discover. That so many remained selectively interested in Romanticism is clear evidence of a persistent commitment to the historical outlook that keeps haunting the textual analyses as their bad conscience.[31]

In the first place, "invention" refers to the fictional status of the generation that de Man calls his own. It is not what invented or produced him, but what he "has chosen to invent." If, as he explains, this means that the genealogical narrative he provides apparently has no referent, his identification of its fictional—indeed fabular—status does not lead him to abandon this narrative. Rather, as soon as he dismisses its referential function and claims this narrative a fable or invention rather than an accurate report, he also produces the referent that he denies. He renders—in a manner that runs counter to expectation—an account of "the study of romanticism [that] would also necessarily be a reflection on our own historical predicament, our history."[32] De Man's fable refers at the very instant that it invents. His dismissal of the referential truth of his narrative occurs within a narrative that recovers his dismissal of this "generation" as an invention without referent. It generates the referent whose existence it denies. This specular (self-referential or autobiographical) structure neutralizes the interruptive power of de Man's claim to invention and allows the narrative of generation to proceed without incident. With his generation, de Man demonstrates what Jacques Derrida has called the "invention of the impossible," the impossible invention, as the only invention possible.[33]

In fact the failure (and fable) of this invention—it is a failure because what he claims has no referent is reflected in the text that claims to invent it—can be understood to constitute the "double bind" in which, de Man goes on to explain, "this generation" finds itself. This "generation" emerges as an invention not because it lacks a referent (it is self-referential: the text enacts the predicament de Man reports), but because it is the (textual) emergence of the unprecedented (which may be another way of calculating fiction). Here, invention is a coming into existence rather than (as, and despite) the denial of existence. Invention (the invention of a generation, of this generation) cannot maintain the purity of its fictional or fabular status.[34]

What matters here is that the double bind—the "tension"—that de Man renders and describes (i.e., that he invents) bears upon teaching.[35] For de Man, this double bind, far from being a reflection of the "authoritative voice" that he describes at the essay's opening, instead "produced frustrating books and teachers"—books and teachers that remain "inconclusive" rather than synthetic or summative, books and teachers trapped in the double imperative of close textual analysis and a conflicted yet "persistent commitment to the historical outlook."[36] While these scholars over and again discover their own duplicity, they also fail to resolve it. Moreover, their enduring attachment to "the historical outlook" becomes, in de Man's account, inextricable from an attachment to romanticism, and romanticism ("our contemporary") becomes inextricable from the double bind of reading and history. In this respect, the "methodological assumptions that stand behind the choice and the treatment of the topic," and which de Man promised his introduction would explain, are not deliberate or rational. Rather, and this is especially true in the case of de Man's (invented) generation, they are the effect of an irrepressible—indeed, "haunting"—inheritance. Romanticism is the sign of their "bad conscience."[37]

De Man's admission of romanticism as his generation's bad conscience sounds the moral of his tale, and it shapes the lesson that he offers to (and performs upon) his students. Whereas romanticism signals the unexamined residue of "genetic or monumental patterns of history," which is to say, whereas the enduring study of romanticism in the work of his intellectual contemporaries indicates the enduring romanticism of their work and thus the bad conscience of close reading, de Man explains, in conclusion, that what is striking about the papers that he presents here is their apparent *freedom* from the disarticulations of neurotic attachment.[38] He explains:

> The papers in this issue of *Studies in Romanticism* are remarkably free from this feeling of guilt. They perform their parricide with such a light touch that the target may not even realize what has hit him. The scope is certainly not wider, far from it. . . . The selective corpus grows smaller and smaller and gets stuck, at times on a sentence, a title, or a word. But far from causing anxiety, the authors wrest their best findings from these obsessive interrogations. Techniques of rhetorical, as opposed to thematic, analysis are used with remarkable ease, with none of the nervousness which, speaking for myself, makes me feel as if someone were looking over my shoulder whenever thematic assertions can be shown to be subservient to rhetorical overdeterminations.[39]

Here de Man accounts for two forms of guilt: on the one hand, the guilt suffered by those who remain attached to "the historical outlook," the guilt indicated by a continued attachment to the romantic canon, despite the insistence of rhetorical reading; and, on the other hand, the guilt that attends a rhetorical reading in which "thematic assertions can be shown to be subservient to rhetorical overdeterminations." These two sources of bad conscience are directly at odds: one is ordered by attachment; the other by disavowal. It becomes clear that the competing tensions they produce would amount to frustration and paralysis. Yet, de Man attributes *this* work's graceful, rather than awkward, paralysis to an *absence* of guilt, a clear conscience that would follow from faithfully executing the de Manian lesson; and he attributes its ease and elegance, but above all its "best findings," to this capacity to remain stuck without any anxiety whatsoever. While *his* anxiety follows from breaking both too much and too little from his teachers, the essays here, unlike the "frustrating books" of his generation, emerge as the work of good students, burdened neither by the inheritance of history nor the pressure on their inheritance that their readings produce. Nevertheless, the paralysis that marks the papers in this issue—coupled with the serenity of their limited scope—signals, as de Man implies, not the fulfillment, but the betrayal of a legacy.[40] The assumption of a legacy masks the extent to which this legacy is betrayed. This is what de Man's introduction shows. Indeed, de Man implies that the confidence with which the essays carry out his project of reading and pedagogy relies upon genealogy rather than close reading.

De Man criticizes this work in words *almost* indistinguishable from praise—for example, "The selective corpus grows smaller and smaller and gets stuck, at times on a sentence, a title, or a word. But far from causing anxiety, the authors wrest their best findings from these obsessive interrogations," or "Tropes are taken apart with such casual elegance that the exegeses can traverse the entire field of tropological reversals and displacements with a virtuosity that borders on parody"—and implies that close reading in these essays stands only as a moment within a dialectic of understanding, rather than its disruption.[41] Thus, de Man points out that the "clarity," calmness, and "casual elegance" of these papers takes the place of the "awkwardness," "lopsidedness," and "inconclusiveness" that marked the work of his generation. He implies that, rather than being merely an improvement upon the work of their predecessors in the resolution of that work's difficulties, these papers continue to discover difficulties. But, because these authors recognize difficulty as the ambition of reading, their work continues on, nonplussed. In this absence of a struggle with the difficulty that they uncover, the papers fail to emulate the models "held up to them." However, their failure also is the outcome of their responsiveness to their models and teachers. Close reading does not leave these papers struggling, but, to the contrary, as de Man says of Carol Jacobs's book, in them "the demonstration of . . . necessary incoherence becomes a remarkably sound narrative."[42] De Man suggests that this absence of anxiety should lead to a second anxiety, the anxiety that he admits to feeling "whenever thematic assertions can be shown to be subservient to rhetorical determinations."[43] Yet, the absence of this anxiety—the authors' apparent freedom from the fear that this work could be an assault against their teachers, rather than a respectful elaboration of their teachers' work—is evidence of disruption rather than continuity. This disruption, however, seems for the most part never to interfere with the essays' grace or narrative coherence.

Indeed, the "ease, lightness, and grace" that de Man recognizes in these papers makes them appear like the "unfortunates" who dance with prosthetic limbs in Kleist's "On the Marionette Theater."[44] It is perhaps no accident that these papers seem to move with the fabricated legs that replace the awkward and unsightly immobility of amputation with "a virtuosity that borders on parody."[45] Yet de Man reminds us that this grace, as if the effect of prosthesis, signals only more broken legs—and in the French of Jacques Derrida rather than the English of Kleist's artists or these young authors—broken legs that are a broken legacy. The essays' incomparable grace, like the prosthesis that substitutes for a mutilation, hides the break of which it also is the evidence.

The violence hidden and demonstrated by elegance is what de Man calls a "parricide," and this death (a broken leg, broken legacy) seems de Man's own. Blind to the violence that they wield against their elders, unaware that their essays are not the fulfillment of an inheritance but rather its disarticulation, and unburdened by the guilt or anxiety that their unconscious violence *should* command, these authors, de Man admits, keep their victim—a victim of their grace—oblivious as well. Like all death, this parricide remains an event foreign to consciousness and without proper witness. It remains unknown and unfelt by those good students whose imagined loyalty hides, but does not protect them from, acts of violence against their teacher; it also remains unknown, indeed unfelt, by the accusatory dead man who "may not even realize what has hit him."

Whereas de Man invented a generation in order to account for his relation to his teachers, he invents a parricide in order to account for his legacy. When de Man figures these essays' violence as a parricide (not just murder, but murder of the father), he also admits the filiation (through violence and its prosthetic remedy) that he reads them to shatter. Moreover, while de Man establishes that the parricide will have taken place and recognizes that it is the actual, deadly outcome of this issue, he also acknowledges that it cannot take place, and remains what cannot be known to have taken place. As soon as he accuses these essays of violence, he also reestablishes (in a negative mode) their inheritance, their legacy as a broken legacy, and their generation. Thus, the accusation and recognition of a parricide becomes inseparable from the recovery of filiation, the production of guilt, and the insistence of an inheritance. By bearing witness to his own death, to a murder of which only he—and hence no one—is aware, de Man replaces the death he invents with the impossibility of dying.

It is in this sense that de Man appears like the Wordsworth he so famously describes. Proleptically speaking from beyond the grave and thus failing to recognize or know death in the moment when he claims to have suffered it, de Man presents the work of his students by accounting not for his influence on or generation of it (his "pulling the strings"), but for his own death through it. And yet, if in not killing the father, one kills him; if in killing the father one only fails to kill him—and leaves him living on beyond the death that never will have "hit" him—this is also because the murderous progeny (like Oedipus, blind in enterprise, and like the dancing amputees, graceful beyond measure) remain just as oblivious as he.

This recovery of filiation in parricide has its parallel in the more general return of history and ethics that de Man recognizes in these essays (and claims is their "most interesting occurrence of all").[46] As he describes:

> At their strongest moments, the shape of another critical discourse begins to emerge, and the critical analysis of the figuration gropes for its own context. This is often accomplished by ways of psychoanalytical schemes of understanding that are no longer ego-centered or by performative modes disencumbered of ethical considerations. The most interesting occurrence of all is that, at the far end of this ongoing enterprise, the question of history and of ethics can be seen to reemerge though in an entirely different manner, no longer predicated, as it was for us, on identifiable evasions of complexities. It would be preposterous to try to state succinctly, in paraphrase, how this reemergence of history at the far side of rhetoric can be said to take place, as if one could spare oneself the labor of reading accomplished in these papers. They deserve at least to have some of their own rigor applied to themselves. Such a reading would reveal that the question of Romanticism can no longer be asked in the manner to which we are still accustomed and that, by extension, the genetic and monumental patterns that are commonly associated with Romanticism have lost much of their authority. The new problems that appear as a consequence are not less redoubtable, but it is exhilarating to capture the moment at which the emancipation is taking place.[47]

For all the grace of these essays, their power coincides with their lost footing, and emerges when the analysis no longer "traverse[s] the entire field of tropological reversals and displacements," but, stumbling, "gropes for its own context." What the papers demonstrate, then—indeed what a reading of them would "reveal"—is *not* "what a poetics of literature and a theory of reading could be on the far side of literary history," but, rather, that the "reemergence of history at the far side of rhetoric" is the disruption of grace *and* the recovery of de Man's legacy.[48] It is the return of history as interruption. And while rhetorical reading may abandon "the question of romanticism" (and not just the answers to this question, as de Man claims was the case for his generation), and while it may displace the "authority" of "genetic and monumental patterns"—of genealogy and generation, and of romanticism as their sign—this abandonment, de Man argues, also recovers the question of history and ethics. It returns the question with which this issue is concerned: the question of legacy and of the possibility of the de Manian legacy.

The return of the question of history and of ethics "at the far side of rhetoric" emerges as both the failure and the invention of this generation. In guiltlessly performing their disarticulation of texts, these essays display the negativity and the violence of romanticism. However, this negativity—and its difficulty—conceals the negativity and the difficulty that remain unmanageable. This residual negativity—the blind underside of elegance—coincides with the return of the question of history and ethics beyond rhetorical reading, and, in this respect, proves indissociable from the question of the relation of these works (and these authors) to the work and the teaching of Paul de Man. Rather than having *overcome* the anxiety that attends simultaneously violating and suffering an inheritance, rather than leaving behind, once and for all, the question of history and ethics, as the trauma and the sign of an inheritance (and of the unavoidable violence of pedagogy), these essays are numb both to the violence they endure and the violence they enact. Yet, they are not, de Man suggests, as free as they seem. As they apparently follow his lesson, they murder the paternal figure. In this sense, the question of legacy remains. It remains as the anxiety that this introduction cannot fail to produce and the filiation that it does not fail to recover. "The legacies of Paul de Man" coincide with the irremissibility of ethics and history, which, in de Man's own account, means his death and the impossibility of his dying. Yet the consciousness of this impossibility also remains another form of blindness, which is to say that this legacy bears the structure of an event.

* * *

It would have been tempting here, and at many points in this reading, to have considered de Man's essay—its association of history and guilt, its account of his generation's relation to the previous generation, and its apparent understanding of a certain approach to literary study—as being symptomatic of de Man's personal bad conscience, and to read this introduction as a rare but undeniable instance in which de Man, in accounting for his guilty attachment to romanticism *and* his guilty demonstrations of aesthetic ideology, might also be accounting for his own historical and political guilt. Read in this manner, the introduction then would seem to provide evidence—often sought—of the bearing of de Man's wartime journalism upon his later literary criticism, and, by extension, on the work of his students. Depending upon the reader's desire or stance, this text would allow either for the indictment of literary theory and rhetorical reading (ahistorical, violent, etc.) *or* the discovery of a covert admission of guilt, one that would somehow allow us to understand de Man, not as having deceived his students, but as having forced them—already in 1979—to confront their teacher's bad conscience. Both of these scenarios would rely upon the same information and upon equally fallacious, which is to say, ideological, perspectives. It is tempting to read de Man's allegory of invention (which, as Derrida suggests, indicates an allegory of allegory and which we could extend to incorporate, to reflect and invent, the entire de Manian corpus) as a discreet allegory of *his* history. However, the non-possibility of appropriating this allegory to redeem or to kill (once again) Paul de Man also indicates the other side of this legacy: the endurance of the question of history and ethics beyond guilt and confession and their possible allegories, and beyond death—including the impossible murder that de Man here witnesses, the death by cancer that he suffers four years later, and the public outrage, confusion, and awkwardness that accompanies the discovery of his wartime journalism.

Professing Literature: John Guillory's Misreading of Paul de Man

Marc Redfield

Both the title and the overall rationale of this essay—a review-essay focused on a book, John Guillory's *Cultural Capital*, that appeared a good decade ago—merit a word of explanation. My subtitle, chosen for clarity, will have its pugnacious thrust slightly (if only slightly) muffled over the following pages, which thematize "misreading" not, or not only or primarily, as a mode of contingent error, but rather as a condition of all interpretation, especially forceful interpretation that ends up making a difference. Whether Guillory's book has genuinely made a difference—whether it may truly be said to constitute an event in an intellectual or institutional history that we find ourselves required to confront as our own—is no easy question; but *Cultural Capital* has certainly proved an important and influential book in the ordinary sense we give to such adjectives, to the point of becoming a canonical text within ongoing debates about the "canon" and the role of literary study at the university. With regard to the reception of de Man, its contribution is harder to characterize. Guillory's book has no doubt lent succor to those who have sought, and still seek, to consign de Manian theory to the outer darkness—as an outdated, erroneous, ultimately superficial (if always strangely threatening) "discourse of mastery"[1]—but apart from that negative role, *Cultural Capital* cannot be said to have left much of a mark on de Man studies, within which, barring a few exceptions, it has received little notice. Though Guillory's book has at times been critically reviewed, neither the accuracy of his account of de Man nor the filiations linking that account to his book's broader claims about literary canon-formation have been carefully examined.[2] And that is a pity: not just because serious mischaracterizations (and there are quite a number in Guillory's representation of de Manian theory) ought to be corrected, but because Guillory's interesting and influential broader theses about the literary institution arguably cannot be fully evaluated unless one accounts for his long, passionate chapter on de Man—the longest and by a good degree the most polemical chapter in the book. Furthermore, at the risk of sounding more paradoxical than one ought in an introductory paragraph, I want to suggest that Guillory's polemic manages to be at one and the same time unoriginal and brilliant. His de Man chapter speaks with a voice that, without exaggeration or malice, we may characterize as an *institutional* voice, yet what it says allows us, against its own intention and manifest argument, to read the degree to which de Man was a theorist of institutionalization and institution ("of" here to be taken as governing both a subjective and an objective genitive). Guillory's genius cannot be teased apart from his conventionality, nor (as the de Manian figure has it) his insight from his blindness. Put less metaphorically: his chapter on de Man is driven by his book's aesthetic-ideological agenda, and offers us a finely symptomatic example of aesthetic-institutional resistance to theory. Yet this chapter's violent reduction of de Manian theory to sociological symptom releases a truth that more timid or technically "accurate" accounts of de Man are likely to overlook.

I

Let me first do my best to recall Guillory's overall project, and draw attention to some of his argument's vectors and fault-lines. *Cultural Capital*'s fundamental proposition, which has deservedly claimed readers' attention and has known considerable influence, is twofold: first, that the "canon debate" has been "misconceived from the start," and second, that this misconceived debate symptomatically registers a "crisis in literary study."[3] The debate is misconceived insofar as it reduces the problem of canon-formation to a question of representation, falsely rendering symbolic representation in the canon analogous to political representation in a polity. Guillory rightly observes that "those members of social minorities who enter the university do not 'represent' the social groups to which they belong in the same way in which minority legislators can be said to represent their constituencies. The sense in which a social group is 'represented' by an author or text is more tenuous still" (p. 7). Such a representational notion of the canon makes the canon into "a hypothetical *image* of social diversity," and this politics of the image renders invisible the institution within which canon-formation actually occurs—"the school, and the institutional forms of syllabus and curriculum" (p. vii). Furthermore, it hampers a critical inquiry into the category of "literature" itself. Literature is a form of "cultural capital," and it is the school's function to regulate and distribute cultural capital, and thereby reproduce the inequities of the social order.[4] Here we encounter, as the book's main thesis, the "crisis in literary study":

> The overarching project of the present study is an inquiry into just this crisis, one which attempts to explain why the category of literature has come to seem institutionally dysfunctional, a circumstance which I will relate to the emergence of a technically trained "New Class" or "professional-managerial class." To put this thesis in its briefest form, the category of "literature" names the cultural capital of the old bourgeoisie, a form of capital increasingly marginal to the social function of the present educational system. (p. x)

Over five meaty chapters, Guillory seeks to make good this claim. Chapter 1 directly engages the canon debate and its shortcomings, emphasizing that the university, though certainly a place of "real power," is "not in itself a *representative* place" (p. 37). Mimetic notions of the canon as mirror of social diversity efface the true sociological role of the school by way of a quasi-sociological conception of literature as "expressive of the author's *experience*. . . . The author returns in the critique of the canon, not as the genius, but as the representative of a social identity" (p. 10). What the school is really about is access to literacy (literacy in the sense of "the systematic regulation of reading and writing," which is "a question of the distribution of cultural goods rather than the representation of cultural images" [p. 18]); it is in this way that the school reproduces unequal social relations. And what literature is really about is "linguistic differentiation as a social fact" (p. 64): literature is the production of a (socially) marked language within (written forms of) the vernacular. The decline of literary study in the schools in the late twentieth century responds to the fact that language marked "literary" no longer functions as "the privileged agent of ideological subjection."[5]

Chapters 2–4 make up a section Guillory calls "Case Studies," and compose a broadly historical trajectory with three focal points: the historical origins of the modern category of "literature"; the mid-twentieth-century professionalization of literary criticism as close reading; and the late-twentieth-century doubling of the literary by the "theory" canon. Chapter 2 reads Gray's *Elegy* as an exemplary "'translation' of classical literacy into an anthology of quotable vernacular phrases" (p. x), and thus as a vehicle for examining the emergence of "literature": under this lens, literature is revealed as "the discursive category devised to accommodate vernacular works in the schools" (p. 87). Chapter 3 focuses on the New Critical revision of the canon: according to Guillory, the technique of close reading produced for the university a new kind of literary language, and thus a new articulation of social distinction, by way of which "the cultural capital of literature" could be "set against a 'mass culture' which at once reveres and neglects the monuments of High Culture" (p. xii). Chapter 4, "Literature after Theory," is the de Man chapter we shall be engaging at length below: here Guillory argues that the "moment of theory is determined ... by a certain defunctioning of the literary curriculum, a crisis in the market value of its cultural capital occasioned by the emergence of a professional-managerial class which no longer requires the (primarily literary) cultural capital of the old bourgeoisie" (p. xii); symptoms of this crisis include the appearance of an alternative "canon" of theoretical texts, and above all—for reasons to be discussed—the exemplary phenomenon of de Manian rhetorical reading.

The final chapter, "The Discourse of Value: From Adam Smith to Barbara Herrnstein Smith," is set off from the rest of the book under the heading "Part Three: Aesthetics." In this section Guillory takes issue with pragmatists such as Herrnstein Smith who negate aesthetic specificity by discovering "use value" in art, thereby conflating economic and aesthetic "value." In response, Guillory offers a history of the notion of value: he rehearses the origins of modern aesthetics in eighteenth-century political economy, arguing that Bourdieu's description of "the emergence of aesthetic production as a 'relatively autonomous' field of cultural activity in the eighteenth century" offers a less reductive and more historically attentive approach to aesthetics than the neopragmatist reduction. He concludes with a ringing endorsement of aesthetic judgment, and with a utopian "thought experiment" that imagines the "transformation of cultural capital into pure 'symbolic distinction'" (p. 339):

> Even were such an [idealized] educational system no longer to regulate access to cultural capital in the grotesquely unequal way it presently does, cultural producers would still compete to have their products read, studied,

looked at, heard, lived in, sung, worn, and would still accumulate cultural capital in the form of "prestige" or fame. But social distinctions reinstated on such an aesthetic basis would have to be expressed in social relations as distinctions in "life-style," in other words as a vast enlargement of the field of aesthetic judgment. . . . The point is not to make judgment disappear but to reform the conditions of its practice. If there is no way out of the game of culture, then, even when cultural capital is the only kind of capital, there may be another kind of game, with less dire consequences for the losers, an *aesthetic* game. Socializing the means of production and consumption would be the condition of an aestheticism unbound, not its overcoming. But of course, this is only a thought experiment. (pp. 339–40)

Cultural Capital thus concludes with a fantasy about an Aesthetic State: a manifesto hedged about with signs of fictionality (as, we may note, such aesthetic-political manifestos traditionally are, from Friedrich Schiller onward: "But does such a State of Aesthetic Semblance really exist? . . . [A]s a realized fact, we are likely to find it, like the pure Church and the pure Republic, only in some few chosen circles.").[6]

This brief recapitulation of a rich book allows, I hope, enough of a sense of its overall project to allow us to understand Guillory's need to confront the work of Paul de Man. *Cultural Capital* offers food for thought and debate along many lines, and I obviously cannot do justice here to many of the questions that any reader of this text will need to ponder; on the plus side, though, the text's main threads tend to intertwine, and a good pull on one of them can help us gauge the strength of the ensemble. For the most part we shall have to leave aside questions such as whether Guillory's hypothesis of a new "professional-managerial class" is as useful as he makes it out to be, whether literature has become straightforwardly outdated cultural capital, how one might best characterize the contemporary relations between "high culture" and "mass culture," and so on. It would be hard to disagree with the claim that literature, like the rest of the humanities, has lost ground within the "school" (to employ Guillory's favored synecdoche)—and by no means just in the United States; at present writing, many of the traditional Western humanistic disciplines are being barely taught in certain areas of the globe. But if one is going to analyze this phenomenon adequately in terms of First-World circulations of "cultural capital," one will arguably have to develop a more fluid model than Guillory provides: a model capable of registering, on the one hand, increasing concentrations of cultural capital in elite Western institutions (above all in the schools, where a smattering of literary study remains part of the process by which these institutions mark their product *as* elite), and, on the other hand, ongoing, highly mediated diffusions of this very same cultural capital in the "mass cultural" mode of allusion, citation, simplification, parody, revision, and so on, a phenomenon sporadically observable throughout the entertainment industry, from Disney products to cult television programs such as *The Simpsons*.[7] I leave these interesting questions aside, but to some extent, as we shall see, they tangle into the questions that obsessed de Man, and which we shall pursue more steadily here—the mode of being of language and literature, the illusions and coercions of aesthetic discourse.

These are questions that for the most part Guillory seeks to flatten, with a force that betrays a deep anxiety, into answers. Language must reduce to a sociological phenomenon, literature to a socially marked linguistic practice. This imperative leaves visible scars in Guillory's fine-grained analyses. If I had world enough and time to track even this (seemingly) circumscribed theme of language and literature throughout the whole of *Cultural Capital*, I would spend more than a passing sentence wondering whether Guillory is justified in ascribing the popularity of Gray's poetry to an "unexpected transparency of the poem's language at the historical moment of its composition" (p. 124), or, conversely, crediting the prominence of Eliot and Stevens in the New Critical canon to, in the last analysis, the university's need for a marked language. That literature functions as a socially marked linguistic practice is obvious; the question is whether that is *all* literature, or language, is or does. Guillory manages uncertainty on this front in two ways: by chastising and expelling as "de Man" the possibility of language's irreducibility to communication and meaning, and by granting the category of the aesthetic its traditional role of absorbing or muffling (within the totality of the human) this same irreducibility—this *technicity*, as we shall be calling it, of language. Let me say a word more about that latter gesture before going on to examine the former.

Eliot and Stevens are difficult poets, perhaps, but *on en a lu d'autres*: there remains the question of what draws us to *these* difficult poets, and here, as my citations from *Cultural Capital*'s fifth chapter indicate, Guillory's sociological reduction develops a complicating fold. Though, on the one hand, "there is no realm of pure aesthetic experience," on the other hand, there is a *"specificity* of aesthetic experience that is not contingent upon its 'purity'" (p. 336). Pressuring this difference between the pure and the specific, Peggy Kamuf, in her 1995 review of *Cultural Capital* in *Diacritics*, wonders whether a certain purity is not being smuggled through the sociological customs-house, and whether Guillory's utopic conclusion does not ultimately promise "a relation that is no-relation . . . a specificity and a property of 'the cultural' without the admixture or contamination of 'the economic'"—or, to recall Guillory's master terms, "a reclaimed, integral humanities curriculum able to pose itself independently of the technical training required by the 'professional-managerial class.'"[8] Kamuf argues—and I shall be confirming her diagnosis in the pages that follow—that Guillory's project is driven by a desire to "'reimagine' the object of literary study as nontechnical, autonomous, or specifically aesthetic" (Kamuf, p. 69), and that in consequence he needs to expel the specter of deconstruction, which has "from the beginning and without reprieve, insisted on the *technicity* of the idea, on the iterability of the proper, on the divisibility of any mark of division, and therefore on the necessary contamination of any posed or supposed purity" (Kamuf, p. 64). This is also to say that Guillory reifies the notion of institution: "there is no institution of any sort," as Kamuf notes, "and first of all no institution of meaningful signs, and of course no 'literature' and no 'cultural,' without iterability. Or rather, iterability is what we mean by institution" (Kamuf, p. 65). Guillory's reification of institutionality yields as its precipitate both an incorrect characterization of deconstruction as "simply *against* institutions as such" (Kamuf, p. 67), and, ironically, a return of the very antiinstitutional, antitechnical idealism that he had objectified and expelled as "deconstruction" within his own discourse. What is really being cast out, as Kamuf notes, is the technicity of the sign and the necessary precontamination of the proper; what is lost, in consequence, is the deconstructive insight that "the possibility of a certain exteriority, or difference" constitutes "institutional space" (Kamuf, p. 67). And what is being affirmed, strongly if necessarily ambivalently, is the presence-to-itself of humanity as a social totality. Guillory's neo-Schillerian dream of the Aesthetic State is, from this perspective, his most overt and daring negation of the possibility that, as Ernesto Laclau and Chantal Mouffe put it, the social "has no essence" and is neither "totally possible" nor "totally impossible."[9] The ancient aesthetic dream of harmony, of a consensus-in-the-lastinstance that is the horizon of the human itself, animates and subtends the dream of an "aestheticism unbound." It must be added that, to the student of aesthetic discourse, Guillory's turn in his final chapter does not come as a surprise. As I have argued at length elsewhere, aesthetics, in its main line of development—from Schiller and Matthew Arnold to the earlytwentieth-century New Humanists, the mid-twentieth-century New Critics, and the pragmatists and New Historicists of the present day—has never been about an escape from the social world. Disinterestedness (here rendered as a "specificity of aesthetic discourse" that slides away from a "purity of aesthetic experience") is always a detour on the way to what I have termed here "sociological reduction," but which one may more generally term the "referential horizon of the human."[10] Small wonder, then, that *Cultural Capital*, as an eloquent and intelligent text well within the broad Arnoldian tradition, has known such uncomplicated success within the professional bureaucracy it chastises.

We may now turn to Guillory's confrontation with the thought, figure, and legacy of de Man. Kamuf, whose main concern is to dispute Guillory's strategic conflation of "deconstruction" with "de Man," offers little help here; indeed, one gains the impression that she feels it necessary to re-key the discussion to a Derridean idiom if deconstruction is to stand revealed as a thinking of institutionalization.[11] But to ignore Guillory's engagement with de Manian theory is to ignore the heart of his book. Guillory is a powerful writer at all times—allowing oneself to be borne up and along by his rolling, organ-toned prose is one of the regular pleasures of reading him—and in chapter 4 his writing, while losing none of its eloquence, achieves a new level of intensity and aggressivity. We approach here what a phenomenologically minded critic might describe as *Cultural Capital*'s imaginative center and origin: the spur or irritant or trauma around which the text grew.

II

Guillory's chapter on de Man begins with a legible, if perhaps not entirely conscious, effort to account for its own passion, for its first step is to identify de Man as a symptomatic figure, a stand-in for "theory" per se. He suggests (rightly, I think) that, however erroneous it may seem at first glance, the journalistic equation between "theory" and "deconstruction" merits serious consideration as a *symptom*—as does the concomitant association of the name "de Man" with "deconstruction" as "theory":

> The immense symptomatic significance of the *figure* of de Man has been indisputably confirmed by the paroxysm which passed through the entire critical profession in the wake of the revelations concerning de Man's wartime journalism. It would not have been necessary for so many theorists and antitheorists, de Manians and anti–de Manians, to "respond" to these revelations if *theory itself* were not perceived to be implicated in the figure of de Man. The easy condemnation in the media of theory along with de Man only confirmed a symbolic equation already present in the profes-

sional imaginary. A symptomatic reading of the de Manian corpus will elucidate this equation along the axis of imaginary identification: theory-deconstruction-de Man. (pp. 178–79)

Noting that de Man's essay "The Resistance to Theory" offers a (de Manian, theoretical) version of the same "imaginary" sequence of identifications (theory as deconstruction as rhetorical reading), Guillory sets out to characterize de Manian theory as the essence of the symptom, as it were—and as the effect of a sociological cause. The argument pursues a triple movement. In a first move, Guillory reworks and develops the link between de Man and theory by arguing that theory "objectif[ies] the charisma of the master teacher as a methodology" (p. 179). Theory, in other words, "is" the transference—the transfer of the transference from the master onto the master's theory, which is in fact what the master desires. In the second phase of the argument Guillory shifts attention to the theory itself, arguing that "the equation of literature with rhetoric" constitutes an ideology that has as its rationale an institutional defense of literature: "Literary theory as a version of rhetoricism defends literature from its half-perceived and half-acknowledged social marginality" (p. 180). This second phase also involves an argument that characterizes theory's "rhetoricism" as a covertly theme-driven enterprise: rhetorical reading is a "linguistic determinism" driven by a master-theme of "determined indeterminacy" (p. 230). Finally, in a third and finely synthetic move, Guillory argues that deconstruction offers an "imaginary reduction of the social to an instance of the linguistic" (p. 237). Rhetorical reading's "thematic of fate" becomes the "rigor of methodology" (p. 231), which, as the pathos of rigor—the cathexis of boredom itself—functions as an unconscious recapitulation of contemporary "conditions of institutional life" (p. 245). That is, "the adjustment of critical practice to new socioinstitutional conditions of literary pedagogy is registered symptomatically within theory by its tendency to model the intellectual work of the theorist on the new social form of intellectual work, the technobureaucratic labor of the new professional-managerial class" (p. 181). Theory is thus revealed to be a symptom of, and a defense against, the increasing marginality of literary culture, and the increasing bureaucratization of the professoriat. Theory reinvigorates the ideology of professionalism by reasserting charismatic authority in a technobureaucratic context, which is why, Guillory claims, de Man's disciples imagine their master to be "outside" the institution, and teaching a doctrine subversive of the institution. As Guillory summarizes near the end of his chapter, de Manian theory registers at the heart of its terminology the historical moment of the fusion of the university teacher's autonomous "professional activity" with the technobureaucratic organization of intellectual labor. Within the larger discourse of "theory," rhetorical reading has the important symptomatic function of figuring a rapprochement with the institutional conditions of criticism, by acknowledging the loss of intellectual autonomy as a theory of linguistic determinism—at the same time that autonomy is continually reinvested in the figure of the master theorist. But this is an autonomy which exists only on the imaginary *outside* of the institution, as an "anti-institutional" charisma. (p. 259)

It is a brilliant argument, and, in its wide-ranging acquaintance with de Man's texts, an impressively detailed one. For once (one is tempted to say, "finally!") a critic hostile to de Man has had the requisite obsessive energy to read through de Man's work, as well as the talent to displace it forcefully. I know of no comparably impressive attempt to dominate (and thus, in the end, annihilate) de Manian theory. It will thus be well worth the effort to retrace our steps more slowly now, so as to begin the work of evaluating the claims and interpretations making up this argument.

Guillory's account of de Manian charisma and de Manian discipleship, while not entirely unprecedented and ultimately not without its limitations, is in many respects quite powerful.[12] All pedagogy activates transferential relationships, but de Man's ability to inspire love and emulation—an *excess* of transference—is part of the record (which is also to say the legend or phantasmatics) of his reception. The question is what to make of this phenomenon. Guillory's answer has its problems, as we shall see, but his description of the skewed love between disciple and master and of the disciple's transference of the transference onto the theory of the master could hardly be bettered. It is all there: the charisma of the master, whose professed indifference to the disciple's love causes the disciple to work endlessly for the master's ever-withheld recognition; the disciple's transfer of the transference onto the theory that the master embodies, to the point that the disciple imitates the master "at the micro-level of style" (p. 199); the master's investment in this transfer, which allows pedagogy to survive as doctrine; the extra spin put on all these maneuvers by a theory that, even more stringently than psychoanalysis, identifies transference and resistance. (For de Man, we recall, theory, in its very transferability or teachability, *is* its own resistance to itself: resistance inheres both in the movement of theoretical thought from the specificity of a reading to the generality of a conceptual claim, and in the personifying dynamic whereby intersubjective relations come to substitute for linguistic ones. Both master and disciple, according to this account, move within endless loops of resistance.) I remarked earlier that *Cultural Capital* has known little impact in deconstructive circles, but it is of interest that in at least one case a putative de Man "disciple," Thomas Pepper, has testified to the force of this section of Guillory's text, confessing that "it is astonishing for me to see many of the insights it took me years to glean from closer readings of de Man's text presented by Guillory in the thick description of an institutional context." Indeed, Pepper then goes on to displace some aggression onto the fantasized figures of *other* disciples who haven't submitted to Guillory's discipline: "Unfortunately, his work has remained unread by those whose predicament is best described in it."[13] This is the sort of thing de Manians often say about de Man himself ("his work has remained unread," particularly by "those whose predicament is best described in it"); and if for a brief moment Guillory comes to resemble or even replace de Man in Pepper's discourse, one must at the very least credit Guillory's analysis with the power necessary to reimpose a mild version of the very phenomenon it studies and seeks to demystify.

And if power, as that formulation hints, is not necessarily purchasable without loss of knowledge, one has reason to ask whether Guillory's study of the "transference of the transference onto theory" can really claim to have mastered its object of study. There are, as I have said, limits to his approach. Though Guillory notes in passing that transferential effects can happen at a distance, he focuses his account entirely on the seminar, and on the kind of transference that most lends itself to being characterized (which is really to say, denounced) as "discipleship." The graduate student who loves the teacher, and by extension the teacher's texts and the texts the teacher loves—this is the sole paradigm of "influence" here. The result is that Guillory, on the one hand, writes very well (if very aggressively) about a certain kind of student that de Man is famous for producing—the graduate student who imitates the teacher's style, writes again and again about the bits of Rousseau or Wordsworth that de Man himself wrote about, and so on—and, on the other hand, has little or nothing to say about more mediated forms of theory's transmission, or about the wider ripples caused by the impact of de Manian thought.[14] Why Guillory has limited his focus in this way is not hard to apprehend. This is the first installment of a polemic that sets out to reduce the content of de Manian theory to the charisma of its teacher, thereby restricting the reach of this theory to a certain place and time and a highly defined pedagogical context. To adapt one of Guillory's favored turns of phrase, we may say that he thus commits himself to an *imaginary reduction to the seminar* of the pedagogico-scientific institutions in and through which theory is replicated and disseminated. His analysis forecloses the larger context of de Man's reception—and that of "theory" itself; for however much one might agree with Guillory that de Man has phantasmatically embodied theory for the professoriat, theory—even as "deconstruction"—is of course not *simply* equivalent to de Manian rhetorical reading. The considerable and diffuse, if erratic, influence of Jacques Derrida's work on the academy has obviously not travelled primarily by way of the seminar. De Man's association with the seminar is powerful, and deserves scrupulous analysis, but it is in the end an *imaginary* association, and forms part of the phantasmatics of a "de Man effect" that we are, arguably, far from being in a position to dominate and understand.

"No legacy without transference," Derrida proposes;[15] and indeed, Guillory's imaginary reduction of theory's dissemination to the seminar is itself our first and largest clue that his analysis is itself being distorted by the transferential effect it describes. I have characterized the writing in this chapter as passionate, and shall in a moment begin tracking some telling distortions; for the moment let us simply register the more trivial observation that in this chapter citations from de Man salt Guillory's prose with a readiness of reference that many a "disciple" might envy—to the point that a quotation from "Semiology and Rhetoric" is even given the last word, directing and capping the chapter's closing sentence ("One may predict, without resorting to prophecy, that such reconceptualization will become 'the task of literary criticism in the coming years'" [p. 265]).[16] One need not be a critic of particularly deconstructive or psychoanalytic stripe to feel that such strenuous wrestling with a "master," in conjunction with an analysis that gets a good deal of rhetorical mileage out of relegating the master's students to the anonymity of "disciplehood" (a fratricidal fantasy all the more satisfying when one recalls that many of these "disciples" were Guillory's graduate school and junior faculty colleagues at Yale), tends to cast the agonist as, in Guillory's own words, a "disciple who struggles heretically with the master" (a kind of discipleship, he adds, "I will not discuss here") (pp. 198–99). But if Guillory "knows," as we say, his own oedipal predicament, that knowledge is complicated by the negative transferential passion with which he denies knowledge to others—to the other disciples, of course, who in this account are little more than bright-eyed dupes, but above all to the master himself. That is the whole point of this section of the chapter, and the locus of its most startling distortions.

Guillory's project throughout is to roll de Man up backwards, as it were: systematically to reverse the thrust of his texts and thereby render "theory" a symptom—an effect of processes beyond theory's self-knowledge, which is to say beyond the theory *qua* theory. If de Manian theory subordinates the theorist to an impersonal linguistic imperative, Guillory will reverse the poles and discover the theorist in advance of the theory, just as he will eventually discover the institution in advance of the theorist. The charisma-and-discipleship phase of the argument, therefore, as noted above, sets out to reduce theory to the person of Paul de Man. On the one hand—I shall come back to this ambiguity—Guillory's project is not to "disprove the argument of deconstruction" but merely to study the "symptomatology of the de Manian oeuvre" (p. 179); on the other hand, he is seeking to destroy the theoretical claims made by that oeuvre, and it thus becomes all-important to show that the oeuvre, as symptom, is blind. He thus faces the fantastic task of showing that de Man is blind to the transference. Working his way around de Man's claim in "The Resistance to Theory" that "teaching is not primarily an intersubjective relationship between people but a cognitive process in which self and other are only tangentially involved" (*RT*, p. 4), Guillory suggests that de Man "forecloses" the psychoanalytical, adding with a telling abruptness that "if psychoanalytic terms nevertheless pervade [de Man's] essay," this "results from the threatening public prestige of psychoanalysis" (p. 191). It is a sign of weakness to come. The actual argument deserves more attention than I can accord it here (I am willing to inflict a good number of pages on readers, but there are limits)—Guillory is proposing that de Man's notion of the self is phenomenological rather than psychoanalytic, that his transfer of the cognitive function from the self to language shunts aside the properly psychoanalytic notion of the subject, and that his displacement of psychoanalytic terms into rhetorical ones actually works to "preserve the phenomenological self of self-reflection" (p. 194). That argument is, I believe, manifestly wrong (language, in de Man, is not centered in self-reflection: it is torn apart at its origin by the divergence between its performative and cognitive dimensions), but it is at least an argument, and one worth having. But that flashing, bizarre moment of sociologico-personalistic reduction (*public* prestige? of *psychoanalysis*?) registers the extremity of Guillory's need to evacuate de Man's text of self-knowledge. The de Manian blindness to the transference needs to be total, uncontaminated by even glimmers of insight: "What de Man has no patience for at all, not even the patience to name, is the notion of transference" (p. 193). "The one analytic concept which cannot be named within this displaced terminology is transference itself, which orchestrates the severance of affect from agency" (p. 194). "The doctrinal insight into the 'linguistic predicament' needs to be read at every moment as symptomatically blind to the *necessary* relation between theory and discipleship" (p. 207).

The problem Guillory faces is that de Man's texts talk about transference constantly. This is, after all, a theory that sets out to say something about figurative language—and "transference," whatever else it means, irreducibly means figuration: the "movement" of figurative transfer. Out of that linguistic black hole (or *mythologie blanche*) spiral any number of narrative lines in de Man's work that address the kind of phenomena Guillory has in mind. De Manian theory is certainly well equipped to explain such phenomena as the master's charisma, the "transfer of the transference onto theory," and the loving obsessiveness of discipleship. The pseudodialectic of *Allegories of Reading* derives such phenomena from the predicament of reading that theory theorizes: the deconstruction of referential systems of language generates the "deconstructive passion of a subject" as an illusory center of authority (*AR*, p. 199). This master-subject is precisely the revered object of fantasy, the *sujet supposé savoir*, that Guillory has analyzed; he is "as far beyond pleasure and pain as he is beyond good and evil, or, for that matter, beyond strength and weakness. His consciousness is neither happy nor unhappy, nor does he possess any power. He remains, however, a center of authority to the extent that the very destructiveness of his ascetic reading testifies to the validity of his interpretation" (*AR*, pp. 173–74). This is, perhaps, merely a dry moment in an allegory of reading; but elsewhere de Man's allegories undergo vivid narrative embodiment. One thinks of the ephebe in Kleist's *Marionettentheater*, whose gracefulness is "not an end in itself, but a device to impress the teacher": "[W]hat the young man is ashamed of is not his lack of grace but the exposure of his desire for self-recognition. As for the teacher's motives in accepting to enter into these displacements of identity, they are even more suspect than those of the younger person, to the precise extent that sadism is morally and socially more suspect than masochism. Socrates (or, for that matter, Winckelmann) certainly had it coming to him." (*RR*, pp. 278). One might also point to the tricky remarks on institutional and generational succession in the introduction to the special issue of *Studies in Romanticism*, or in the foreword to Carol Jacobs's *The Dissimulating Harmony* (*CW*, pp. 218–23).[17] My object here is not to read and do justice to these various texts, but simply to provide a bit of documentary backing for the observation that de Man understood the "linguistic" as something that affects our lives. (Guillory will later admit this, by way of accusing deconstruction of an "imaginary reduction of the social to an instance of the linguistic" [p. 237].) If for de Man it is possible "that the entire construction of drives, substitutions, repressions, and representations, is the aberrant, metaphorical correlative of the absolute randomness of language" (*AR*, p. 299), this does not mean that we ever leave drives, substitutions, repressions, and representations behind. It is actually hard to think of a critic who is *more* alive to the finer shades of complicity, desire, guilt, ruthlessness, and so on than de Man; whatever else one thinks of his analysis of Rousseau's purloining of the ribbon, it is certainly not a reading easily accused of psychological naiveté.

Guillory's account of de Man and transference culminates in a truly strange attempt to strip de Man's discourse of its self-irony. He quotes de Man's comments on Bakhtin's seductiveness in "Dialogue and Dialogism," which I reproduce here:

> [T]he circulation of more or less clandestine class or seminar notes by initiated disciples or, even more symptomatic, the rumored (and often confirmed) existence of unpublished manuscripts made available only to an enterprising or privileged researcher and which will decisively seal one mode of interpretation at the expense of all rival modes—at least until one of the rivals will, in his turn, discover the real or imaginary counter-manuscript on which to base his counterclaim. What in the context of our topic interests us primarily in this situation is that it is bound to engender a community tied together by the common task of decrypting the repressed message hidden in the public utterance. As the sole retainers of an esoteric knowledge, this community is bound to be small, self-selective, and likely to consider itself a chosen elite. (*RT*, p. 108; cited in Guillory, pp. 206–7)

And here is Guillory's commentary: "De Man's contempt for Bakhtinian discipleship is so completely without irony as to constitute the purest form of negation, a simulacrum of irony." One hardly knows what to do with such a hyperbolic claim; as in the following sentence, in which we are told that de Man is "merely venting a contempt for discipleship as imitation" in this passage (p. 207), one's attention is forced away from the peculiarities of the primary text by those of the secondary one.

III

It is of course not enough to reduce the theory to a person, a charismatic master, since the master's blindness signifies his subordination to forces beyond his control. The critique will have to move on. It is not yet done with him, however—it will never be done with him: the momentum of personification demands that he be credited with a certain knowledge and a range of intentions, generally negative ones, of course, in a scenario such as Guillory's. We have seen Guillory's de Man displacing Freudian terminology because of "the threatening public prestige of psychoanalysis"; later de Man's critique of aesthetic ideology will be said to represent a last-ditch attempt "to preempt the second wave of 'left' reaction to deconstruction" (p. 239). What makes Guillory's book exceptional is that such comments—subsociological in their eagerness to return phenomena to the cunning and fear of an individual—pop up within tenacious, sophisticated arguments far more ambitious in scope than the personifications to which they have recourse. It is this blend of finesse and brutality that we shall need to interpret if we are to develop Guillory's polemic into something closer to a genuine reading of de Man's relation to the pedagogical institution.

The theorist and his theory, as said, will have to yield authority to historical and sociological narrative. Yet for these reductions or substitutions really to be able to occur, the theory will have to be decertified as theory. Such is the ambiguity of symptomatic reading that I noted earlier. Theory must be shown to be *wrong*, for otherwise the critique will lose its traction: theory, after all, can be ahistorical, elitist, taught by a charismatic master, propagated by blind disciples, akin to bureaucratic styles of work, et cetera, and still be truth incarnate. The reduction of the theory to the theorist or to sociological reality remains willful so long as the theory itself remains untouched. The encounter can be delayed but not avoided, and Guillory does his best, in this section of his chapter, to prove theory wrong. His occasional protestations to the contrary ("the indistinction of style and doctrine . . . falls short of invalidating the doctrine's truth" [p. 202]; "it is not my intention to prove that such a reduction [of rhetoric to trope] is not possible, only that it has not been demonstrated" [p. 218]; "I shall not be concerned directly with the validity of [de Man's] reading [of Proust]" [p. 221]) form part of an ongoing rhetorical strategy, which intends to empty de Manian discourse of its authority by insisting on that discourse's symptomatic status. But the epistemological question lurks, and Guillory addresses it as he seeks to reduce rhetorical reading to thematic narrative.

I shall therefore have little to say about the first half of this section of the chapter, in which Guillory offers an interesting and informed account of the history of rhetoric, and of the emergence of the discursive categories of literature in the eighteenth century, and linguistics in the twentieth.

His purpose here is of course to historicize de Man's interest in rhetoric and literature, suggest de Man's unawareness of the historicity of these discourses, and thereby once again insist on the theory/theorist's blindness ("his theorizing of rhetoric elides the historical conditions that produced the category of the literary out of the very obsolescence of poetics and rhetorics in the school system" [p. 214]). Later I shall gloss one error in this section—Guillory's claim that de Man conflates "the referentially disruptive trope with the Saussurian signifier" (p. 211)—and I shall also come back to the question of what the notions of "literature" and "literariness" mean in de Man. But for the moment let us pass to the claim that "the rhetorical terminology in de Man" is "a covert thematic" (p. 221).

It is a crucial claim: ultimately everything hangs on it, and Guillory offers here his most sustained, patient, and careful engagement with a de Manian text. He chooses as his object de Man's reading of Proust in *Allegories of Reading*—a shrewd choice, for it is one of de Man's earliest efforts at "rhetorical reading," and its heavy reliance on a Jakobsonian opposition between metaphor and metonymy offers Guillory opportunities. I shall take the liberty of assuming broad familiarity with de Man's interpretation (which is distributed between chapters 1 and 3 of *Allegories*), though of course it will be necessary to do at least some pacing over this well-trodden ground. Guillory focuses on de Man's reading of Marcel reading—reading in his room. Here is the passage from Proust's *A la recherche*, in de Man's translation:

> I had stretched out on my bed, with a book, in my room which sheltered, tremblingly, its transparent and fragile coolness from the afternoon sun, behind the almost closed blinds through which a glimmer of daylight had nevertheless managed to push its yellow wings, remaining motionless between the wood and the glass, in a corner, poised like a butterfly. It was hardly light enough to read, and the sensation of the light's splendor was given me only by the noise of Camus ... hammering dusty crates; resounding in the sonorous atmosphere that is peculiar to hot weather, they seemed to spark off scarlet stars; and also by the flies executing their little concert, the chamber music of summer: evocative not in the manner of a human tune that, heard perchance during the summer, afterwards reminds you of it but connected to summer by a more necessary link: born from beautiful days, resurrecting only when they return, containing some of their essence, it does not only awaken their image in our memory; it guarantees their return, their actual persistent, unmediated presence.
>
> The dark coolness of my room related to the full sunlight of the street as the shadow relates to the ray of light, that is to say it was just as luminous

and it gave my imagination the total spectacle of the summer, whereas my senses, if I had been on a walk, could only have enjoyed it in fragments; it matched my repose which (thanks to the adventures told by my book and stirring my tranquility) supported like the quiet of a motionless hand in the middle of a running brook the shock and motion of a torrent of activity. (*AR*, pp. 13–14)

De Man famously associates this passage's theme of synaesthetic totalization with metaphor, and then argues that the passage ultimately deconstructs its own aesthetic vision by exposing the vision's reliance on, or exposure to, a contingency that de Man associates with metonymy:

[Proust's passage] contrasts two ways of evoking the natural experience of summer and unambiguously states its preference for one of these ways over the other: the "necessary link" that unites the buzzing of the flies to the summer makes it a much more effective symbol than the tune heard "perchance" during the summer. The preference is expressed by means of a distinction that corresponds to the difference between metaphor and metonymy, necessity and chance being a legitimate way to distinguish between analogy and contiguity. The inference of identity and totality that is constitutive of metaphor is lacking in the purely relational metonymic contact: an element of truth is involved in taking Achilles for a lion but none in taking Mr. Ford for a motor car. (*AR*, p. 14)

The "purely relational metonymic contact," however, turns out to underlie and undermine the metaphorical totalization because, de Man argues, the metaphor "torrent of activity" is in fact doubly metonymic: first because, since it is a cliché, "the coupling of the two terms is not governed by the 'necessary link' of resemblance ... but dictated by a mere habit of proximity," and second, because "the reanimation of the numbed figure takes place by means of a statement, ('running brook') which happens to be close to it, without however this proximity being determined by a necessity that would exist on the level of transcendental meaning" (*AR*, p. 66).

Guillory remarks the binary oppositions that seem to line up in de Man's analysis (metaphor vs. metonymy, necessity vs. contiguity) and then asks his leading question: "What if the role assigned to the Jakobsonian tropes were determined from the first by the concepts of necessity and contingency, and tropes were being employed simply as the 'technical' rhetorical names for these thematic notions?" (p. 224). What if, that is, the deconstruction were really being directed by its desire for the pathos of "contingency," for the reassurance, self-aggrandizement, and pedagogical effectivity of an ever-reiterated lesson of self-loss in language? Guillory leans heavily on de Man's idiosyncratic use of rhetorical terminology. The metaphor "does not look at first glance like a metaphor at all since the music of the flies does not substitute for summer in its absence. The music is not *like* the summer; it is as much a part of the summer as the quality of the light, or renewed vegetation" (p. 224). The relationship is one of association rather than analogy, and of part (the flies) for whole (the summer). Guillory notes that de Man has in fact had to call the trope of the flies a synecdoche, and append a footnote admitting that "classical rhetoric generally classifies synecdoche as metonymy." However, "the relationship between part and whole can be understood metaphorically, as is the case, for example, in the organic metaphors dear to Goethe. Synecdoche is one of the borderline figures that create an ambivalent zone between metaphor and metonymy" (*AR*, p. 63). For Guillory this means that "it is simply at de Man's own discretion whether to assimilate synecdoche to metonymy or metaphor, and the grounds for the choice have little to do with how tropes actually work. Synecdoche is moved across the border into the domain of metaphor only because the concepts of identity, totality, and necessity have already been imputed to metaphor as its defining attributes" (p. 225). And if what de Man calls "metaphor" is a vexing issue, what he calls "metonymy" is even more so, since "torrent of activity" is on the face of it a metaphor. It is reanimated by its proximity to the "running brook," but; Guillory objects, "*there is no metonymy*, unless the actual syntax of the sentence, without which no sentence could exist, is being conflated with the trope of metonymy" (p. 226). Because the Proust passage "contrasts not a metaphor and a metonymy but a metonymy (or synecdoche) 'understood' as a metaphor and a metaphor 'understood' as a metonymy," Guillory concludes that "what de Man called the 'metafigural' level of the text was never anything other than a preexistent thematic, now superimposed upon the figural language of the text." The names of the tropes are indeed important, but only, or precisely, as red herrings: "they permit the methodology to advertise itself as rigorously rhetorical or nonthematic, and therefore to displace its thematic to the unconscious of its own terminology" (p. 227).

Guillory is certainly right at least to this extent: anyone attempting to normalize de Man's use of tropological terms will be in for many a sleepless night. De Man reads the text of rhetoric as violently as he does any other text—but that is not quite to say that he simply reads willfully. Let us, yet once more, go over the Proust passage and its tropes. The chamber music of the flies is certainly a synecdoche of summer, but its immediate figurative task is more local: the flies' music, like Camus' hammering, conveys to Marcel "the sensation of the light's splendor" in the dark room. The music is a synaesthetic substitution for the light, or more precisely for the splendor of the light, a substitution enabled by the fact that both the flies' music and the light's splendor are synecdoches of summer. The music and light, therefore, are part of a chain of synecdoches linked to each other like terms in a metaphor (they share the proper meaning "summer," just as Achilles and the lion share the proper meaning "ferocity" or "strength"). De Man's reading here, while certainly not akin to anything a classical rhetorician would produce, does not seem sheerly an exercise of his "own discretion" either. As for the "torrent of activity": it is of course a ("dead") metaphor, and the question is whether de Man is in any way justified in sticking onto the deadness of the metaphor and the proximity of the brook the rhetorical label "metonymy." The Jakobsonian heritage weighs heavily here, as Guillory says, but need not propel us all the way down to "the actual syntax of the sentence, without which no sentence could exist." Proximity or contiguity is a rhetorical device among others; any writer of modest ability, let alone Proust, attends to various sorts of associations and crosspollinations (I have just attended to double-s sounds). That is an elementary point, but the de Manian question of whether inherently arbitrary linguistic structures mobilize, and perhaps even generate, thematic or metaphysical associations is not. Relations of contiguity are open to themes of contingency (we may grant repeated s-sounds ornamental value, but if we suspect that a desire for this repetition was the sole determinant of the author's choice of words, we might feel cheated). De Man gets these themes of necessity and chance from Proust's own metacommentary—which is to say, from a broad Western and romantic aesthetic tradition that Proust's text inhabits and to which it contributes. The flies, Proust's narrator tells us, are "necessary," the tune heard "perchance" is not; the flies guarantee summer's "actual persistent, unmediated presence," and the ensemble of mediations of which they are a part offers Marcel "the total spectacle of the summer," as opposed to the "fragments" available to his unmediated senses. The question that de Man raises for us here, and that Guillory's critique does not obliterate, is whether Proust's thematic valorization of totality depends on patterns of substitution that make this theme possible ("metaphor") yet lack semantic or intentional depth ("metonymy"). The *theme* of contingency, to be sure, makes meaning out of something-other-than-meaning. Thematization is unavoidable; but the haunting possibility raised by the long-standing association of associative linguistic pattern with inessentiality or contingency is that *thematization* runs deeper than *theme*—that the making of meaning involves processes that exceed and potentially disturb meaning. (Philosophy's foundational quarrel with rhetoric concerns precisely this possibility.) Pace Guillory, de Man's notion of reading does not—cannot—characterize itself as simply "nonthematic." The de Manian project consists rather in an attempt to register an ungrounded (and thus endlessly thematized, because unthematizable) process of thematization. As de Man noted in a 1972 revision of his 1967 Gauss lecture on Wordsworth, reading, as he understands it, "means that the thematic element remains taken into consideration." A sheerly structural analysis of a text would fall short of a *reading*: "we look for the delicate area where the thematic, semantic field, and the rhetorical structures begin to interfere with each other, begin to engage each other" (*RCC*, p. 200).

Is "metonymy" a justifiable thematic name for nonthematizable linguistic events? Within limits, yes. But we may honor the local power of Guillory's critique here and agree that the strain put on conventional rhetorical terminology in de Man's famous reading of Proust grants Guillory's overall critique more legitimate polemical traction than it achieves anywhere else. My own opinion is that de Man himself found the terminology of the Proust essay unsatisfactory. He did not build any of his other early-1970s essays so squarely over the Jakobsonian metaphor-metonymy divide, and said very little about metonymy over the subsequent decade; the metaphor-metonymy binary opposition, I think, soon came to seem to him misleadingly totalizing, no matter how violently one spun and shook it. It is intrinsic to de Man's methodology to devour its own metalanguage; but some terms and oppositions proved more useful to him than others.

Over the course of the 1970s de Manian rhetorical reading was to develop along lines of thought opened most forcefully in an essay he wrote about the same time as the Proust essay, "Theory of Metaphor in Rousseau's *Second Discourse*," which became chapter 7 of *Allegories of Reading*, the first in the sequence of Rousseau chapters making up the second half of the book.[18] I can do no more than point toward this dense (and much commented upon) reading of Rousseau's fantasy of a primitive man's encounter with another primitive man, whom he fears and thus perceives and names as a "giant"; for our purposes we need only recall that de Man argues that according to this particular "allegory of reading," at least, metaphor, in coming into being, obliterates its own precondition: radical uncertainty. The other primitive man may or may not be dangerous; this is undecidable; "the metaphor [i.e., 'giant'] is blind, not because it distorts objective data, but because it presents as certain what is, in fact, a mere possibility" (*AR*, p. 151). In becoming a figure, the figure dis-figures itself, generating a stable difference between literal and figurative meanings by foreclosing the truly figural, if impossible, "state of suspended meaning" out of which it originated. What de Man means by rhetoric presses in a sense "beyond" what we ordinarily think of as "language," since the rhetorical reading generates as its allegory of the reading predicament a story about the constitutive (and thus also deconstructive) violence *of* language. Language thereby ceases to be merely an object in the world, a constituted entity we can learn or use or study. Though such uses of language are on their own terms perfectly necessary and legitimate, they are *uses* that presuppose that language "is"—and "is not": language, a nonentity that "is" only in its relation to that which it "is not," becomes a name for what Derrida calls the *perhaps*.[19] *Perhaps* it is a giant; it *is* a giant: both at once, impossibly. The *perhaps*, endlessly effaced, endlessly returns, haunting the meanings and referents it makes possible. This story about "language," which, according to itself, inevitably mistakes itself as a story about an object (hence de Man's mobile and violent hyperobjectifications of language-terms), is inevitably thematic and universalizing, which is why theory is the resistance to theory, even as it tells the story of the possibility that themes depend upon non-theme-driven linguistic motions. The imperative-to-theme is in advance of theme; yet what this "means" is that thematization—the making of meaning—is driven by an imperative "prior" to meaning. And thus, what the rhetorical reading *does* is never quite in line with what it *says*, even though such a nonconvergence of saying and doing *is* what it says.[20]

Guillory does not discuss de Man's quite idiosyncratic displacements of the Austinian notion of the performative, or his equally emphatic revision of a Fichtean idiom of positing or positionality. When Guillory offers a summation of rhetorical reading's procedures, he casts rhetorical reading as thematizing a straightforward triumph of cognition over persuasion: "In the metanarrative of deconstruction, tropes are said to have seductive powers of persuasion but never fail, by virtue of their cognitive dimension, to deconstruct their own persuasive performances" (p. 219). Such descriptions help Guillory characterize deconstruction as a tacit effort to preserve a phenomenological self, but they do not help us understand de Manian theory. For de Man the cognitive dimension of language is endlessly out of synch with its performative dimension. As a well-known dictum from the late-1970s essay "Shelley Disfigured" has it: "Language posits and language means (since it articulates), but language cannot posit meaning; it can only reiterate (or reflect) it in its reconfirmed falsehood. Nor does the knowledge of this impossibility make it less possible" (*RR*, pp. 117–18). Guillory is obviously ready to understand the positing power of language as simply one more theme by means of which rhetorical reading generates and savors the pathos of nonhuman agency, but his swerve away from de Man's thematization of the performative may be taken as symptomatic of his desire to purge the theory of elements that resist being returned to cognition, and thence to self and the pedagogue's charisma, and thence to a social world.

The project of annihilating theory *qua* theory becomes legibly violent as Guillory turns from his strenuous examination of de Man's reading of Proust to debunk the notion of "materiality" mobilized in de Man's late work. Many an essay, at this point in time, has addressed itself to the question of what de Man means by "materiality"; clearly it is a concept or quasiconcept that attentive readers have been able to describe in various ways.[21] What the word surely does *not* mean, however, is a materialism that "reconstruct[s] contingency as another kind of necessity, one that is not metaphysical but *physical*, a determinate indeterminacy in which the process of signification is subject to the random causality of chance" (p. 228; emphasis in the original). It is of note that Guillory launches this claim at de Man from a considerable distance; fortified by his close, hard reading of de Man on Proust, he does not even glance at, let alone examine carefully, any of the relevant de Manian texts. We have reached a certain bedrock of intransigence in Guillory: a site of resistance where interpretative labor cedes to starkly willful misrepresentation. For whatever "materiality" means in de Man, it does not mean physical presence. De Man uses the words "materiality" or "materialism" rather rarely, and almost always in conjunction with the words "form," "inscription," and "letter." In "Hypogram and Inscription," he writes of the "materiality of an inscription" (*RT*, p. 51), and has a few similar phrases in the two late essays on Hegel (e.g., *AI*, pp. 102, 108–9); in the two Kant essays, arguing that "radical formalism . . . is what is called materialism" (*AI*, p. 128), he uncovers a "formal materialism" at the heart of aesthetic judgment (*AI*, p. 83), and subsequently refers to the "materiality of the letter" (*AI*, p. 90). Let us gloss that last phrase briefly. As Saussure showed, there is no such thing as a letter in sheerly phenomenal terms—as an unmediated presence-to-self of a perception. A letter can only be read (as opposed to ink on paper being seen) because of its constitutive difference from other letters (I may write my "I" quite variously, so long as something distinguishes it from "J," "i," "l," etc.). When Kant's text, in de Man's reading, crumbles into letters, it is crumbling into minimal units of form—form as the product of difference and iterability—within the context of an act of reading. The "letter" here is neither the physicality of ink nor the molecules or atoms of physical reality, and has nothing immediate to do either with pre-Kantian materialism or with the noumenon or *Ding-an-sich*. Derrida offers the formula "a materiality without materialism and even perhaps without matter" over the course of his commentary on de Manian materiality: a frustratingly cautious phrase, perhaps, but it nonetheless serves our understanding far more faithfully than does Guillory's claim that de Man invests "the word as material object" with "the same numinous agency evacuated from the subject" (p. 229).[22] Guillory understands "material" here as physical or phenomenal—the word in its presence to perception—but that is precisely what materiality in de Man is not, as even a brief look at what he actually wrote can make clear.[23] Without getting into the complications of de Man's reading, in "Hypogram and Inscription," of Michael Riffaterre's reading of (among other texts) Victor Hugo's poem "Ecrit sur la vitre d'une fenêtre flamande," we can glance at the end of that essay:

> Every detail as well as every general proposition in [Hugo's] text is fantastic except for the assertion, in the title, that it is *écrit*, written.... The materiality (as distinct from the phenomenality) that is thus revealed, the unseen "cristal" whose existence thus becomes a certain *there* and a certain *then* which can become a *here* and a *now* in the reading "now" taking place, is not the materiality of the mind or of time or of the carillon [which are all personifications in Hugo's poem—M.R.]—none of which exist, except in the figure of prosopopeia—but the materiality of an inscription. (*RT*, p. 51)

Scratches on a pane of glass, like ink marks on paper, can be perceived as phenomena, but to the extent that they are *read* they are being supported not just by a literal pane of glass (that would be, perhaps, the "physical" materiality Guillory has in mind) but by what de Man tropes here as an "unseen 'cristal,'" a glass beyond seeing: the *inscription* as the self-difference and iterability that allows these words to be read "here" and "now," a here and a now that are always, in their actual and potential reiterations, other and elsewhere.

IV

Though Guillory's chapter has a good third of its length yet to go, and though I shall of course have a few remarks to make about the final movement of his argument, readers will perhaps be relieved to hear that it is no longer necessary to linger over the minutiae of his struggle with de Man. We have reached a point in our analysis where it becomes possible to offer some general observations.

Looking back over the trajectory of Guillory's argument, we may substantiate the claim I made in my introduction about the *institutional* flavor of Guillory's critique. If his portrait of a de Man flinching at shadows, glued to the publicity barometer, anxiously manipulating his disciples, and venting contempt in his essays has less to do with the biographical narrative one might plausibly construct as "Paul de Man" than with the stereotypes of antitheoretical discourse, this is congruent with the overall project of the chapter. All of the tools Guillory employs to retrofit de Manian theory into a symptom of the marginalization of the humanities in the new technobureaucratic world are familiar; they are the clichés of the resistance to theory, animated by the skill and passion of a first-rate polemicist. We have heard it all before, so very many times: de Man invented his theory to defend elite literature; to gain personal prestige; to corrupt the young. His theory waters down the true Continental vintage in order to obey "the agenda of a specifically American apparatus" (p. 238). His theory's unhappy success was, thankfully, soon followed by its "waning" (p. 255). Deconstruction is over now; it can be brought to book and historicized. And if de Man's theory had, in its day, at least a shred of originality about it as, precisely, *his* theory, woe betide the "disciples" who reproduce it: in doing so they become no more than nameless, meaningless pawns. And so on. It would accord with the momentum, though not the poised intelligence, of Guillory's critique to add to these commonplaces the most journalistic and bizarre of them all: that de Man invented his theory so as not to feel guilty about having written his youthful wartime journalism. To refresh one's sense of the strangeness of all this it suffices to note how rarely one hears equivalently aggressive polemics launched against some other critic or theory. Derrida, it is true, can inspire a similarly fevered resistance, though arguably even Derrida's reception has been less traversed by hurricanes than de Man's. Other comparanda are rare; one has to go to the fringes of the academy—to, say, remarks of Camille Paglia's about Foucault—to find hostility akin to that which the name "Paul de Man" has routinely inspired over the past thirty years. Guillory is absolutely right to discern a symptom at work here, but his analysis exactly repeats the symptom's own grammar and terms. Recycling the personification of theory as "de Man," he alternately ignores or dismisses theory's critique of personification (personification, that is, as an inevitable but endlessly unstable trope), and necessarily repeats in negative form the fetishizing gesture of the transference. The result is that odd blend of originality and ordinariness that I have wondered about more than once in these pages. One might risk the somewhat fanciful diagnosis that, in wrestling with de Man, Guillory manages to internalize and incorporate anti–de Manian commonplaces so successfully that they become indistinguishable from his own particular, and in many ways very laudable, accomplishment. I shall say more about what I find laudable about Guillory's reading, but first let me try to bring into sharper focus the outline of his resistance to theory—which, as noted, is not simply "his" resistance.

Peggy Kamuf was right, in the review I cited earlier, to diagnose as *Cultural Capital*'s sticking-point the deconstructive insistence "on the technicity of the idea, on the iterability of the proper, on the divisibility of any mark of division, and therefore on the necessary contamination of any posed or supposed purity." Throughout his reading of de Man, Guillory works to separate the technical from the ideational and render the former an ornament of or supplement to the latter. We are told that the de Manian disciples do not really imitate the master's doctrine, which is a contentless content: "What is imitated rather is the form of the doctrine's iteration, in other words, its style" (p. 201). Style separates from content, and becomes, on the one hand, a sheer principle of mechanical reproducibility, and on the other hand *l'homme même*—a mechanical reproduction of *this man*'s style. The "form of the doctrine's iteration" is thus at once expelled from meaning and subordinated to personality. When Guillory turns from the institutional propagation of theory via discipleship to the theory itself, he repeats a version of the same gesture: tropes become technical ornaments separate from, and subordinate to, the "themes" of rhetorical reading. Earlier I noted but did not comment on Guillory's claim that de Man conflates trope with the Saussurian signifier; let me say a word about that error now. Despite the proximity between the notions of trope and signifier (they are translatable: one can describe a trope as a signifier, and one can describe the relation between signifier and signified as a trope) the two concepts are not equivalent (the translation, that is, leaves a residue). Tropes, for de Man, always raise epistemological questions because they put into play the difference between literal and figurative meaning; thus, given that they perform semantic displacements, tropes involve the "signified" as much as they do the "signifier." Tropes are disruptive for de Man precisely because they twine together meaning (the "signified") and the principle of meaning's articulation (the "signifier") while disallowing a stable link between the two. Guillory identifies trope and signifier as part of his overall, tacit effort to segregate themes from their "technical" expression.

The fallacious translation of trope into signifier is symptomatically reiterated later in the chapter in the form of an atypical terminological mistake. Guillory usually gets his terms right, but as noted his discussion of materiality is conducted at some distance from the pertinent texts, and when he speaks of the "materiality of the signifier" (p. 229) he targets a phrase that de Man never used. The mistake is small but telling: it forms part of Guillory's emphatic refusal to dwell with de Man's notion of materiality, which, as we have seen, more closely resembles the Derridean non-concept of *différance* than traditional philosophical materialisms. Guillory goes so far as literally to naturalize de Manian materiality by way of a rapid jab at "Shelley Disfigured": "The linguistic Atropos cutting the thread of Shelley's text produces the pathos of indetermination (accident) out of the simple determinism of a material causality (in this case, bad weather)" (p. 229). What Guillory himself means by "material" here is somewhat obscure (if one's vocabulary is Aristotelian, "bad weather" could be termed the efficient cause of Shelley's death, but hardly the material cause), and one is forced to conclude that Guillory has assimilated the material to something like "the real" in a precritical sense—the natural world as physical force and phenomenal experience. That reduction is of a piece with all the others. The guiding thread is an affirmation of *presence*: of the professor to the seminar participant, of meaning to the mind, of objects to experience. And as we have seen, this logocentrism must endlessly condemn and expel what we may call the technicity of language: technicity, here, signaling not just "mechanical" iterability, but the irreducibility and irreducible unpredictability of *mediation*.[24] "There is no deconstruction," Derrida affirms, ". . . which does not begin by again calling into question the dissociation between thought and technology. . . . This is why this deconstruction, at the very moment when it puts into question the hierarchical division between thought and technology, is neither technicist nor technological."[25]

It is with this caution in mind that we may now turn to the most original element of Guillory's argument: its powerful final reduction of de Man and de Manian theory to symptoms of institutional and social crisis and change. The technical plays an important role in this argument: having characterized de Man's tropological terminology as a sheerly technical excrescence on a pathos-driven theme, Guillory claims to have discovered a "valorization of the technical" in de Man: "just as the rhetorical terminology exists for the sake of the determinist thematic, that thematic in turn offers a means of recharacterizing the rhetorical terminology as technical or rigorous in *contemporary* terms" (p. 232). No longer a *technê rhêtorikê*, this new, late-twentieth-century art of rhetoric thematizes its technicity as "rigor." De Manian rigor is of course, for Guillory, a sham, an excuse for the pathos and the lurid figures it generates;[26] but the de Manian mastertrope of rigor "facilitates an imaginary reduction of the social totality to the structure of trope," allowing "rhetorical reading to function as a political theory just by virtue of being *no more than* a theory of literature" (p. 236). This "imaginary reduction of the social to an instance of the linguistic" in turn allows the disciples to 1) respond to the desire that criticism have political effect in a way that imposes "a *limit* to curricular revision, a limit intended to preserve theory as *literary* theory" (p. 237); and 2) imagine de Man as external to and subversive of the institution.

As to the first claim, which seeks to bring home the traditional leftwing antideconstructive argument that de Manian theory "defends" a high-literary canon, we may note that Guillory, who knows well that this theory offers (via its "technical" focus on rhetoric) "an extension of the category of the literary" that "removes any logical grounds for distinguishing between literature and any use of language whatsoever" (p. 212), depends heavily upon his reduction-to-the-seminar and his restriction of the reception of de Manian theory to "disciples," who like their master read "a very select set of texts within the Romantic tradition" (p. 216), in order to make his argument. Indeed, he goes on to note (with perhaps a touch of annoyance) "de Man's relative lack of interest in this consequence of his theorizing" (p. 212). De Man, that is, writes on canonical texts but seems uninterested in affirming the virtues of the canon. Only by granting a canonical sense to various de Manian references to "literature" and ignoring statements that set out in a contrary direction (such as the broad definition of "literariness" in "The Resistance to Theory" [*RT*, pp. 9–11]) can Guillory link de Man to a conservative canonical agenda. It is, of course, true that de Man wrote almost exclusively about certain high-literary texts; it is almost certain that de Man, like Derrida or Blanchot, should be read as affirming the interest and power of the post-eighteenth-century discursive category of literature; it is furthermore highly probable that, in the context of his own training and tastes, and his own particular mandate as a pedagogue, de Man thought it his job to teach "literature." (Guillory—and we—will have more to say about de Man and professionalism in a moment.) It is also true, however, as Guillory rightly points out, that de Manian rhetorical reading in no way requires of its practitioners that they focus on Wordsworth or Hölderlin. This set of facts does not add up to an "aporia" or a "conceptual catachresis," as Guillory claims (pp. 215, 216); there is no logical impasse here—nor even a pragmatic or institutional one, as becomes obvious as soon as we broaden our horizon and look at the diverse kinds of critical projects that de Manian theory has in fact inspired over the last twenty years. If critics have drawn on the idiom and procedures of rhetorical reading to address "texts" such as trauma theory or journalism or the rhetoric of war, this is because in de Manian terms neither literariness nor the aesthetic are fundamentally "high-cultural" phenomena.[27] They are aspects of language; and "language" is not, for de Man, a positive object among others, but is perhaps better thought of as the catachretic name for the possibility that understanding cannot catch up with—cannot understand—its own mediations.

I shall not comment much on Guillory's distortion of various remarks that de Manians have made about de Man being "outside" the institution; it is of course not the case that any competent deconstructive critic has ever imagined de Man to be simply or fundamentally external to the institutions of criticism and pedagogy. (The deconstructive position, as we saw Kamuf pointing out earlier, is that "the institution," despite having a fundamental power to exclude and include, is not a homogenous space that texts or textual practices can simply *inhabit*.) We may pass on to consider what Guillory considers to be the ideological freight of such imaginings: they serve, in his reading, a dream of autonomy, via an ideology of professionalism. Within a bureaucracy, professionalism is the ideology by means of which "the charisma of the master theorist appears to constitute a realm of *absolute* autonomy, and therefore, as we have noted, an 'other scene' of politics" (p. 254; emphasis in the original). De Manian theory thus reasserts charismatic authority in the face of "technobureaucratic dominion" (p. 256); but at the same time, in and through the valorization of the technical as "rigor," it transforms the work of reading into "an *unconscious mimesis* of the form of bureaucratic labor." "Rigor" supports a dream of autonomy even as it recapitulates, as positive qualities, the "boredom, monotony, predictability, and unpleasantness" of bureaucratic existence. "Just as the transference transferred in the pedagogic sphere imparts to 'rigor' the eros, the sexiness, of the master teacher, so in the bureaucratic sphere it signifies a *charisma of routinization*, the cathexis of routine" (p. 257).

Now, on the one hand, as we have seen, every brick making up this massive conceptual edifice is a friable mixture of untruth, half-truth, hypothesis, or assertion. The seminar of the charismatic teacher, no doubt important enough in its way, is an imaginary reduction of the real technobureaucratic conditions for the propagation of theory. As for the theory being propagated: it is not blind to the transference; it does not rediscover the cognitive mastery of the subject as linguistic determinism; it is not securely theme-driven; it does not isolate trope from theme; it does not, except as deployed within very specific institutional contexts, "defend literature." Its practitioners no doubt imagine what they do to be irritating to the institution, but do not, if they are competent practitioners, labor under the illusion that either their discourse or that of anyone else, including the "master," occupies "a realm of *absolute* autonomy." Deconstruction has its suspicions about absolute autonomy.

But, on the other hand, Guillory's argument, marked at every turn by a negative transference and a determination to preserve the metaphysical hierarchies and conceptual distinctions that theory puts into question, makes visible the degree to which de Manian theory reflects on its own institutional conditions. We have noted how this theory builds into its allegory of itself a gloss on the transference and the moral ambiguities of pedagogy; we may now, prodded along by Guillory, credit de Man's discourse with a sustained allegory of its institutional unfolding. The discourse is not an "unconscious mimesis of the form of bureaucratic labor" (a claim that makes clear the degree to which the sociological critique ultimately relies upon an uncritical metaphysics of reflection); it is a registering and a reading of the technobureaucratic scene of theory's production. The empirical specificity of the historical event of theory ("pragmatically speaking, then, we know that there has been, over the last fifteen to twenty years, a strong interest in something called literary theory" [*RT*, p. 5]) may indeed be aligned, as an empirical phenomenon, with the technobureaucratic development of the university within the wider regime of late capitalism and modern technics. Derrida, whose texts thematize such matters far more explicitly than de Man's, affirms as much: "it is not by chance that deconstruction has accompanied a critical transformation in the conditions of entry into the academic professions from the 1960s to the 1980s."[28] Rigor signals, among other things, the imperative to *produce readings*, and thus refers itself, as Guillory says, to the reader-producer as employee within a scientific-bureaucratic organization. Rhetorical reading implicitly incorporates and reflects on its own institutional conditions of production, not in order to condemn its own institutionalization or celebrate its own professionalism, but because the imperative to read is infinite, and these conditions of production form part of the text to be read. The production of readings may then be characterized as a bureaucratic task that—whether or not the nominal topic is traditionally high-literary—in a very broad sense works performatively to "defend literature" (just as Guillory's book or any other field-relevant academic publication does, sheerly by virtue of its contribution to criticism as an institution); but arguably no critical approach more consciously addresses itself to the complexities besetting its own performance than rhetorical reading. We return to a classic hermeneutic and deconstructive insight: the reading—here, the Guillorian interpretation, to the extent that it has traction enough to *be* a reading—is not something we add to the text from the outside, but constituted the text from the beginning (the beginning, that is, of the reading). The de Manian text stands revealed not as blind to its own institutional conditions of production, but rather as remarkably well-equipped to register them.

Rigor is indeed a charged figure in theory's production and propagation, but Guillory's analysis cannot stand in the form he offers it. There *is no* unambiguous "valorization of the technical" in de Man, as any careful inspection of "Aesthetic Formalization in Kleist" or the "Confessions" chapter of *Allegories of Reading*—to name only two particularly obvious texts—shows. Technical and aesthetic formalization in de Man is not just inhuman; it is potentially damaging to humans (to Rousseau, entranced by the metal rolls [*AR*, p. 298]; to the mutilated man in Kleist's story who dances like a marionette [*RR*, pp. 288–90]). Formalization obtains inhuman, machine-like powers of iterability in these de Manian readings, and formalization is all the more dangerous when it has been aestheticized and thereby rendered, fallaciously, a property of the "human" or a principle of political order. Rhetorical reading cannot help fetishizing "rigor," but is also a rigorous critique of rigor. Avital Ronell has argued that "Paul de Man's work is essentially engaged with and inflected by the question concerning technology";[29] what Guillory calls theory's ideology of rigor is a dimension of that engagement. Even as theory's invocation of rigor triggers the pathos and thrills of technical formalization, it enacts the imperative to read the uncertainties, the violent derivations and deviations of formalization.[30]

It is telling that, as his chapter approaches its end, Guillory's assaults on de Man grow conflicted, particularly in the orbit of some lines he cites from de Man's interview with Stephano Rossi:

> So, personally, I don't have a bad conscience when I'm being told that, to the extent that it is didactic, my work is academic or even, as it is used as a supreme insult, just more New Criticism. I can live with that very easily, because I think that only what is, in a sense, classically didactic, can be

really and effectively subversive. And I think the same applies there to Derrida. Which doesn't mean that there are not essential differences: Derrida feels compelled to say more about the institution of the university, but that is more understandable within the European context, where the university has such a predominating cultural function, whereas in the United States it has no cultural function at all, here it is not inscribed in the genuine cultural tensions of the nation. (*RT*, p. 117)

Guillory attacks immediately, in the hyperbolic mode we have encountered before: "No proposition could be more blind to its own meaning than the claim that the American university has no 'cultural function.' A claim of this sort would be hardly credible about any social institution" (p. 241). But then comes—rather unexpectedly given the overall tone of this chapter—the next sentence: "Yet this is not to say that de Man's assertion has no basis whatsoever." The semi-retraction is perhaps partly spurred by embarrassment over having pounced ravenously on a crumb (for obviously de Man, improvising in an interview, offers a loose phrase here, which he then follows with a tighter one); but as we read along it becomes apparent that part of Guillory's problem is that de Man is saying something uncomfortably close to what Guillory is saying, as Guillory eventually half-admits: "What de Man considered to be the cultural irrelevance of the university describes a real condition, perhaps, not of the university but of the literary curriculum" (p. 264). In between these two moments in his essay Guillory has exempted de Man from the "outside-the-institution" fantasy that Guillory attributes to the disciples: "So far from inhabiting a space exterior to the institution, de Man proposes that fully implementing a deconstructive pedagogy would transform 'departments of English from being large organizations in the service of everything except their own subject matter into much smaller units, dedicated to the professional specialization that Professor [Walter Jackson] Bate deplores' (*RT*, pp. 25–26)" (p. 247). Guillory presses that citation toward a de Manian requirement that "the methodology of rhetorical reading be *identified* (how closely, we shall see) with the institution and its strictly institutional agenda"; but a few sentences later he nonetheless finds it necessary to distinguish de Man from the "aggressively 'professionalist' polemic" of a pragmatist such as Stanley Fish (p. 247). Here, for a small magic moment, de Man seems to float free, an inch or two above the clutches of polemic. De Man, we are told, "*identifies*," in italics, his theory with the institution—but he also doesn't quite. Guillory has come as close as he is able in this text to registering de Man's double or deconstructive reading of institutionality (and of the technically or rigorously or classically "didactic") as *both* determining and unstable, coercive and liberating.

Looking back over this long chapter, and then over this powerful and important book, one has the sense of having watched a champion archer, shooting over vast distances, clump arrows around but never quite in the bull's-eye—itself an extraordinary feat, and one perfectly capable of transforming our sense of the target by reframing it and allowing us to see it anew. We learn a great deal from Guillory, precisely because the lessons he teaches are the sort that conscientious students need to modify. If Guillory's persuasive critique of the "canon debate" should have led him to be leery of the temptations of personification (the trope that allows minority authors to become "representative" of experiences and constituencies, thereby effacing the institution through which this "representation" occurs), the fact that he repeats so fiercely the personifying gesture in his chapter on de Man suggests that no genuine account of canon-formation—and, for that matter, no adequate history of literary theory—can be achieved in the absence of a fundamental rhetorical critique. As regards de Manian theory per se, most of Guillory's characterizations and propositions, as we have seen, offer at best secondary or derivative truths. The legendary transferential effects of de Man's seminar did indeed play an important if necessarily limited role in the diffusion of de Manian theory. One can hardly deny that de Man was a charismatic figure, and it would be nearly as hard to deny that the "rigor" of his method facilitated many of the transferential and ideological effects that Guillory describes. It is always tempting to imagine one's beloved teacher "outside" the institution, even if one knows better; and when the sociological context is one in which full-scale humanities instruction has largely retreated to elite enclaves and is being carried out—at best, in these enclaves—by a two-tier staff of bureaucratically integrated professionals and an increasingly proletarianized casual workforce (this latter category including, of course, the master teacher's students so long as they are literally *students*), it becomes all the easier for the participants in this drama to reimagine the master's singularity as "absolute autonomy." But de Manian *theory* does not license these phenomena; it predicts and in a sense exploits, and after a fashion repeats them, yet only in order to come to grips with and critique them.

In his heart, perhaps, Guillory knows this, and perhaps we know he knows. That is why we are not, perhaps, completely taken by surprise when, on the final page of this chapter, Guillory offers us a half-smothered confession of impotence, telling us "how nearly impossible it is to imagine what lies beyond the rhetoricism of literary theory, and hence beyond the problematic of literariness" (p. 265). That near-impossibility spurs a formulaic gesture toward some future moment, when "a much more thorough reflection on the historical category of literature" will allow us to "conceptualize a new disciplinary domain." The signifier "history," here, as so often in contemporary academic criticism, points toward salvation from history and from the "disciplinary domains" within which we find ourselves. It is not de Man's project but rather Guillory's that, in the last analysis, turns away from the task of understanding the historical conditions of literary criticism, and the various institutions of the aesthetic.

This swerve from history by way of a messianic historicism returns as a hyperbolic investment in the aesthetic at the end of *Cultural Capital*, as we have seen. As its final offering, Guillory's book proffers, anxiously and self-consciously, as the prize of its anti–de Manian polemic, the dream of an Aesthetic State in which the violence of social inequity is transformed into "pure 'symbolic distinction'" (p. 339). On the purity of that pure distinction, that difference between literal and figurative violence, the vision depends utterly. Guillory is right to argue, against the pseudohistoricists and neopragmatists, that aesthetic judgment cannot be evaded; just as little, however, can one evade the rhetorical critique that locates in the radical singularity of aesthetic judgment the impossible but necessary condition of suspense between literal and figural meaning that de Man saw as the predicament of reading. Aesthetic humanism does not give up its dream easily; indeed, it perhaps cannot be given up at all—even by those who pursue their bureaucratic careers as practitioners of "theory." And thus criticism continues to twist in the turns of aesthetic discourse, while periodically registering its fascination and anxiety with regard to the critic who most severely and strangely followed out those turns. It is likely that this predicament will remain that of "literary criticism in the coming years."

IV.

Theory, Materiality, and the Aesthetic

Thinking Singularity with Immanuel Kant and Paul de Man: Aesthetics, Epistemology, History, and Politics

Arkady Plotnitsky

Proceeding from Immanuel Kant's third *Critique*, *The Critique of Judgment*, and Paul de Man's reading of Kant, this essay will discuss certain specific concepts, first, of singularity, and, second, of the relationship between the individual and the collective, based on this concept of singularity. While emerging from Kant's analysis of *aesthetics*, this conceptuality entails a radical form of *epistemology* and, correlatively, a radical form of *historicity*. This conceptual and epistemological configuration, however, also translates into a *political* concept of community or, as I shall call it here, "parliamentarity." The genealogy of the conceptuality and epistemology in question may itself be in part political, insofar as the actual practice of politics may have served, deliberately or not, as one of the models of this epistemology. On the other hand, Kant's analysis of the aesthetic *expressly* offers a model for this conceptuality and epistemology, cognition in general, or historicity, and establishes the aesthetic (in his sense) as the condition of possibility of their emergence and functioning in contexts other than the aesthetic.[1]

As a result, aesthetics, epistemology, history, and politics become interconnected, and each becomes in turn conceptually refigured through these interconnections. Indeed, the interpenetration among these determinations is irreducible: once we enter any of the domains thus designated, we can bypass others only provisionally or conditionally, but not in principle. One might say that each corresponding situation involves a "detour" through others as part of its emergence. Furthermore, these interconnections inevitably, and ultimately uncontainably, extend to other determinations, such as ethical, or new definitions and denominations, proliferating within a given domain, for example, to different varieties and subspecies of the aesthetic.

This field, however, involves not only conjunctions and interactions, but also disjunctions and heterogeneities, and cannot be seen as fully unifiable or containable by means of a synthesis, dialectical or other. As such, it is governed in part by an epistemology analogous (although not identical) to the epistemology of singularity and of the relationships between the individual and the collective to be considered here. As de Man's reading of both Kant and Hegel makes apparent, such disjunctions often appear at the very point of an attempted synthesis. According to de Man: "We would have to conclude that Hegel's philosophy, which, like his *Aesthetics*, is a philosophy of history (and of aesthetics) as well as a history of philosophy (and of aesthetics)—and the Hegelian corpus indeed contains texts that bear these two symmetrical titles—is in fact an allegory of the disjunction between philosophy and history."[2] An argument of this type would apply to Kant's philosophy as well, just as many key points (including those to be discussed here) of de Man's reading of Kant to Hegel's.[3] Kantian or, conversely, Hegelian, specificity remains, of course, important. My main concern here, however, is a certain fundamental underlying problematic set into operation by Kant's philosophy, especially in the third *Critique*, and brought out by de Man's reading of Kant.

Singularity, Universality, and Freedom in the Judgment of Taste

I take as my point of departure paragraph 5 of the third *Critique*, in "Analytic of the Beautiful," where Kant distinguishes between "the agreeable or merely likable [*das Angenehme*], the beautiful [*das Schone*], and the good [*das Gute*]."[4] The section immediately precedes and leads to Kant's "Explication of the Beautiful," as "inferred from the First Moment," that of "a Judgment of Taste, As to Its Quality," which extends from Kant's "definition of taste" as "the ability to judge the beautiful."[5] "*Taste*," Kant *infers*, "is the ability to judge an object, or a way of presenting it, by means of liking or disliking *devoid of all interest*. The object of such a liking is called *beautiful*."[6] These are familiar commonplaces of the third *Critique*. Or rather, these statements are made into commonplaces by abstracting them from the arguments from which they are inferred as conclusions and thus depriving them of their complexity and their essentially un-commonplace-like and even (philosophically) idiosyncratic character. They can only be given an adequate reading if the richness of the conceptual and textual fabric of Kant's elaborations is brought to bear on Kant's argument, for example, by reaching what de Man calls "linguistic" understanding.[7] According to Kant:

> A judgment of taste, on the other hand [i.e., in contrast to the agreeable and the good], is merely [*bloß*] *contemplative*, i.e., it is a judgment that is indifferent to the existence of the object: it [considers] the character of the object only by holding it up to our feeling of pleasure and displeasure. Nor is this contemplation, as such, directed to concepts [as in the case of the good], for a judgment of taste is not a cognitive judgment (whether theoretical or practical) and hence is neither *based* on concepts, not directed to them as purposes. . . . Hence the agreeable, the beautiful, and the good designate three different relations that presentations have to the feeling of pleasure or displeasure, the feeling by reference to which we distinguish between objects [*Gegenstände*] or between the ways of presenting them. . . . We call *agreeable* that which *gratifies* [*was ihn vernnügt*] us, *beautiful* that which gives us just *feeling of liking* [*was ihn gefällt*]; *good* what we *esteem* [*geschätz*], endorse [*gebilligt*], that is, for which it is possible for us to posit [*setzen*] an objective value. Agreeableness holds also for animals without reason; beauty only for human beings, i.e., beings who are animal and yet rational, though it is not enough that they be rational (e.g., spirits) but they must be animal as well; the good, however, holds for every rational being as such, though I cannot fully justify and explain this proposition until later. We may say that, of all these three kinds of feeling of liking [*Wohlgefallen*, "inclination toward something"], only that involved in the taste for the beautiful is disinterested and *free*, since we are not compelled to give our approval by any interest, whether of sense or of reason. So we might say of the term *Wohlgefallen*, in the three cases [*Fällen*] just mentioned, refers to *inclination* [*Nciung*], or to *favor* [*Gunst*], or to *respect* [*Achtung*]. For *favor* [*Gunst*] is the only *free* form of liking [*Wohlgefallen*]. Neither an object [*Gegenstand*] of inclination, nor one that a law of reason enjoins on us as an object of desire, leaves us the freedom to make an object of pleasure for ourselves out of something or other. All interest either presupposes a need or gives rise to one; and because interest is a determining ground for approval [*Beifall*], it no longer makes the judgment about the object free. (translation modified; my emphasis)[8]

It is tempting to read these passages at an abstracted logical level, and it has been done, often with disastrous consequences. One can easily miss both a more complex conceptual architecture and subtle textual workings (sometimes against Kant's own grain) of Kant's "Analytics," and, especially, the incessant reciprocity between them, such as those of the signifier "*fall*" in this passage and elsewhere in Kant, which I shall discuss later in this essay. It is not merely a matter of paying close attention to Kant's German, although this is obviously necessary, since rigorously no translation is possible, but only a reading, a reading always determined by Kant's German but not contained by it. For example, one might prefer to read Kant's definition of the beautiful, cited above, in a more Heideggerian vein as "what stands in appearance in front of us as we are immersed in this feeling of being inclined toward it is called *beautiful*." Most fundamentally, however, it is a matter of reading the *irreducibly idiosyncratic* language and concepts of Kant's *irreducibly idiosyncratic* or *singular* philosophy. It goes without saying that the task of such a reading is not easy, and the present reading of Kant, or of de Man, too, might fail, and to some degree is bound to fail.

If, however, one can refer to a number of remarkable readings of the Kantian sublime, such as those by de Man and his followers, the beautiful remains an as-yet-*unread* enigma, especially if one speaks of reading in de Man's sense.[9] It is doubtful that any rigorous reading would remove the enigmatic from either the beautiful or the sublime in Kant, and the best such a reading may hope for is to *read* them as enigmas. Both the beautiful and the sublime may be best seen as defined by the enigmatic character of their emergence in certain types of processes of human (individual and collective) existence. The situation may be seen as follows. At certain points and under certain conditions, such processes produce certain types of effects, such as those of the beautiful and the sublime, while themselves remaining, in their *ultimate* nature, inaccessible to any knowledge or even conception in any terms or concepts available to us. "Ultimate" is a crucial qualification, since intermediate levels of the overall efficacious dynamics in question may be accessible, again, in terms of certain effects of the more remote and ultimately inaccessible parts of such processes. At least, the beautiful and the sublime may need to be configured in these terms for the purposes of theorizing them, which entails what I call "nonclassical" theory, to be discussed in the next section.

This type of epistemology, which links what can be known to what cannot be known or even conceived of, extends Kant's epistemology, introduced in the first *Critique*, *The Critique of Pure Reason*, and developed by him in all three *Critiques*. It also provides arguably the most fundamental connection between them, especially through the third *Critique*, which develops the ultimate model for the working, or at least underpinning, of both pure and practical reason. The beautiful and the sublime offer the well-known parallels with, respectively, understanding and reason, famously invoked by Kant.[10] These parallels, however, do not in themselves amount to the model in question, nor are they sufficient to build up this model. Rather they are made possible by virtue of this model.[11]

While this model is essentially *epistemological* in nature, it also defines a certain *political* model, a model of community, although one might also, and more rigorously, argue that both models reciprocally define each other. For the reason to be explained below, the political model may be called "parliamentary." This model, along with the reciprocity in question, is at work already in "The Analytic of the Beautiful," rather than only in Kant's analysis of the sublime, where Kant directly appeals to the idea of community and where most commentators trace the political problematic of the third *Critique*.

Kant sets the stage with his contention that "in their logical quantity all judgments of taste are *singular* [*einzelne*] judgments" and they emerge as such within "the entire [phenomenal] sphere of each *judging person*" (translation modified).[12] As he explains at the same juncture: "For example, I may look at a rose and make a judgment of taste by declaring it to be beautiful. But if I compare many *singular* [*einzelne*] roses and so arrive at the judgment, roses in general are beautiful, then my judgment is no longer merely aesthetic, but is a logical judgment based on an aesthetic one" (my emphasis).[13] It follows that, according to Kant, in offering an aesthetic judgment, one can say "this rose is *beautiful*," but one cannot, rigorously (in everyday life we do all the time, of course), say, in conveying as aesthetic judgment, "this is a beautiful *rose*." The "rose-ness" of any given rose, which is or essentially a linked concept (of "rose-ness"), is irrelevant. Contrary to Gertrude Stein's famous tautology, in Kant's aesthetics, as a beautiful object, "a rose is not a rose, is not a rose, is not a rose."

Most crucially, while implying a possibility of a certain repetition, a judgment of the beautiful and the object (or, in the sublime, a certain unobject) involved, are singular, each time unique, in every case. In this respect they are not unreminiscent of death, as de Man must have realized, as is apparent, for example, in his reading of Shelley's *The Triumph of Life*, to be discussed later in this essay. One is also reminded of Emmanuel Levinas's and Jacques Derrida's appeal to this type of singularity, including in ethical and political contexts, as in Derrida's title, "The End of the World, Each Time Unique." In short, in Kant the universality of such a judgment rigorously pertains to the moment at which it is made, and involves some community that is actually or potentially present at this moment. This community would, at this moment, relate and might, hopefully, accept this judgment, or come to the same judgment, by involving "the entire [phenomenal] sphere of each *judging person*."

As we have seen, Kant also argues that "the *favor* [*Gunst*] is the only *free* feeling of liking [*Wohlgefallen*]." If, however, such is the case, we *must*—for, otherwise there would be no freedom!—allow that our (always singular) claim for, or offer of the possibility of, the same kind of feeling concerning a given object on the part of any other person could be just as freely rejected as it could be freely accepted.[14] This must be the case, even though one has the bestowal of the highest possible favor upon an object or (as in the sublime) un-object in mind, as the German *Gunst* could suggest here, as it did to Heidegger in his reading of Nietzsche.[15] By the same token, *Gunst* appears to indicate a certain randomness and uniqueness or singularity of such a feeling. In short, the condition of the possibility of *sensus communis*, which Kant famously invokes in "The Analytic of the Sublime," is also the condition of the possibility of the failure of *sensus communis* to emerge in any given case. I would argue that it is this essential possibility of failure of *sensus communis* that defines the *universality* of the judgment of taste concerning the beautiful, or of the judgment (which cannot be seen as that of taste in Kant's scheme) concerning the sublime, most fundamentally. The universality, or at least a sufficiently large collectivity, defining the possibility of the beautiful or the sublime, could best be seen as an assemblage of irreducible singularities, each of which emerges, enigmatically, from something that, along with the process of this emergence itself, is not subject to the law(s) defining this collectivity. As will be seen, this enigmatic emergence also entails a special form of historicity.

From this perspective one might speak of a certain parliamentary model of the aesthetics and the political alike, and thus of a model for parliamentary politics, defined by Kant's conception of aesthetic judgment, and, again, reciprocally serving as a model for aesthetic judgment concerning the beautiful or the sublime. This type of reciprocity is suggested by Kant himself in a different, but related, context of human communication and sociability *under laws* in his appendix, "On Methodology of Taste," to "The Analytic of the Sublime" (*CJ*, p. 321). The model is defined by the circumstances, just described, of a possible failure of a possible consensus or (in principle, interminable) negotiations, possibly never fully cohering, in the manner of the sublime, and sometimes with feelings similar to those in experiencing the sublime, although outright frustration is more common.

In politics, the situation becomes even more complex (if this is possible) when one takes into account the broader field of judgments entertained, often simultaneously, by different individuals or parties, including political parties in their conventional sense. In fact teleological judgments (governed by concepts) are also subject to an analogous economy, although the possibility of freedom entailed by aesthetic judgments might well be unique, and it might have been seen by Kant as unique. Leaving the earlier history aside, one could trace the significance of this dynamics from Kant's fellow critical philosophers to Jean-François Lyotard's postmodernist vision of politics and justice, and beyond, with a great many thinkers in between.[16] It would also be difficult to dissociate these Kantian problematics from the political history of modernity, specifically the history of parliamentarity, from the Enlightenment onward.

One can easily see, now, how and why aesthetics, epistemology, historicity, and politics form a complex interactive network in Kant, and, with Kant, in general. The considerations offered so far still amount mostly to a logical and a content-oriented reading. Ultimately we must analyze and understand this machinery in textual terms, including by means of what de Man calls "linguistic terms," in particular as this machinery relates to the sequence of *gefallen, gefällt, Fällen, Beifall, Wohlgefallen,* and so forth, or the "*fall*-sequence," as one might call it, for reasons to be explained later. This analysis will proceed here through de Man's reading of Kant and such figures as Schiller, Kleist, and Shelley, and aesthetic, epistemological, and political models developed by de Man on the basis of these readings. Before I undertake this analysis, however, I shall, in the next two sections, outline more formally the epistemology in question.

Nonclassical Theory and Nonclassical Epistemology

It may be useful to backtrack briefly to the first *Critique, The Critique of Pure Reason,* and to Kant's *things in themselves,* a decisive step on the road to nonclassical epistemology, even if, at least short of the supplementary economy of the third *Critique,* not quite reaching the nonclassical limit. According to Kant:

> We have no concepts of the understanding and hence no elements for the cognition of things except insofar as an intuition can be given correspond-

ing to these concepts, consequently . . . we have cognition of no object as a *thing in itself*, but only insofar as it is an object of sensible intuition, i.e., as an appearance [phenomenon]; from which follows the limitation of all even possible speculative cognition of reason [*Vernunft*] to mere objects of *experience*. Yet the reservation must also be noted, that even if we cannot *cognize* [*kennen*] these same objects as things in themselves, we at least must be able to *think* [*denken*] [about] them as things in themselves. To *cognize* an object, it is required that I be able to prove its possibility (whether by the testimony of experience from its actuality or a priori through reason). But I can *think* whatever I like, as long as I do not contradict myself, i.e., as long as my concept is a possible thought, even if I cannot give any assurance whether or not there is a corresponding object somewhere within the sum total of all possibilities. But in order to ascribe objective validity to such a concept (real possibility, for the first sort of possibility was merely logical) something more is required. This "more," however, need not be sought in theoretical sources of cognition; it may also lie in practical ones.[17]

One might illustrate Kant's point by the example of the human body, which is crucial both to Kant and to de Man's reading of Kant. When we think of our bodies as having a certain shape or organization, defined by such features as the head, the arms and the legs, and so forth, we think of it on the basis of (phenomenal) appearances. The very concept of the body is defined by this way of looking at it, possibly with inner organs, such as the heart, the liver, the brain, and so forth, added on. When, however, we think of the body as constituted by atoms or elementary particles, even if we think of the latter classically (in terms of physics or epistemology), we think of the body as a (material) thing in itself.[18]

Kant himself proceeds next to an example of the freedom of the human soul, crucial to his analysis in all three *Critiques*, including in the present context, given the centrality of the question of freedom in aesthetic judgment, as discussed earlier. This example is also significant insofar as it refers to *mental*, rather than material, things in themselves. Although one might think more readily of things in themselves as material *objects* (also in Kant's sense of "noumenal object," correlative to "thing in itself"), for Kant the concept equally refers to mental objects and distinguishes them from appearances or phenomena, although in this case both the objects and the phenomena are mental. This view has major implications for our understanding of the nature of thinking, specifically understanding, logical or other, and reason, also in Kant's sense of *Vernunft*, and then for Freud's and Lacan's understanding of the unconscious as thinking.[19] It may be argued that Kant, too, ultimately assigns reason and the processes responsible for our sense of freedom, for example, that of aesthetic judgment, to the unconscious—to the unknowable, if not unthinkable, regions of the mind, even if, to put it in (early) deconstructive terms, without quite saying so or against himself, and against the history of philosophy. For philosophy has always (or just about) associated reason with consciousness and self-consciousness.

Nonclassical thinking moves us beyond the limits defined by Kant's conception of things in themselves in the first *Critique*. The case becomes more complex when we move to the third *Critique*, especially when our reading reaches the level of textual or "linguistic" understanding, as explored by de Man. While unknowable, Kant's things in themselves are still thinkable, at least at the logical-conceptual level of analysis. They are thus theorized as classical in the present view and may indeed be seen as defining classicality. That is, a *classical* theoretical account would, at least in principle, determine all of its objects, which may be called "classical" in turn, as knowable or, on the model of Kant's things in themselves, at least as thinkable. By contrast, the objects of nonclassical theories are configured, at least *as the objects of the theory*, as *irreducibly* unthinkable, ultimately even as objects in any conceivable sense, such as things in themselves, or as anything at all. I use the term "object" as designating that with which a given theory concerns itself and that it may, accordingly, idealize from other entities, and possibly idealize as unknowable or inconceivable. Thus, either Kant's noumenal (things in themselves) or phenomenal objects, such as the human body (which can, again, be conceived of as either), would be "objects" of a classical theory in the present neutral sense of "object," and Kant's definition of either defines them as such, at least up to a point and at a certain level of reading. On the other hand, an "object" of a nonclassical theory, say, "the human body," would be configured as unthinkable within the theory, including as "body" or as anything "human," whether such an object can or cannot be linked to a thinkable or even knowable entity outside the theory, or possibly by a different theory. This type of link would be bracketed by the nonclassical theory in question as well. Is the human body *ultimately* (this qualification is, again, crucial) knowable or unknowable, thinkable or unthinkable? Do we have a rigorous theory, philosophical or scientific, to do so? These are as-yet-unanswered questions, either at the level of the ultimate material constitution of the body (say, as a conglomerate of elementary particles) or at the level of our phenomenal, cum linguistic, understanding of it.

While, then, a classical theory could *think* or *theorize* the unknowable, a nonclassical theory may, at least for the purposes of the theory, configure as unknowable or even as unthinkable the entities that could in principle be thinkable or knowable, or could become such in other contexts, by means of other theories, and so forth. If such is the case, the nonclassical theory in question would, in its own context, *disregard what can be thought or known* about such entities. In other cases, the unknowable or unthinkable character of nonclassical objects may extend beyond the context(s) of the theory where these objects are defined as objects. A stronger claim concerning their inaccessibility would be made upon the entities idealized by the theory as its nonclassical objects, either from within the theory or even beyond it. A nonclassical theory may see its objects, as the objects of that theory, as inaccessible not only by means of this theory but also by other means, possibly by any means, even though it may allow for the existence of entities that, while idealized nonclassically by the theory in question, may be configured classically by other theories. Or it can extend its nonclassical claim by arguing that such entities are equally inaccessible by any rigorous theory.

In other words, a nonclassical theory constructs a particular type of theoretical idealization, in which the ultimate objects of the theory are conceived of or idealized as ultimately inconceivable. This idealization may allow one to infer the existence of something in nature, mind, or culture that is manifest in and is, at least in part, responsible for certain knowable phenomena considered by the theory but that is irreducibly beyond anything we can experience or beyond anything we can possibly conceive of. By the same token, however, such inconceivable entities are seen as the ultimate *objects of the theory and not as objects of nature, mind, or culture*. This view actually leads to a more radical form of nonclassicality. For, whatever exists in nature, mind, or culture as being responsible for the knowable phenomena considered by the theory might be beyond even this idealization and may, accordingly, prove to be something else: either something nonclassical-like or something classical-like in character, or something altogether beyond this type of scheme. (As such, it may be subject to alternative theoretical accounts.) A nonclassical theory can thus be defined by an epistemological double rupture, which would lead to the most radical form of nonclassicality. The first rupture is that between itself as a theory and its ultimate objects, placed beyond the reach of the theory itself or any possible conception, and, the second, between this scheme and the possible constitution of nature, mind, or culture, which defines the first rupture as a theoretical idealization.

A nonclassical *situation* usually proceeds from a given theory, which may be demarcated either more or less determinately or more or less loosely. The *nonclassical* character of the theory is defined by the fact that this theory places certain objects it considers, usually the ultimate objects in question in the theory, beyond the reach of the theory or, at the limit, beyond all knowledge or any possible conception, at least, again, if these objects are considered as the objects of the theory. Such objects, which I shall call "nonclassical" in turn, are, accordingly, treated by the theory as unthinkable, in the literal sense of un-thinkable, as being beyond the thinking of theory, ultimately including objects in any conceivable sense, such as, for example, that of things in themselves. It is essential that unthinkable entities are rigorously defined by means of this theory, rather than merely postulated, and are rigorously correlated with or even derived on the basis of what is thinkable or knowable and indeed known within the field of the theory. As a result, the unthinkable is placed *inside* and is made, as the unthinkable, a constitutive part of this theory, rather than positioned beyond the purview of or otherwise *outside* the theory.[20]

By the same token, the presence of unthinkable objects and the fact that they are unthinkable are essential to what the theory can do in terms of knowledge, explanation, prediction, and so forth. These objects are the constitutive part of the efficacious processes responsible for what (certain effects, events, and so forth) is thinkable and knowable and indeed known by the theory, and from which the existence of the unknowable and the unthinkable involved in the theory is derived or with which it is properly correlated. A nonclassical theory thus does not say that one is not concerned with knowing or thinking about the nature of nonclassical objects, but that the theory, in principle, excludes, or, in the radical cases of nonclassical theorizing, *precludes* the possibility of knowing, saying, or thinking about the nature of such objects. All that the theory can say about such objects is that they exist or, more accurately, as the objects of the theory, relate to something that exists, while this "existence" itself may not be conceivable in any specific form available to the theory or even to our thinking.

By definition, however, nonclassical theories contain classical and indeed strictly knowable strata as well, if one assumes, as I do here, that the existence of nonclassical objects and processes is not merely postulated or imagined, or even thought of, but is rigorously derived by a nonclassical argument. For such a derivation cannot be possible otherwise than on the basis of, or at least in relation to, something that could be and is known, and yet must also be seen as impacted by what is not and cannot be known or thought of. We *know* of or configure the existence of nonclassical objects and *know* (rather than only think) and specifically configure them as unthinkable through their effects upon the knowable, and only through these effects. Accordingly, nonclassical knowledge and thinking could only concern effects produced by nonclassical objects upon other, knowable, and hence classical, objects, in contrast to the Kantian situation, as considered above, whereby we aim to think the unknowable things in themselves.

In the language of Georges Bataille, who gave the nonclassical efficacious processes one of his most famous names, "un-knowledge [*nonsavoir*]," "it would be impossible to speak of unknowledge [*nonsavoir*] [for example, as 'unknowledge'] as such, while we can speak of its effects." Reciprocally, however, "it would not be possible to seriously speak of unknowledge independently of its effects."[21] Hence, while always unknowable and inconceivable, in each instance these effect-producing processes may indeed be different and unique, singular, as, and reciprocally, each effect produced. The field itself of the unthinkable may be different as well depending upon the theory in which it is established, even though it is, again, always established as a field of the unthinkable. Nonclassical epistemology is the epistemology of *knowable* effects whose *ultimate* (but, again, only ultimate) efficacious processes—or, one might say, "history"— are configured by a given theory as irreducibly, in principle (rather than only in practice), *unknowable* and, furthermore, as *inconceivable*, without, however, assuming any mystical agency, divine or human, governing the situation. Hence, the term "history" may only be provisional here and is, ultimately, no more adequate than any other terms or concept.

Accordingly, as understood here, nonclassical theory is essentially materialist. "In principle" is, again, a crucial qualification. For, in most classical cases, too, while it may not be possible to *know* such efficacious dynamics in practice, it may be possible at least to conceive of them, as things in themselves, in principle on one model or another. It follows that, nonclassically, these efficacious dynamics cannot be seen as causal, since causality would be merely one of conceivable attributes, which cannot be assigned to the ultimate processes involved in these dynamics any more than any other attribute.

While, then, the existence itself of such processes or, more accurately, of what is idealized accordingly, is assumed by a given nonclassical theory, the character of these processes may be inconceivable by the theory or, for the purposes of that theory (or possibly even beyond it) in any terms that are, or possibly will ever be, available to us. "Existence" and "nonexistence," are, too, among these terms, as are "efficacious" or "process," along with the possibility or impossibility to "conceive" of it, or "possibility" or "impossibility," or "history," or "it" and "is," to begin with.[22]

These terms just listed or any other terms are not merely inadequate but are strictly inapplicable at the ultimate level, thus introducing a radical, irreducible discontinuity into any representation of these processes. The extent of this inapplicability may, again, vary depending on the scope of (the claim of) of a given nonclassical theory.

As will be seen, this discontinuity is epistemologically analogous to that of de Man's allegory and irony (there are further differences between both tropes), which serve de Man in his engagement with nonclassical epistemology, taken by him to, I would argue, just about the furthest reaches of its claim. It is true that de Man often associated allegory (or irony) with discontinuity, also in juxtaposition to the continuity of the symbol. In view of the considerations just given, however, we may more properly think of this relation as neither continuous nor discontinuous, or in terms of any conceivable combination of both concepts, or, again, in any given terms. In this sense, de Manian discontinuity is more radically "discontinuous" than discontinuity itself, that is, than any form of the discontinuous we can conceive of. De Man's emphasis on the discontinuity of allegory conceptually and strategically points in this direction, away from the continuity of the symbol or of aesthetic ideology. Both continuity and discontinuity are retained at the level of "effects," and the effects of discontinuity are indeed more crucial to allegory (or irony). It must, however, be seen as an effect of a more complex efficacious machinery, which is itself neither continuous nor discontinuous, nor is, again, accessible by means of the theory developed by de Man or, it appears, according to de Man, any terms or concepts available to us, whether by means of other theories or otherwise. As a bridge to a more textually oriented discussion of nonclassicality in and via de Man's work, I shall, in the next section, introduce a model of the nonclassical epistemological situation by considering collectivities and organizations of nonclassically conceived individual elements or singularities.

Organization of Singularities and the Parliament of Taste

As we have seen, according to Kant, "all judgments of taste are *singular* [*einzelne*] judgments," at least "in their logical quality" (my emphasis). They are such by virtue of emerging through extraordinarily complex processes, which are not governed by concepts or possibly even by cognition in its usual sense (such as that of *kennen*, used by Kant in the first *Critique*, as cited above), but instead by a certain economy of "feeling," a very complex conception in turn. The famous *de gustibus non disputantum est* is a commonsense reflection of this singularity and uniqueness, and of the complexity of the constitution and emergence of the singular. How each such judgment comes about appears to be too complex to analyze or even to conceive of at the ultimate level of its constitution, at least in practice, but possibly in principle. If the latter is the case, these processes may and perhaps must be theorized nonclassically (again, in relation to the ultimate level of their functioning and constitution). Then, how such judgments cohere into a universal consensual field or, in any event, a sufficiently large consensual field, would be at least as enigmatic or mysterious as how each such singular judgment of the beautiful or the sublime could emerge. How could we possibly agree or even negotiate our judgments of taste, and within what limits, given the irreducibly singular and irreducibly random nature of each? Or, how can we, proceeding from a singular judgment, postulate the possibility of such an agreement, which must also, indeed by virtue of the singular character of each judgment, entail the possibility of the rejection of our judgment? In a nonclassical account the enigmatic, but, again, not mystical, nature of these processes at the ultimate level of its operation would be taken as a given, at least as concerns the purview of the theory. A nonclassical account would take for granted the impossibility of theorizing the ultimate nature of such processes, in both cases: that of the history of each individual judgment, and that of a collective coherence of such judgments. It would proceed instead to an analysis of effects and, through such effects, implications of these processes, possibly leaving a more complete (by classical criteria) account to a future theory.

Collectivities of nonclassical singularities are, by definition, assemblages of singular elements such that the emergence or history of each is nonclassical, is subject to a nonclassical theory and epistemology. Under certain circumstances (such as those of the beautiful and the sublime in Kant), however, although not always (for example, not in the case of aesthetic judgments other than those of the beautiful or the sublime), some among such assemblages may allow for *organized* or cohering relations between their individual elements. Such circumstances may be rare. It is enough, however, that they occur sometimes, and that they do is remarkable, given that each such judgment is singular in its logical quality, that is, each follows its own logic, which, however, allows one to take the nonclassical view of the situation and use it as a nonclassical model in any given domain. Such situations disallow us to establish, or possibly even conceive of, the ultimate nature of the emergence of these (organized) relations, just as they do already in the case of the emergence of each individual element involved, whether, again, these belong to organized collectivities or not.

Singularity may be defined by the property of *manifest* lawlessness of an object or an event in relation to a given law, or to law in general. Here this definition applies more specifically when this property arises in a single or point-like fashion—physical, as in the case of black holes, although the latter may have (inaccessible) inner structure; mathematical (a "singular" point of a function, or a "singular" solution of an equation); phenomenal; historical; and so forth.[23]

Nonclassically, then, the history of each *individual* judgment concerning the beautiful or the sublime would be singular and, in relation to this context, random (it may be causal in the context of this individual history), even though collectively these judgments may cohere together into a certain pattern or be (nearly) identical to one another. These circumstances would always pertain to the case of the beautiful or the sublime, but not necessarily otherwise, in which cases we have random, rather than organized, collectivities, while the nature or history of the individual elements involved is equally nonclassical in both types of collective situations. This is why that two types of collectivities, random and organized, may result is essential to the model in question.

It follows that when organization, order, or law apply in organized collectivities comprised by singularities, they apply only at the level of the *effects*, to the collectivities of effects, involved but not to the ultimate efficacious dynamics responsible for these effects. One could hardly be surprised to encounter random collectivities, whether governed by usual statistical laws (which are quite different from the regularities we encounter in nonclassical cases) or not. By contrast, that the irreducible randomness of individual events may cohere into an order is enigmatic or else paradoxical. One avoids the paradox, although not the enigma, by theorizing the situation in terms of nonclassical epistemology: we do not and cannot possibly know, or possibly even conceive of, how this is possible. On the other hand, in accordance with the nonclassical view, neither the singular and/as lawless nor, by the same token, nonclassical efficacious processes that produce them as effects (along with ordered collectivities that these singular effects comprise) is seen as something that is excluded from a given domain or a system governed by a singularized collectivity. Neither is seen as an outside or an *absolute* other of the system, but, joined together, as the constitutive, essential part of it and as fundamentally responsible for its constitution. In conformity with nonclassical theory, we now deal only with certain effects and certain particular configurations of effects, without addressing their (in this context noncausal) histories, which, however, allows us to theoretically handle ordered organizations of singularities.

It is worth stressing that it is not merely the question of the impossibility of applying organization or law to the history of *certain* exceptional individual entities (elements, cases, events, effects, and so forth) within a given multiplicity. The history of *every individual* entity that belongs to an organized collectivity of singularities is not subject to the organization and law involved, or to organization and law in general.[24]

In some cases, each such (in its emergence) random individual entity may possess a rich structure of its own, possibly in turn governed by a nonclassical organization of singularities, as would indeed be the case in any individual judgment of the beautiful or the sublime. That "inner" structure may, furthermore, become involved in the set-up of the relationships between the individual and the collective, as is, again, the case in assessing each individual judgment of the beautiful or the sublime. The ensuing renegotiation can in turn lead to a reorganization of a given collective negotiation of such judgments, and lead to a new singularized collectivity or make one reconfigure a classical collectivity nonclassically (or, in certain cases, a nonclassical one classically). Leibniz here might have spoken of monads, which may be seen as minimal or atomic (in the original Greek sense of not divisible any further), as *thinking* entities, even though at least their bodies, if not their souls, may be seen as, in a certain sense, composite. The essence of monads as thinking elements or atoms in Leibniz remains crucial, however, and is especially pertinent in the present context. The concept of nonclassical organization of singularities may be seen as a critical, post-Kantian response to, or as a nonclassical rereading of, Leibniz's monadology, which makes it, if one is permitted so monstrous a term, into "singularology." In contrast to Leibniz's scheme, while the nonclassical efficacious dynamics responsible for collectivities of singularities may produce effects of both types, collectively organized and individually lawless, these dynamics are, by definition, not thought and possibly cannot be thought of in terms of a single underlying governing "wholeness" (that of the World as a whole), in relation to which Leibniz places his monads. Nonclassical efficacious dynamics cannot be seen either as single in governing all of their effects or as multiple in the sense of allowing one to assign a specific separate efficacious dynamic to each individual effect. They must, however, be seen as irreducibly multiple in the sense that the efficacious processes involved that give rise to each individual effect are each time different. In other words, as I have indicated, the efficacious dynamics of any given effect are each time as unique, singular as, and reciprocal with, the effect they generate, and yet are, each time, also ultimately inconceivable.

From the nonclassical viewpoint, then, one may offer the following understanding, possibly more radical than Kant aimed at, of Kant's argument that "in their logical quality all judgments of taste are *singular* [*einzelne*] judgments," while, at the same time, allowing for a possibility of the universality, or at least sufficiently large consensus concerning, the beautiful or the sublime. One can establish partial and intermediate links between such judgments and even must do so in order for them to work, even as singular judgments, but especially in the case of the consensus demanded by the beautiful and the sublime, in the cases of which Kant traces experiential (phenomenological, psychological, or social) commonalities that help the consensus. There may, however, be no possibility to *theorize* either the ultimate efficacious dynamics or/as history of each or, in spite of the commonalities just alluded to, their correlations as leading to the beautiful or the sublime. Nonclassical theory would replace "there may be no possibility" with "there *is no* possibility," at least from within the nonclassical framework that one could apply. On this view, the events in question are irreducibly random, or, given the ascertainable commonalities between them, each involves irreducibly random elements, which elements (rather than only the commonalities) are, nevertheless, also part of the correlations between aesthetic judgments of the beautiful or the sublime. The ultimate character of this organization of, in their separate histories, random events may be bound to be beyond our grasp.

Accordingly, the primary difference between the classical and the nonclassical view of the situation would be as follows. A classical theory of a consensus shaped by and shaping aesthetic judgments, such as those of the beautiful and the sublime, would view the emergence of this consensus in terms of the phenomenological, psychological, or cultural experiential commonalities of the judgment involved. That any aesthetic judgment offering itself to a consensus, for example, as that concerning the beautiful or the sublime must be accepted freely and, hence, could be rejected just as freely, would be handled as follows. This "freedom" would be seen as determined by the phenomenological, psychological, or cultural experiential commonalities, more or less innate and more or less developed (or even enforced through ideological apparatuses of one kind or another), that is, by a certain underlying necessity. This freedom could then be analytically approached classically, even if in terms of unknowable but thinkable things in themselves, which—or the question of freedom in general—is the main subject of Kant's epistemology in the sphere of the human mind. These aspects of the situation are significant and must be taken into account by a nonclassical view of this situation as well, either as part of a nonclassical account (which inevitably involves classical strata) or by way of complementing it with a classical account. Nevertheless, a nonclassical account would see the emergence of this "consensus" as due most essentially to the inscrutable correlations of singular, random judgments, even if the latter are seen in this way only provisionally, due to the complexity of the history and the constitution of each such judgment.[25] Even this would be enough to change the shape of the theory. As de Man's work suggests, however, in aesthetics and elsewhere, stronger forms of nonclassicality may be possible or become necessary.

Allegory and Nonclassicality in de Man

De Man's concepts of allegory and irony, and the theoretical models developed by de Man with the help of these and related conceptions, might be argued to conform to the nonclassical paradigm in, I would further argue, its stronger version. For de Man's claim of the nonclassical inaccessibility of the ultimate objects in question in theoretical models appears to extend beyond the inaccessibility by the means of these models and to place absolute limits upon the power of our knowledge and thought—or language, since the question of language plays an essential role in de Man's work.

This epistemology was initially discussed and deployed by de Man, in particular in "The Rhetoric of Temporality," primarily in the context of literary history by exploring the relationships between more nonclassically oriented allegory and irony, on the one hand, and the more classically oriented symbol, on the other. Even in this earlier work, however, but especially in his later work, this problematic extends well beyond this literary context, important as it remains throughout, while allegory becomes arguably the dominant rubric under which de Man's argumentation is developed. His formulation in "Pascal's Allegory of Persuasion" captures the nonclassical epistemology of allegory in its radical form: "the difficulty of allegory is rather that this emphatic clarity of representation does not stand in the service of something that can be represented."[26]

De Man does not say that this something cannot be represented by means of a *given* allegory; nor does his argument in the article suggest this more limited claim. Instead, he appears to refer to that which is unrepresentable by any means, at least from the viewpoint of the theory, which, as we have seen, may be an epistemologically stronger claim, making the unrepresentable in question unrepresentable even as unrepresentable, unknowable even as unknowable, unthinkable even as unthinkable, and so forth. Accordingly, one might say that the emphatic clarity of representation in allegory stands in the service of something that, while it enables allegory itself and its emphatic clarity, cannot be represented by any means.

It is hardly surprising, in view of the preceding analysis, that the question of singularity and of assemblages of singularities becomes significant in de Man's work, especially in his *reading* of Kant.[27] This reading proceeds in part in conjunction with his readings of Kleist, juxtaposed to Schiller and his (mis)reading of Kant, and, perhaps more unexpectedly but logically, Shelley, and de Man, importantly, speaks of the "models" that he has "been developing on the basis of texts," and, one might add, a certain type of texts.[28]

Nor it is surprising that the question of history acquires a special significance at this juncture. De Man defines "history" in terms of allegorical discontinuity in juxtaposition to "temporality," at least if the latter is seen, as it is by de Man, in terms of continuity and, hence, classically in the present sense. The discussion, and the very concept, of allegory in "Pascal's Allegory of Persuasion" is linked to this question, via the question of narrative and irony. As de Man says there: "The (ironic) pseudoknowledge of this impossibility, which pretends to order sequentially, in a narrative, what is actually the destruction of all sequence, is what we call allegory."[29]

This is a subtle way to look at the situation. This statement implies that allegory in de Man's sense also involves a production of a certain, perhaps pretended, classical configuration, superimposed on a nonclassical assemblage of events (either random or organized nonclassically), which cannot itself be rigorously read classically, except by way of a misprision, blindness, or pretence. The nature of this misprision, blindness, or pretence in relation to the nonclassical dynamics in question must be analyzed, in de Man specifically via the texts, such as Kleist's or Shelley's, which, in de Man's words, "analytically thematize" various aspects, classical and nonclassical, of allegory.[30]

History in de Man's sense can be seen in terms of nonclassically singular events, as considered here, whereby we are irreducibly and, as de Man stresses, irreversibly deprived of any possibility of conceiving of how these events could be linked and, it follows, theorized as continuous with the ultimate processes responsible for their emergence. Collectively, such events may exhibit certain organizations, either sequentially or in parallel. But this organization, too, is nonclassical and, as such, disallows the possibility of establishing how the (nonclassical) correlations between such events came about. Hence, "the [ultimate] destruction of all sequence," whereby we can, with "(ironic) pseudoknowledge," at most only "pretend" to order this dynamics and this emergence "sequentially, in a narrative." By the same token, while history itself is thus seen in terms of such events, as effects, each of which "has the materiality of something that actually happens, that actually occurs," the nonclassical processes themselves responsible for these events cannot be seen in terms of history any more than in any other terms.[31]

De Man describes this view of history most explicitly in "Kant and Schiller." He addresses, first, the irreversibility of the passage from cognitive or tropological to performative, and then invokes a trap into which he had fallen in approaching this concept of history. He says: "When I was asked the other day whether I thought of history as a priori in any sense, I had to say yes to that. Then, not knowing quite into which trap I'd fallen, or what or whether I had fallen into a trap or what's still behind it . . ." (*AI*, p. 133). "Trap" and "fall" are persistent tropes in de Man's approaches to this problematic. He explains his concept of history itself as follows:

> History, the sense of the notion of history as the historicity a priori of this type of textual model which I have been suggesting here, there history is not thought of as a progression or a regression, but thought of as an event, as an occurrence. There is history from the moment that words such as "power" and "battle" and so on emerge on the scene. At that moment things *happen*, there is *occurrence*, there is *event*. History is therefore not a temporal notion, it has nothing to do with temporality, but it is the emergence of the language of power out of a language of cognition. An emergence which is, however, not itself either dialectical movement or any kind of continuum that would be accessible to a cognition, however much it may be conceived of, as would be the case in a Hegelian dialectic, as a negation. (*AI*, p. 133)

It follows that the ultimate processes responsible for "events" are seen in radically nonclassical terms: they are inaccessible, first, by means, and in terms, of de Man's model in question and, second, beyond this model, in terms of any available or conceivable terms, including in terms of negation of terms, concepts, and predicates. As such they would be inaccessible even as inaccessible, unrepresentable as unrepresentable, unknowable as unknowable, inconceivable as inconceivable, and so forth. Accordingly, the separation in question allows for "no mediation whatsoever," dialectical or other, as de Man further explains in the context of the historical relationships between the performative and the cognitive or the tropological, to which he applies his historical model, including the model of irreversibility, as considered earlier. "The performative," de Man says, "is not a negation of the tropological. Between the tropological and the performative there is a separation which allows for no mediation whatsoever. But there is single-directed movement that goes from the one to the other and which is not susceptible of being represented as a [continuous or causal] temporal process. That is historical and it doesn't allow for any reinscription of history into any kind of cognition."[32]

The material and cognitive irreversibility of these dynamics is an essential aspect of the situation. The material irreversibility is due to the fact that nonclassical processes are, by definition, irreducibly irreversible in relation to the individual events they produce as their effects, or the nonclassical correlations between such events. In "Kant and Schiller," de Man speaks of "[the] problem of the question of irreversibility, of the reversibility in the type of models which I have been developing on the basis of texts. And this is linked to the question of reversibility, linked to the question of historicity."[33] I would argue these models to be essentially nonclassical.

It is true of course that history conceived on a classical model is also irreversible in actual sequences of events or occurrences that one considers. The nonclassical irreversibility is, however, more radical epistemologically or cognitively by virtue of the nonclassical nature of the processes responsible for the events in de Man's sense. For, while such processes are responsible for the events in question, they also, in principle, disallow one to trace back—*cognitively*, rather than only *actually*, "reverse"—a causal or continuous historical trajectory leading to these events or even to presuppose the existence of such a trajectory, in the way it would be done in classical historical or temporal models. The models of such situations are, de Man also argues, *performative*, rather than *cognitive*.[34] As a result, the question of historical repetition of such events takes the new dimensions as well.[35] In other words, classically, while we cannot reverse history materially, we can, at least in principle, follow its trajectory back in order to arrange the events in question "sequentially, in a narrative." Nonclassically, this is impossible, and it is this impossibility that leads to irreversible (a)cognition or allegory as "the (ironic) pseudoknowledge of this impossibility," even though the historical events may, in spite of their individual singularity, collectively exhibit certain organizations, sequential or parallel. This organization, however, is nonclassical and, as such, allows for no possibility to represent or even to conceive of, especially in continuous or causal terms (causality is itself a form of conceptual continuity), the processes responsible for this organization, and hence no classical wholeness behind it either. As other nonclassical models, these, too, necessarily involve classical elements or models at the level of effects, in accordance with the analysis given earlier.

The same type of historical model is applied by de Man to the very history of reception of the third *Critique* and reading (or not reading) Kant from Schiller onward, specifically as the history of aesthetic ideology.[36] These applications carry certain inflections concerning the functioning (cognitive, discursive, cultural, or political) of the concept and practice of historicity and history. Similar moves and inflections are found in de Man's reading of, among others, Rousseau, Kleist, and Shelley, where the history of romanticism is also at stake. These texts are, then, read by de Man as allegories of the processes in question. The model itself is, however, very general in nature. Indeed, it may be applied to temporality (which is given a more continuous meaning at the particular juncture in question) and the rhetoric of temporality as well, as has been done by de Man himself from "The Rhetoric of Temporality" onward, or aesthetics and politics, along the lines considered earlier. At the ultimate level, any event is either itself unique and singular in the nonclassical sense or, however ordinary or un-eventful it is or appears to be, is decomposable into the sum of such nonclassical events, whether nonclassically organized or not.[37] In this case (the relationships between the classical and the nonclassical may take other forms), any classical organization or a classical view of each event could only be superimposed upon, and is itself an effect of, the nonclassical dynamics governing the situation.

De Man arguably makes his strongest epistemological claim in the famous elaboration closing "Shelley Disfigured." He says: "*The Triumph of Life* warns us that *nothing*, whether deed, word, thought or text, *ever* happens in relation, positive or negative, to anything that preceded, follows, or exists elsewhere, but only as a random event whose power, like the power of death, is due to the randomness of its occurrence" (my emphasis).[38] In the present terms, we may speak of the radical, irreducible singularity and discontinuity of random events, into which any given event or historical trajectory would always ultimately *decompose* itself, just as, to use a fitting image here, any human body will ultimately do, at least after "death." This decomposition or this death, however, begins much earlier, although the effects of death to which we give a particular sense in the context of what we call "human existence" are of course significant, not least in providing a model for other conceptions of death. Life is always death, but death is not always life. As it makes allegory irreducible in any representation, phenomenalization, knowledge, and so forth, death or life-death becomes a model for—or, better, an allegory of, and perhaps *the* allegory of—the ultimate structure of *every* event of life. Given de Man's conception of allegory in his essay on Pascal, cited earlier, it would, as elsewhere in nonclassical theory, be difficult to speak of the underlying efficacious dynamics of such random events as themselves random, any more than causal, or any more discontinuous than continuous, or, again, in any given or even conceivable terms. At the same time, this view leaves the space to the corresponding effects—such as (these are often parallel) those of randomness and causality or those of discontinuity and continuity, or any other we might or must need, in a way nearly all terms classical theories of the situations in question would use.

Such literary texts as those of Kleist, Keats, or Shelley, or such philosophical texts as those of Kant and Hegel, offer us new, nonclassical, models of singular events—hence of un-patterning, unordering, and un-lawfulness—and new ways in which these relate to patterns, order, and law. But are order, organization, or coherence actually possible, given de Man's view of history, literary or other, as just outlined, or, returning to the Kantian situation considered above, in politics? Are they possible in the world, which *The Triumph of Life* analytically thematizes and in which we must live and die? Are they possible in the world where *ultimately*, "*nothing* [and not only certain things], whether deed, word, thought or text, *ever* [and not only sometimes] happens in relation, positive or negative, to anything that preceded, follows, or exists elsewhere, but only as a random event whose power, like the power of death, is due to the randomness of its occurrence"? Yes, they are possible, but at a cost, which one unavoidably pays in the epistemological economy of gains and losses of nonclassical theory. De Man does not close "Shelley Disfigured" with the randomness of death as the final warning of Shelley's poem. Instead, he adds:

> [The poem] also warns us why and how these events [and at bottom the ultimate events constitutive of any event] *then* have to be reintegrated in a historical and aesthetic system of recuperation that repeats itself regardless of the exposure of its fallacy. This process differs entirely from the recuperative and nihilistic allegories of historicism [or aestheticism]. If it is true and unavoidable that any reading is a monumentalization of sorts, the way

in which Rousseau is read and disfigured in *The Triumph of Life* puts Shelley among the few readers who "guessed whose statue those fragments had composed." Reading as disfiguration, to the very extent that it resists historicism [or aestheticism] turns out to be historically more reliable than the products of historical archeology [or aesthetic ideology]. To monumentalize this observation into a *method* of reading would be to regress from the rigor exhibited by Shelley, which is exemplary because it refuses to be generalized into a system.[39] (my emphasis)

In accordance with de Man's view of history in "Kant and Schiller," considered earlier, there is a complex stratification, with interactive classical and nonclassical strata, to the historical or, interactively, aestheticoideological processes in question. As in de Man's reading of Kant, this multicomponent and multilevel machinery is also applied to the history of reading Shelley's poem itself or, via Shelley, romanticism. All of these are "analytically thematized" by Shelley's poem, which as a reading of (the figure of) Rousseau, among others, and the history of literature and culture, is already a history of romanticism and reading romanticism, a nonclassical history and, as such, is more reliable than its classical alternatives. Shelley's reading of Rousseau, especially cum de Man's reading of Shelley (or of Rousseau elsewhere in his work) thus also transforms into a nonclassical register our understanding of biography as well, or how biography and history are related nonclassically, conjunctively or disjunctively.[40]

First, then, there is a nonclassical history of singular, random events, "whose power, like the power of death, is due to the randomness of its occurrence." Second, there is, under certain circumstances, a nonclassical history of organizations of such singular events, or organization of singularities, including a historical organization of them as events. Finally, there is a history, in turn nonclassical, of "reintegrating in a historical and aesthetic system of recuperation that repeats itself regardless of the exposure of its fallacy," in a process that "differs entirely from the recuperative and nihilistic allegories of historicism." This history, I argue here, is also a (nonclassical) history of the nonclassical processes that give rise to classical forms of historicism as one of its effects. These effects (or other classical elements nonclassical approaches involve) sometimes lead to an ideologizing misreading of the analysis or enactment of these processes in such texts as those of Kant, Hegel, Kleist, and Shelley. It is, then, by this multileveled nonclassical process that a more reliable history, including (as is clear from the passage) in its classical sense, may be achieved, and is achieved by Shelley's poem. In other words, by rigorously putting the irreducible "loss" in historical accessibility, representation, knowledge, or conception into play, both a greater richness of historical representation, knowledge, or conception, and a greater reliability of a "guess," become possible as well. One can of course only speak of "loss" here if one applies a classical concept of representation. For, we also gain in terms of knowledge that now becomes possible and was not possible classically. But then, as de Man's last sentence suggests, each nonclassical reading may itself be unique, singular. The lessons of such texts or of their grouping together are complicated accordingly. It is still an *educated* guess, which, however, entails a very different type of guessing and a very different type of education (the subject to which I shall return presently).

The allegory of the human body in the form of the fragmented statue, introduced at the outset in de Man's epigraph (courtesy of Thomas Hardy) is, again, a decisive vehicle of de Man's analysis.[41] The essay also alludes to the body of romanticism, conjoined with many a dead body found in key romantic texts, and with the disfigured dead body of Shelley himself.[42] I would like, in closing, to link the preceding discussion, via the question of the body, to the question of "linguistic understanding" of Kant's argument on the sublime according to de Man. This understanding brings Kant's third *Critique* even closer to nonclassical epistemology, at least at the textual level, if not in terms of its logical argumentation (to the degree that we separate these).

This, epistemologically more radical, reach of Kant's text is suggested by de Man's reading of Kant's architectonics, via the question of the body, toward the end of "Phenomenality and Materiality in Kant." We must, de Man says, consider "our limbs," formally, "in themselves, severed from the organic unity of the body." "We must, in other words, disarticulate, mutilate the body" and hence enact "the material *disarticulation* not only of nature but of the body, . . . [which] moment marks the undoing of the aesthetic as a valid category."[43] Any arrangement of such parts— phenomenological, conceptual, or linguistic—is ultimately a form of allegory and is subject to its nonclassical epistemology (with inevitable and indispensable classical effects), just as is the body of a given text, history, or aesthetic field, as discussed above in the context of "Shelley Disfigured." Some of these effects can serve to construct partial and ultimately inadequate (classical) "allegories" of the materiality of the "body" in question, both that of the manifest effects or of the irreducibly inconceivable efficacious processes responsible for these effects. The initial (wherever we begin) "parts" or "limbs" are already such allegories, derived from the classical view, and hence as supplementary as the body itself. Accordingly, a more radical disarticulation and disfiguration (in either sense) of the (un)body is at stake, even at the level of manifest effects. The efficacious processes behind these effects are, again, inaccessible in any way, no more by means of disarticulation, however radical, than by means of articulation. With respect to these processes, the dismemberment and disarticulation in question (at the level of the effects) itself reflects only this inaccessibility, not the character of the processes themselves. This disarticulating dismemberment of the body will be linked to the linguistic understanding of materiality and specifically to the disarticulation of tropes, as indeed the term (figure? trope?) "disarticulation" suggests.

De Man, accordingly, extends and radicalizes the complexities of the concept of the body, as considered above, along the Kantian lines—as demarcated in a more limited, let us say, physical-physiological register, whereby our conception of the constitution of the body could proceed from the phenomenal, to the noumenal, and ultimately to the nonclassical level—and related them. The *linguistic* dimensions (in de Man's sense) of this question, which sometimes (but not always!) could and even must be bypassed in this register, inescapably bring the nonclassical register of this question into play.[44] Kant's text itself, linguistically, shows this, as do both those of Kleist and Shelley, or, perhaps more accurately, de Man's reading of these texts puts this machinery of disarticulation to work, which allows him to build the model(s) in question "on the basis of texts," and readings of those texts, as he said.

In "Aesthetic Formalization: Kleist's *Über das Marionettentheater*," de Man, again, proceeds from Schiller:

> I know of no better image of a beautiful society than a well-executed English dance, composed of many complicated figures and turns. A spectator located on the balcony observes an infinite variety of criss-crossing motions which keep decisively but arbitrarily changing directions without ever colliding with each other. Everything has been arranged in such a manner that each dancer has already vacated his position by the time the other arrives. Everything fits so skillfully, yet so spontaneously, that everyone seems to be following his own lead, without ever getting in anyone's way. Such a dance is the perfect *symbol* of one's own individually asserted freedom as well as of one's respect for freedom of the other.[45] (my emphasis)

This is, in present terms, a classical description, and as such is also a classical philosophical concept of political community, as well as, as noted above, of education and educated guesses and calculated risks, mitigated by the classical (aesthetic) ideology and model of education, all part of the history of ideologizing misreadings of both idealism and romanticism. Gasché sees de Man's argumentation as a possible, or possibly impossible, alternative to this program. According to Gasché, "[T]he legacy of [de Man's] endeavors consists in attempting to think a notion of community that would not represent a higher whole of relations, whose public stature would not be grounded in a universal form of mediation, and that would escape altogether the *dialectic* of universality and individuality. It is a formidable task, undoubtedly, at the limit of the possible perhaps, but therefore an assignment for thinking" (my emphasis).[46] I would argue that, if this task, perhaps less impossible than Gasché suspects, is to be approached, one way of proceeding is to relate the individual, as unique and singular, and the collective ("community") along the lines of the analysis offered here. I would also argue that de Man travels rather further on this road than Gasché appears to suggest. The resulting conception is, by definition, nondialectical, since it is not grounded in the synthesis in which the parts and the whole are harmonized after dialectically negating each other. But, as the preceding analysis suggests, it is more radical and complex than only this.

De Man juxtaposes both Kant and Kleist, especially Kleist's nonclassical allegories (as against Schiller's "symbol" and the classical aesthetical-political ideology it entails) to Schiller's vision, and to Schiller's reading of Kant, along the aesthetic, epistemological, and political lines of singularity and nonclassicality. After a complex analysis, which cannot be addressed within my limits here, de Man arrives at a dance that is very different from the "strictly ballroom" dance and calculus of Schiller:

> We have traveled some way from the original Schiller quotation to the mechanical dance, which is also a dance of death and mutilation. The violence which existed as a latent background in the story of the ephebe and of the bear now moves into full sight. One must already have felt some resistance to the unproblematic reintegration of the puppet's limbs and articulations, suspended in dead passivity, into the continuity of the dance: "all its members (are) what they should be, dead, mere pendula, and they follow the law of pure gravity."[47]

The invocation of Newton's law of gravity, the paradigmatic classical physical law, is of much interest and significance here. Both the question of the classical laws of physics, and thus the formalization of nature, specifically via differential calculus (an important connection here), are at stake. A more Newtonian Kant, against himself, makes Kleist and (it is easier after Einstein) de Man think beyond Newton, who is about to appear next. I shall return to the question of falling, physically defining gravity.[48] De Man writes next:

> The passage is all the harder to assimilate since it has been preceded by the briskly told story of an English technician able to build such perfect mechanical legs that a mutilated man will be able to dance with them in Schiller-like perfection. "The circle of his motion may be restricted, but as for those [movements] available to them, he accomplishes them with an ease, elegance and gracefulness which fills any thinking mind with amazement." One is reminded of the protests of the eyeless philosopher Saunderson in Diderot's *Lettre sur les aveugles* when, to the deistic optimism of the Reverend Holmes, disciple of Newton, Leibniz and Clark, he opposes the sheer monstrosity of his own being, made all the more intolerable by the mathematical perfection of his highly formalized intellect: "Look at me well, Mr. Holmes, I have no eyes. . . . The order (of the universe) is not so perfect that it does not allow, from time to time, for the production of monsters." The dancing invalid of Kleist's story is one more victim in a long series of mutilated bodies that attend on the progress of enlightened self-knowledge, a series that includes Wordsworth's mute country-dwellers and blind city-beggars. The point is not that the dance fails and that Schiller's idyllic description of a graceful but confined freedom is aberrant. Aesthetic education by no means fails; it succeeds all too well, to the point of hiding the violence that makes it possible.[49]

At stake, then, is the possibility of organization, aesthetic or other, under the condition of the radical singularity and deformity—monstrosity—that are manifest, materially and phenomenally, as effects. De Man further explores the economy of "the mutilated body" in his analysis of the Kantian architectonics in "Kant's Materialism" and "Phenomenality and Materiality in Kant." In a parallel gesture to his essay on Kleist (cited by him), de Man invokes Diderot's *Lettre sur les sourds and les muetes* in considering the allegorization of the faculties of reason and imagination in terms of both the anthropomorphized dramatic conflict and the sacrificially mutilated body. Then, he proceeds to a reading of Kant's architectonics and its self-de-architectonization in terms of a mutilated body. He writes:

> After lingering briefly over the aesthetic vision of the heaven and the seas, Kant turns for a moment to the human body: "The like is to be said of the beautiful and sublime [found] in the human body. We must not regard as determining grounds for our judgment the concept of the purposes which all our limbs serve [*wozu alle seine Gliedmassen da sind*] and we must not allow this unity of purpose to influence our aesthetic judgment (for it would

not longer be pure) . . ." [. . .] We must, in short, consider our limbs, hands, toes, breasts, or what Montaigne so cheerfully referred to as "Monsieur ma partie," in themselves, severed from the organic unity of the body [or rather of our perception of this unity]. . . . We must, in other words, disarticulate, mutilate the body in a way that is much closer to Kleist than Winckelman, though close enough to the violent end that happened to befall both of them.[50]

It may be argued that de Man is here moving beyond Kant in the radical degree of disarticulation that he proposes, insofar as Kant suspends only "the unity of purpose," while de Man severs the parts from any organic unity. Indeed, a still more radical linguistic and conceptual disarticulation of such "parts" (as *body parts*) is at stake. De Man continues:

> From the phenomenality of the aesthetic (which is always based on an inadequacy of the mind to its physical object, based on what is referred to, in the definition of the sublime, as the concrete representation of ideas—*Darstellung der Ideen*) we have moved to the pure materiality of *Augenschein*, of aesthetic vision. From the organic, still asserted as architectonic, principle of the *Critique of Pure Reason*, to the phenomenological, the rational cognition of incarnate ideas, which the best part of the Kant interpretation in the nineteenth and twentieth century will single out, we have reached, in the final analysis, a materialism that, in the tradition of the reception of the third *Critique*, is seldom or never perceived. To appreciate the full impact of this conclusion one must remember that the entire project of the third *Critique*, the full investment in the aesthetic, was to achieve the articulation that would guarantee the architectonic unity of the system. If the architectonic then appears, very near the end of the analytics of the aesthetic, at the conclusion of the section on the sublime, as the material disarticulation not only of nature but of the body, then this moment marks the undoing of the aesthetic as a valid category. The critical power of a transcendental philosophy undoes the very project of such a philosophy leaving us, certainly not with an ideology—for transcendental and ideological (metaphysical) principles are part of the same system—but with a materialism that Kant's postcrity has not yet begun to face up to. This happens not out of lack of philosophical energy or rational power, but as a result of the very strength and consistency of this power.[51]

"The pure materiality" inherent in this "aesthetic vision," by the time it reaches this stage, would entail a radical dislocation of any possible representation at the level of the efficacious dynamics of the effects or material (or mental) marks phenomenalized by this vision, let alone any organic, systemic, symbolic, or other unity. This (nonclassical) epistemology and aesthetics, or antiaesthetics, are, again, applied by de Man to the text of Kleist's essay itself, as well as to Kant's third *Critique*, which are unexpectedly, but more logically than paradoxically, brought together. Kant's text, too, is now seen in terms of radical textual materiality, structured through "a dismemberment of language." De Man argues that "to the dismemberment of the body *corresponds* a dismemberment of language, as meaning-producing tropes are replaced by the fragmentation of sentences and propositions into discrete words, or the fragmentation of words into syllables or finally letters" (my emphasis).[52]

One thus encounters the workings of radical materiality in de Man's sense in the textual working of Kant, or still more radically, or at least more deliberately, in Kleist and Shelley. This materiality, I argue, *corresponds* to the nonclassical efficacious dynamics of the effects in question, and the accompanying singularities, constituting and disfiguring in constituting, constituting in disfiguring—both in the body (either as the human body or whenever the signifier applies) and in the text. It would, however, be a mistake to see them as merely mirroring or mapping each other (although this happens, too, sometimes), as de Man's usage of "corresponds" here might suggest, but should not.[53] Instead, the following situation obtains. As one approaches the world by way of a text or a (body of the) text by way of reading, one encounters the dismemberment or, we may say, "decoherence" of language—the irreducible and uncontrollable divergence of the meaning of figures, tropes, signifiers, and so forth, of whatever carries meaning. This decoherence, however, signals the irreducible inaccessibility of the efficacious processes that give rise to the body or the text through certain nonclassical configurations of material or phenomenal effects. Accordingly, the (nonclassically) dismembered, decohered language or representation (i.e., the configuration of the corresponding phenomenal effects) does not map or otherwise represent them any more than (classically) "coherent" language and representations do, or more than a reading represents a text. However, decoherent representations or allegories appear to be better suited to relate to the world and life, and whatever bodies one finds there, or to read the kind of texts in question here.

In de Man, this model is developed "on the basis of [reading] texts," in other words, on the basis of (an enactment of) a decoherence of figures and tropes, or of all language, in the text of Kleist, or Shelley, or Kant, if in the latter case against other forces, conceptual or textual.[54] This decoherence defines the functioning of virtually all figures and tropes in these texts. They give the materiality of the signifiers a formal structure we encounter in nonclassical theory. Or rather the materiality of the signifier in de Man's sense is this structure, which then requires a very different form of formalization able to handle the organization of singularities, each of which is random if considered in terms of the history of its emergence. De Man writes:

> [W]hen, by the end of the tale, the word *Fall* has been overdetermined in a manner that stretches it from the theological to the dead pendulum of the puppet's limbs to the grammatical declension of nouns and pronouns (what we call, in English, the grammatical case), then any composite word that includes *Fall* (*Beifall, Sündenfall, Rückfall* or *Einfall*) acquires a disjunctive plurality of meaning.
>
> C's story of the puppets, for instance, is said to be more than a random improvisation: "*die Äusserung schien mir durch die Art, wie er sie vorbrachte, mehr als ein blosser Einfall.*" As we know from another narrative text of Kleist ["*Über die allmähliche Verfertigung der Gedanken beim Reden*"], the memorable tropes that have most success (*Beifall*) occur as mere random improvisation (*Einfall*) at the moment when the author has completely relinquished any control over his meaning and has relapsed (*Zurückfall*) into the extreme *formalization* [my emphasis], the mechanical predictability of grammatical declension (*Fälle*).
>
> But *Fälle*, of course, also means in German "trap," the trap which is the ultimate textual model of this and of all texts, the trap of an aesthetic education which inevitably confuses dismemberment of language by the power of the letter with the gracefulness of dance. This dance, regardless of whether it occurs as mirror, as imitation, as history, as the fencing match of interpretation, or in the anamorphic transformations of tropes, is the ultimate trap, as unavoidable as it is deadly.[55]

In introducing "the dismemberment of the body" in "Phenomenality and Materiality in Kant," de Man speaks of the word *Glieder* in Kant as "meaning members in all the senses of the word, as well as, in the compound *Gliedermann*, the puppet of Kleist's Marionettentheater."[56] "Fall" is a decisive figure and concept in Kleist, not least in defining any stability, formal—linguistic or mathematical—or physical, for example, monumental. It is curious, however, that, perhaps focusing on "The Analytics of the Sublime," de Man missed or omitted the Fall-sequence at the outset, at least at the level of linguistic understanding, of "The Analytics of the Beautiful," and thus the very concept of judgment. The initial sections, in particular, section 5, with which I began this essay, of the third *Critique* contain virtually all of these signifiers and hence entail the critical epistemology in question, although one might need Kleist and his reading of Kant (all Kleist's works are readings of Kant) to see it.

On this point, one would need to undertake yet another "romantic" rereading of Milton's attempt "to *justify* the ways of God to man" in *Paradise Lost*, which brings together, now in English, the Fall and judgment, or justice, and the modern, post-Copernican world, defined by the incessant fall of planets toward the Sun. It would not be possible to address the subject here or consider the relevant physics—for example, the way gravity bends even light itself—that would bring all these figures and texts together in yet another way. These connections must be relevant to de Man's reading, even if only because from Newton, who is uncircumventable in Kant, to Einstein and beyond they changed our sense of fall and thus (they are ultimately the same) the world, via Kant, the creator of the first modern cosmology. One would need to reassess the passages on stars and heaven in Kant's "Analytics of the Sublime," which de Man considers in his essays. I shall only comment on the passage on, as it may be called, the "galactical colossal," which refers to Kant's cosmology.[57] Kant writes:

> Nature offers examples of the mathematically sublime, in mere intuition, whenever our imagination is given, not so much a larger numerical concept, as a large unity for a measure (to shorten the numerical series). A tree that we estimate by a man's height will do as a standard for [estimating the height of] a mountain. If the mountain were to be about a mile high, it can serve as the unity for the number that expresses the earth's diameter, and so makes this diameter intuitable. The earth's diameter can serve similarly for estimating the Milky Way system. And the immense multitude of such Milky Way systems, called nebulous stars, which presumably form another such system among themselves, do not lead us to expect any boundaries there.[58]

While it may be imagined as the mathematically sublime in nature, this picture is not very likely to correspond to the universe given our present knowledge of it, even though Kant deserves much credit for guessing, arguably for the first time ever, that the Milky Way is merely one of many galaxies in the universe. As we see it now, this picture resembles the universe very little, whatever its ultimate geometry will prove to be, consistent with the data we have. The universe, although expanding, may or may not be infinite.[59] Instead, it may well prove to be ultimately inconceivable and as such to become "the unfigurable Universe," as Blanchot calls it in *The Infinite Conversation*: "an unfigurable Universe (a term henceforth deceptive); a Universe escaping every optical exigency and also escaping consideration of the whole—essentially non-finite, disunified, discontinuous."[60] This is a universe, or un-universe, that cannot ultimately be articulated as a body and, rigorously, has to be allegorized otherwise. Kant's figure can offer only a particular, if also aesthetically *universal* enough (and boring enough), model. By contrast, the materiality of the actual universe, as it appears to us at the moment, cannot in fact be visually presented universally, either as beautiful or as sublime, in part because it may not be presented at all. The sublime, in Kant, appears to correspond to a vision of that which always escapes the architectonic, geometrization, and so forth, while appearing to be available to them. We recall that, in contrast to the beautiful, this vision cannot be seen as having an object, but rather as making such an object impossible. Kant's concept of object, *Gegenstand*, however, and the overall economy, including political economy, of the beautiful would complicate the beautiful as well, to the point of the "*material* vision" in question in de Man's analysis of the sublime.[61] Once made "more intelligible," "understanding [the materiality of the sublime] in linguistic terms" also reveals the un-architectonic un-sublime of the beautiful.

This also amounts to saying that, rather than following Kant's cosmology, we might as well conceive of the universe on the Kantian model of the political, conceived on his aesthetic-epistemological model of aesthetic judgment. This model allows us to bring singularities into an assemblage or, at the human level, assembly and community, if not unity, as the effects of the unfigurable, the unrepresentable, the unknowable, the unthinkable—ultimately unfigurable even as unfigurable, unrepresentable as unrepresentable, unknowable as unknowable, unthinkable as unthinkable. It allows us to do so in spite and because of the radical limit it thus places upon our power of figuration, representation, knowledge, and thought. But it also adds to this power.

Seeing Is Reading
Rei Terada

What do we see in reading? It might seem that "see" is a murky word, one whose conflation of sensory perception with cognition makes it a poor lens for the inspection of either. This suggestion, common in the last twenty years' work on lyric poetry, takes its cue from Paul de Man's emphasis on the discontinuity of phenomenal and cognitive processes. In "Phenomenality and Materiality in Kant," de Man proposes that in the Third Critique Kant needs "a phenomenalized, empirically manifest principle of cognition on whose existence the possibility of . . . an articulation [between conceptual and empirical realms of discourse] depends,"[1] but instead registers "a deep, perhaps fatal, break or discontinuity" between "language as a performative as well as a cognitive system" and "the powers of transcendental philosophy" (*AI*, p. 79). This discontinuity "becomes apparent in the text" (*AI*, p. 79) as what de Man calls "a *material* vision," "purely material, devoid of any reflexive or intellectual complication" (*AI*, pp. 82, 83). De Man goes on to propose that the "equivalence . . . in the order of language" of Kant's material vision is "the prosaic materiality of the letter" (*AI*, pp. 90, 89). For Kant's purposes, then, "a material vision" is the very opposite of the "phenomenalized, empirically manifest principle of cognition" that the aesthetic was supposed to provide; material vision is the Dantean hell that de Man invents for Kant as a parody of Kant's desire for "phenomenal cognition." "No degree of obfuscation or ideology," de Man writes, "can transform this materiality into the phenomenal cognition of aesthetic judgment" (*AI*, p. 90). Much discussion of perception after de Man seems to compare and contrast the physiological process of seeing—which might seem to be a transformation of material into cognition—and its metaphoric extension into the idea of "seeing what one means" with the process of phenomenal cognition for which Kant's transcendental aesthetics hopes. From here, it seems reasonable to interpret the metaphor of seeing meaning as a mystified rhetorical strategy of the transcendental project.

De Man distinguishes a linguistic function from "perception" in another way in "Resistance to Theory." Here de Man stipulates that "linguistic terminology"—the terminology of "literary theory"—considers reference to be a function of language and not necessarily an intuition: "Intuition implies perception, consciousness, experience, and leads at once into the world of logic and of understanding with all its correlatives, among which aesthetics occupies a prominent place."[2] De Man is doing a lot, probably too much, in this single sentence. He disarticulates linguistic functioning from all the other capabilities named in the sentence, which are conceived as a network. Reference is not only "not necessarily . . . an intuition" or perception according to de Man, but not necessarily part of the "world of logic and of understanding" either, if that world is construed as a complete set of "correlatives." In this context the discontinuity between seeing and reading would be typical of the always possibly contingent relations between intuitive and nonintuitive mental acts. De Man's reasoning here differs from that of "Phenomenality and Materiality in Kant," but again supports the impression that one should be suspicious of metaphoric uses of "seeing," given the possible differences between linguistic functions and other mental acts.

The contrast between kinds of mental acts, however, is not as stark as it might at first seem. The objects of seeing are perceptual and intuitive; the products of linguistic functions, according to de Man, are "not necessarily" so. By de Man's own logic, I would like to suggest, his carefulness about the nature of linguistic functions should not be taken as a direction to purge the notion of "seeing" from literary theory.[3] "Seeing" does not always function as an aesthetic figure for the phenomenalization of thought; still less does that figure represent what seeing may actually be. The word "seeing," in all its ambiguity, encompasses both perceptual and cognitive, literal and figurative, meanings, and only our own interpretive decision to collapse its inner difference can unify, and hence aestheticize, it. In itself, I'll suggest, it represents what we know—and don't know—of perception and cognition more accurately than the terms "perception" and "cognition" do. Complementarily, attempts to use "seeing" narrowly, over and against "reading," can entangle themselves in aesthetics. Not that there is, after all, "phenomenal cognition" in the aesthetic sense. Rather, whenever we arrive at the place where such magical cognition is needed and missing, we find ourselves in a difficulty for which "seeing," understood as internally and enigmatically divided, can be a rather honest figure, one that does not necessarily resemble aesthetic ideology's appropriation of it.[4]

If we take de Man's readings of Kant seriously, then after his analysis of aesthetic ideology we are called on to go beyond transcendental philosophy's elements. Beyond, and not simply back to naive empiricism: de Man leaves us with a materialism "more radical" than that of empiricism in that it is found at the heart of form (*AI*, p. 121). Although it is compatible with an unredemptive formalism, however, this materialism should not be made to serve retranscendentalizing operations. Frances Ferguson criticizes de Man for describing the mind as always needing to start over, and compares him to Adorno in this respect.[5] She is right to note that he does this, and we should value de Man for the epistemological modesty she attributes to him. Over twenty years after his death, de Man's resistance to transcendental systematization is virtually unique in late-twentieth-century theory, as it cannot be found consistently in the late work of Derrida, and has been succeeded by renaissances in phenomenology and theology. Much recent critical theory argues for metaphysical structures of mind and/or a metaphysical need to refer ourselves to ideals. The cognitively unfinished position to which de Man returns us (from which, he reveals, we have never yet actually budged) is presented by de Man, in contrast, as a routine condition of epistemology that requires no supplementation by regulative ideals or empty universals, and provides no cause for either celebration or disappointment. In tracing the possible impacts of de Man's remarks on material vision, then, we might begin by remembering that for de Man, the foundering of Kant's transcendental system in material vision is a failure of redemption, the nontragic failure of materiality to be transformed. As such, material vision is the manifestation in de Man's late work of his lifelong analysis of renunciation.[6] The long narrative of anticlimax of which de Man's notion of materiality is part provides tonal evidence for how de Man reception might interpret it: The message of the larger narrative is that we are merely what we are, that the world is merely what it is (which is not to say that we know what it is). From

Blindness and Insight onward, de Man describes this reality of our epistemological circumstances steadily and urbanely, without ascending into hysteria or supplementary idealism. He liked to call it "prosaic." This is what the word "prosaic" adds when de Man characterizes material vision as a vision of "the prosaic materiality of the letter" (*AI*, pp. 90, 89). I worry that the current direction of the reception of de Man's ideas about materiality, in contrast, invents a new, philosophically reactionary transcendentalism that erodes de Man's legacy, or at least the attitude of resilient skepticism that is part of what I would like de Man's legacy to be.

I

For the editors introducing *Material Events: Paul de Man and the Afterlife of Theory* (2001)—Tom Cohen, Barbara Cohen, and J. Hillis Miller (Andrzej Warminski does not coauthor the introduction)—the constellation of ideas around "materiality" inspires the project of an alternative to the Third Critique, one that seems not to give up on transcendentalism but to reformulate it. They see opportunities in the a priori. "Whatever *inscription* designates, it conjures sheer anteriority," they suggest; "it does not deliver us to any immediacy of reference, [or] to any historical narrative that presumes to encode such, but to mnemonic programs that appear to precede and legislate these."[7] De Man's work is called "the portal for a wide-ranging interrogation into how the 'event' operates in history, and what intervention in the order of inscription entails" (*CCM*, p. xii). "Intervention" is depicted as the storming and occupation of the imperial palace of faculties: "By way of de Man's late work on 'materiality' a project emerges that relates less to a 'seventies' venture in theory than to still future and proactive investigations of and interventions in the hypertextual relay systems and programs out of which the 'human' (and nonhuman) appears constituted, temporalization produced and managed, the 'sensorium' altered, the virtuality of the present and the technicity of inscription brought to a point of passage or crossing" (*CCM*, p. xiii). Cohen, Cohen, and Miller thus remodel the infrastructure of the Third Critique. De Man appears here as an "*engineer*" who approaches "the archive, the prerecordings out of which experience is projected and semantic economies policed" (*CCM*, p. ix). They cite the career of Benjamin as another example of arche-engineering on the production lot of phenomenality, "where this trajectory finds an ultimate articulation as a radical (re)programming of the (historial) archive out of which the 'sensorium' would be alternatively produced" (*CCM*, p. x). Still, "experience is projected," and "the 'sensorium' . . . produced," out of the engineer's workplace. Engineering has a polemical connotation in the history of literary theory; this engineer seems to be the short-circuiter of structuralism's empirical base in *bricolage*. If Lévi-Strauss is the engineer of inductive reason, assembling significance gradually from observable surfaces, in *Material Events* the engineer enters the studio at night and with a few keystrokes changes what is projected on the screen—the blockbuster known as *Sensorium Redux*. That the archive, and the source code, are external, and that there is no way to infer archive from screen, does not dilute the strictly transcendental nature of the fantasy.

Is de Man's work a "portal" to this project?[8] De Man is fascinated with the a priori often enough, but can be ironic toward it, too. His work on "reference prior to designating the referent" and the "autonomous potential of language" show such an ambivalent fascination (*AI*, p. 133). In "Kant and Schiller" de Man speaks of "the historicity a priori" of the textual event; the ever-expanding motion of the unfolding textual event is pursued to a logical extreme in "Phenomenality and Materiality in Kant." Part of de Man's point in stressing the necessarily one-way movement of language as history, however, is that this is not a wave that can be caught. His vision of "the saturation of the tropological field as language frees itself of its constraints" (*AI*, p. 79) adapts the problem of plenitude in Neoplatonic metaphysics that he considers in his early work. As understood by Neoplatonism, the problem of plenitude is that the infinite generativity that would seem to be required of an infinitely powerful being ends in the existence of everything—a blow to unity and value whose damage, according to Lovejoy, the "great chain of being" is inadequate to repair.[9] In his early essay "Criticism and the Theme of Faust," de Man condenses quotations from Lovejoy to conclude that "'rationality, when conceived as complete, including all arbitrariness, becomes itself a kind of irrationality. . . . The world of concrete existence . . . is no impartial transcript of the realm of essence. . . . It is, in short, a contingent world.'"[10] De Man's narrative here discovers materiality at the end of power: materiality is the anticlimax of an investigation into a priori capacity.

Similarly, a Kantian-sounding passage of "Resistance to Theory" defines "literary theory" by its movement from "meaning" and "value" to "the modalities of production and of reception of meaning and of value prior to their establishment," yet turns back from transcendental aesthetics (*RT*, p. 7). De Man observes that semiotics, as the study of modalities, is, at least in principle, a more theoretical kind of discourse than interpretation. He also concludes, however, that because the telos of semiotics (for example, in the work of a semiotician such as Greimas) is a logic applicable "to the generation of all texts," it rejoins the *aesthetic* project (*RT*, p. 14). Only "reading," de Man writes, rather than any properly critical—in linguistic terms, "grammatical"—investigation, is "a negative process in which the grammatical cognition is undone" (*RT*, p. 17). If semiotics' shift to "modalities of production and of reception of meaning and value" makes it more theoretical, more critical in the Kantian sense, than some forms of literary study, this is not a compliment to semiotics or to literary theory. Rather, it shows that literary theory remains susceptible to aesthetic ideology because of its aspirations to logical totalization. From the standpoint of de Man reception, passages like this one ought to qualify the claim that the enterprise of "proactive investigations" into the general operation or generation of textual events as such "emerges" from the late de Man with his imprimatur. Still less does de Man write about intervening in or reprogramming mnemonic structures and the sensorium. Not only does he not mention the possibility of intervention in mnemonic and sensory structures; it is difficult to reconcile such a possibility with his assertion that what disarticulates the Third Critique cannot be mobilized by any drive.[11]

The notion of the sensorium as film studio, in the head or in the world, replete with engineers, set designers, directors, and projectionists, is one of Western metaphysics' favorite motifs—the fantasy production lot of the aesthetic project. Politically progressive in *Material Events*, it is in any case philosophically regressive. Never advocated by de Man, this motif can be found in the most un–de Manian places—in the startlingly strange perceptual literalism of Elaine Scarry, for example. Scarry takes the position opposite to contemporary deconstruction on "seeing" and "reading": she believes that while reading we "see" mental images that surpass the vivacity of nonliterary imagining, images that "somehow ... acquire the vivacity of perceptual objects."[12] (As she notes, many philosophers and psychologists do not believe that "mental images" exist, but some do, and she does [*DBB*, pp. 258–59n6]). The verbal arts "displac[e] the ordinary attributes of imagining," Scarry asserts in *Dreaming by the Book*: "its faintness, two-dimensionality, fleetingness, and dependence on volitional labor—with the vivacity, solidity, persistence, and givenness of the perceptible world. ... This comes about because we are given procedures for reproducing the deep structure of perception, and because the procedures themselves have an instructional character that duplicates the 'givenness' of perception" (*DBB*, p. 38). In another passage from *Dreaming by the Book*, "imaginary vivacity comes about by reproducing the deep structure of perception. . . . What in perception comes to be imitated is not only the sensory outcome (the way something looks or sounds or feels beneath the hands) but the actual structures of production that gave rise to the perception; that is, the material conditions that made it look, sound, or feel the way it did" (*DBB*, p. 9). In approximating the material conditions of perception, texts make readers feel as though they are having particular perceptions of objects and not just of letters. This feeling is what Scarry calls "seeing" a mental image.

In "Kant and Schiller," de Man shows how Schiller's sublime forms a symmetrical set of chiasmi that allows for safe travel back and forth through the universe. Scarry is extravagantly Schillerian in her attachment to imitation as play and in her calm, symmetrical transfers;[13] flowers (and other small diaphanous things) are her ultimate imaginable objects because they already resemble mental images—they are the entry points to her aesthetic *Paradiso*. Scarry even cites Schiller's *Aesthetic Education* as an authority on this point: Schiller, she notes, "places the flower in the space of passage between material and immaterial," contributing to the "explanation of the easily imagined as something that can enter the mind precisely because it is always already in a state of passage from the material to the dematerialized" (*DBB*, p. 63).

What does Scarry's apparatus have in common with Cohen, Cohen, and Miller's? Surprisingly much, considering their diverse critical lineages and aims. Scarry, too, pursues the post-Kantian project of gaining access to the conditions, or "actual structures," of what she believes to be the sensory effects of perception. Moving from an investigation of textual effects to the conditions of possibility of the sensorium, her argument recalls eighteenth-century arguments from the very existence of multiple senses to a supersense that supports them. For her, the fact that "verbal art, especially narrative, is almost bereft of any sensuous content" only suggests an alternate, subterranean route to sensuous content—"miming the deep structure that brings the sensation about" (*DBB*, pp. 5, 256n6). While she does not believe that we can alter that structure itself, she does believe that we can manipulate it for our own ends. Primary among the methods that Scarry claims enable such manipulation are the suppression of the sense of volition—the imaginer likes being given "direction" by someone, as this makes the content seem "given," therefore real—and a "sequence of coherent steps for constructing the image" (*DBB*, p. 19). Scarry, too, is a programmer. For her, imagining under authorial direction is more than a way of cultivating a mere illusion of sensation. Her version of mimesis is strong enough for virtual worldmaking: it is a repeatable method for stimulating in the body an image that responds to the content of a particular idea. If the methods are sleights-of-hand, they are sleights that provoke physiological responses and specifiable perceptions, and hence become imitations with the substance of realities. For her, the fact that texts have their own sensory properties as ink shapes on paper does not interfere with their power to evoke images related to their semantic content. Rather, the sensory fact of their materiality rubs off on the mental images the words conjure, much as the ongoing sensory experiences of the dreaming body may enhance the reality effects of dream content.[14] Like Cohen, Cohen, and Miller, Scarry organizes her work through cinematic metaphors, down to two of her section titles, "Making Pictures" and "Moving Pictures." For the utterly non–de Manian, indeed aesthetically ideological, Scarry, then, language is again "material production" that elicits a "perceptual outcome" in a "projective space" (*DBB*, pp. 20, 14).

II

In contrast, de Man reads Kant partly in order to give an account of a relatively straightforward attempt at aesthetics, one that does not conceal its failure. In "Kant and Schiller," de Man both points out how Schiller edits Kant's troubled Third Critique into a system that raises fewer questions, and admires Kant for his relative inability to paper over its problems. Just after having discussed Schiller's choreographing of the "organic, sensory," "chaotic," and "concrete" elements of discourse into a symmetrical exchange with order and system, de Man writes:

> Here, the comparison to make with Kant is with Kant's statements about figuration, about *what he calls* hypotyposis, which *is the difficulty* of rendering, by means of sensory elements, purely intellectual concepts. And the particular necessity which philosophy has, to take its terminology not from purely intellectual concepts but from material, sensory elements, which it then uses metaphorically and frequently forgets that it does so. . . . At any rate, hypotyposis for Kant is certainly a problem for understanding, and a very difficult problem that again threatens philosophical discourse; whereas here it is offered by Schiller *as a solution*, again in the form of a chiasmus, for a similar opposition. (*AI*, p. 153; my emphases in line 2)

What Schiller offers as a solution, Kant, to his credit, sees as "the difficulty," which he calls "hypotyposis." The thinking of hypotyposis, then, could be a model for aesthetics' failure as transcendental system and the self-critical registration of this condition.

Literally, hypotyposis is a sketch, an outline, thus "form" with an emphasis on the emptiness, as Rodolphe Gasché observes.[15] The rhetorical tradition uses this spatial figure of outline as an analogy for crisp verbal description. Hypotyposis is "clear explanation and *almost* visual presentation of events *as if practically* going on," writes Cicero.[16] The only thing that becomes clear in such definitions is that hypotyposis is as thin referentially as a term of art could be. The invocation of hypotyposis implies exactly nothing about how hypotyposis gets done. Nor do we even know exactly what its effects are, for hypotyposis is a figure whose effects are themselves described figuratively, with an "as if." In that way, it is close to what I mean by "seeing" and, as I will explain below, what de Man means by "materiality." These are placeholders in language for something we do not know anything about—not least whether it actually exists or not.

In §59 of the Third Critique, "On Beauty as the Symbol of Morality," Kant glosses hypotyposis as "exhibition [*Darstellung*], *subiectio ad adspectum*."[17] He also specifies what hypotyposes are not: "mere *characterizations*, i.e., designations of concepts by accompanying sensible signs [*bloße Charakterismen, d.i. Bezeichnungen der Begriffe durch begleitende sinnliche Zeichen*]," such as "words, or visible (algebraic or even mimetic) signs [*Worte, oder sichtbare (algebraische, selbst mimische) Zeichen*]." Hypotyposes have intuitive content: they are schemata or symbols. A schema, in turn, is what mediates the assimilation of intuitions by concepts of understanding. And what is a schema? It is a rule. So far, the analysis of hypotyposis simply gives exhibition in general, as opposed to description, and explains what counts as exhibition only circularly. What *kind* of a rule is a schema? Well, it is, for example, the rule that effects must follow causes in time, or the rule that substance has to have duration. Schemata are the rules of the classical natural world: if concepts are linked to intuitions through schemata, they are linked through their common fitness for that world. (A schematic hypotyposis might be, for example, a Euclidean proof.) So we can now say about hypotyposes that when they are schematic, they are natural, that is, they are plunged in space and time and in the natural world. But hypotyposes—I return now to §59—can also be symbolic:

> Symbolic exhibition uses an analogy . . . in which judgment performs a double function: first it applies the concept to the object of a sensible intuition; and then it applies the mere rule by which it reflects on that intuition

to an entirely different object, of which the formal object is only a symbol. Thus a monarchy ruled according to its own constitutional laws would be presented as an animate body, but a monarchy ruled by an individual absolute will would be presented as a mere machine (such as a hand mill); but in either case the presentation is only *symbolic*. For though there is no similarity between a despotic state and a hand mill, there certainly is one between the rules by which we reflect on the two and on how they operate. This function has not been analyzed much so far, even though it very much deserves fuller investigation; but this is not the place to pursue it. Our language is replete with such indirect exhibitions according to an analogy, where the expression does not contain the actual schema for the concept but contains merely a symbol for our reflection. Thus the words *foundation* (support, basis), to *depend* (to be held from above), to *flow* (instead of to follow) from something, *substance* (the support of accidents, as Locke puts it), and countless others are not schematic but symbolic hypotyposes; they express concepts not by means of a direct intuition but only according to an analogy with one, i.e., a transfer of our reflection on an object of intuition to an entirely different concept, to which perhaps no intuition can ever directly correspond.

Kant's examples of the equally symbolic corporeal and machinstic presentations of monarchy might be said to reveal that symbolic hypotyposis all too conveniently imports qualities from the presentable to the unpresentable through merely poetic association. The question arises why, in that case, Kant thinks symbolic hypotyposis counts as hypotyposis at all. What is it about the symbolic that merits comparison to the schematic, and makes it a kind of intuitive presentation? A monarchy, an animate body, and a "hand-mill" are unlike; a monarchy is not an entity whose properties are completely definable. While it is fair to say that a monarchy must be answerable to the laws of physics, it is also fair to say that we do not know exactly how, because "monarchy" itself is an approximation—if not an opaque name, then one that is dark around the edges. If someone tells us that a "monarchy" is at least an organization of bodies, however, then when we imagine its workings, we do so by using our concepts of other organizations of bodies. We do not have to know, or be able to know, what tyranny is in order to be able to understand if someone tells us (wrongly or rightly) that, like a pepper-grinder, it is operated by a single will.[18] The hypotyposis indicates the schema to which disparate concepts are connected as an otherwise unpresentable cause is to its effects. Kant's text even illustrates hypotyposis by hypotyposis: His verbal comparison between the comparison between tyrannies and pepper-grinders, on one hand, and symbolic and schematic hypotyposes, on the other, suggests by symbolic hypotyposis how symbols and schemata are both hypotyposes. The proof concerning demonstration is not demonstrated directly: discourse and method occur together, method being talked about in discourse.[19] My point is not that, therefore, all is discourse. It is rather that the virtual meeting-place of symbolic and schematic hypotyposes is the end of the line, and no one can say what, if anything, happens there. Whatever conclusion one draws will be partly a matter of preference. In this place, repeatedly, the philosophy of language takes a leap of faith, and claims to plug into natural science: it bids to become a natural science of language, grounded in necessity, as in Descartes, Russell, early Wittgenstein, or Chomsky. This is the place where philosophers start saying, with regard to analogy, that it *really seems*.[20]

One's degree of faith in the realism of analogy is not so much an interpretation as a decision. Hypotyposis, or any construct that serves its place-holding function, is a black box. For de Man, I would suggest, such a construct is not a solution but a "difficulty of rendering." We do not know what is there, or whether anything is there that is not a mere artifact of the terms of the problem; we do not know what real seeming consists in, or whether it consists in anything or not. We can only agree with Kant that *if* it is somewhere, *there* is where it should go.

Now, Derrida argues in "Typewriter Ribbon" that "materiality" is, like hypotyposis, a word to put down when one can go no further. In "Phenomenality and Materiality in Kant," de Man casts his characterization of Kant's description of the ocean as a catachretic act of nomination: "the only word that comes to mind is that of a *material* vision" (*AI*, p. 82). In "Kant and Schiller" de Man again struggles verbally to nominate "something [properly unnameable] which one could call a progression—though it shouldn't be—a movement, from cognition, from acts of knowledge, from states of cognition, to something [again] which is no longer a cognition but which is to some extent an *occurrence*, which has the materiality of something that actually happens" (*AI*, p. 132). Noting de Man's appeals "to what he himself says he 'calls text'" and "'*what is called* [by de Man in *AI*, p. 128] materialism,'" Derrida proposes that materiality for de Man is whatever fills "the place of prosaic resistance," "a very useful generic name for all that resists appropriation," or, going even further, "the name, the artifactual nomination of an artifactual figure. . . . A sort of invention by de Man, one could say, almost a fiction produced in the movement of a strategy."[21] In this case the materiality of language is de Man's X at the spot where aesthetics cannot be completed.

The resort to algebra—"here is where *something* should go"—leads, along one path, to a literature in which indexicals and names become the new foundations of knowledge: a new metaphysics, potentially, or a deconstructive nominalism.[22] It also opens the way to negative theology, a recentering of metaphysics on the void (the path of Lacan and Žižek). Cohen, Cohen, and Miller continue to treat materiality as a realm "out of which experience is projected." They take their difference from Kant to mean that experience would be projected *differently*, and, in this sense, proceed as though the transcendental system could be made to work to new ends. De Man's conclusion at the end of "Phenomenality and Materiality in Kant," however, is that the loss of "the architectonic unity of the system . . . marks the undoing of the aesthetic as a valid category" and "undoes the very project of such a philosophy" (*AI*, p. 89). A forward-thinking literary theory, I would suggest, would not read in this conclusion the possibility of something like a transcendental philosophy persisting but no longer being predictable or unified;[23] or persisting as a negative of itself, refounded on the inevitability of a now transcendental lack; or subsisting in ruins whose debris could be taken up and used for other purposes, or turned against itself. De Man's suggestion is rather that because Kant leaves a question mark at the most important place in his system, the transcendental philosophy has not been something so substantial as to have produced debris, but rather a plan for a system that never got finished and never produced anything. One can keep trying to revise and finish it, but that makes sense only if you wish it worked. If you are relieved that it does not work, the issue is still open, but for the moment, it makes more sense to say: So much for *that*. That way lies a renewed empiricism, not eighteenth-century empiricism, but a radical empiricism strong enough to encompass formalism and skeptical enough to know that it will always be prosaically incomplete.[24]

The attraction of the Cohen-Cohen-Miller model is its speculative liberation theology:

> We will take the position for the sake of argument and because it is interesting to consider, that what remains unengaged in de Man's text addresses the possibility of intervention in the mnemonic, the programming of the "historial," and a treatment of "materiality" that compels a rethinking of technicity and the "sensorium" on the basis of inscription. Among other things it would be an approach, given the "materiality of inscription," to the notion of the "virtual" and toward a rendering virtual—and hence, toward alternative histories to those programmed by inherited regimes of definition and perception. (*CCM*, p. viii)

The appeal of this position lies in the fantasy of reaching into structures that produce history and the sensorium, thereby arriving at a means of generating histories and sensoria. The notion of "the programming of the 'historial'" is stronger than that of the writing of history, as "a rendering virtual" of "alternative histories" is stronger than the practice of revisionary history. The language of virtual intervention intensifies and sensualizes both, and implies that at the end of the intervention we will process alternative histories as new perceptions. Changing the past is a crucial revolutionary desire for which Benjamin is a good keynote. I do not mean to derogate it in the slightest by suggesting that it has been given most serious expression in the mode of impossibility. Rendered possible, it is no longer the same desire, no longer revolutionary but totalitarian. The idea of possibly intervening in regimes of definition and perception is downright frightening (it also opens up the black-comic possibility of a Charlie Kaufmanesque nightmare of botched interventions), and with good reason "remains unengaged in de Man's text." When de Man reconstructs the mechanism of Rousseau's social contract in "Promises" as "a paradoxical juxtaposition of interference of relational networks,"[25] he also stresses Rousseau's differentiation of his view of social system-building from one that models itself on a "'common sensorium'" (Rousseau, *Manuscrit de Genéve*, quoted in *AR*, p. 259).[26] Rousseau makes it clear, de Man writes, that the "synesthetic illusion" of a common sensorium is the "the misleading model after which no sound political system should be patterned" (*AR*, p. 260). By this logic, the Cohen-Cohen-Miller angle on materiality is the wrong end of materialist criticism: it retranscendentalizes materialism, making the difficulty into the solution, rather than understanding materialism as something that detranscendentalizes one's cognitive hopes.

III

In his brilliant *Ends of the Lyric*, Timothy Bahti draws a distinction between "seeing" and "reading" using the example of Shakespeare's Sonnet 43:[27]

> When most I wink, then do my eyes best see,
> For all the day they view things unrespected,
> But when I sleep, in dreams they look on thee,
> And darkly bright, are bright in dark directed.
> Then thou, whose shadow shadows doth make bright
> How would thy shadow's form form happy show

> To the clear day with thy much clearer light,
> When to unseeing eyes thy shade shines so!
> How would, I say, mine eyes be blessèd made,
> By looking on thee in the living day,
> When in dead night thy fair imperfect shade
> Through heavy sleep on sightless eyes doth stay!
>   All days are nights to see until I see thee,
>   And nights bright days when dreams do show thee me.

Bahti notes that some of the poem's chiasmi of repeating words can be noticed even by a reader who doesn't know English, as in line 4: "darkly bright . . . bright in dark." "So far, this is only seeing, not reading," he remarks (*EL*, p. 33). Others depend on semantics, like the first line's "most I . . . eyes best" (*EL*, p. 34). We could say that the chiasmus can be filled in with intuitive or symbolic content—literal or figurative seeing—while the chiasmic form leads us toward understanding ("seeing" in a metaphoric sense), that "dark bright . . . bright . . . dark," is *like* "most . . . I . . . eyes . . . best." But "reading," Bahti asserts, "necessitates the distinction of sense as meaning from sense as the sense-perception of vision, the precise distinction of actual letters seen and actual letters not seen (no longer seen) but read acting" (*EL*, p. 38). He continues, "reading would 'appear' [at the end of the poem] if it were something one could see, but instead one can only read the vanishing of sight" (*EL*, p. 39). Bahti figures reading as seeing *plus* interpreting *minus* seeing, so the end of the process recedes over the horizon, under the line at the end of the column/poem: sublime. Described as though it were given, the perceptual process of seeing is made to provide ballast for reading-in-abstraction-from-seeing, an "end" of lyric in a reading remaining to be seen. There is a double sense of "reading" here: as participle, reading is what we do as we see and interpret; as abstract noun, it is the never-wholly-attained end-product of seeing, interpreting, and learning not to see.

Bahti's assumption is that texts and reading, like tyrannies, are not phenomenal entities and processes, while pages and retinal activities, like pepper-grinders, are. We are so used to thinking metaphysically, whether in deconstructive or in humanistic subgroups—especially those of us who think about lyric—that it is hard to imagine any other way of approaching seeing and reading. But what if texts and tyrannies and retinal activities *were* on the same level—were all alike empirical entities, not aesthetic ones, only subject to more or less complex inspection? If they were, it would become evident that inspection itself is a difficulty all the way down (and up).

Daniel Dennett, in a typically brisk fifteen-page treatment of a vast question, in this case an essay called "Seeing is Believing—or Is It?," asks how we *know* when we have seen something. What Dennett poses as "the nature of 'takings'" is none other than the question of seeing and reading—the question of whether and when "a state of the nervous system" is to count as a "perception."[28] How do we know we have seen something? We remember it, so we believe we have had a perception; or we took a photo, and believe that the photo is a picture of what we perceived. "One of the reasons people tend to see a contrast" between belief and perception, according to Dennett, "is that they tend to think of perceptual states as much richer in content than mere belief states" (*SB*, p. 341). Not always: Scarry, stressing mental images, thinks of ordinary perceptual states as richer than what Dennett calls "belief states" (memories, conjurings), yet thinks of literary belief states as being as rich as ordinary perceptual states. Bahti, stressing texts, understandably thinks of interpretations—belief states—as richer than the perceptual states of seeing mere letters. For my argument, though, it does not matter which way the values go. What matters is the dualism, and its tendency to obscure "what happens in the middle," which in Dennett's opinion is everything. "No sane participant . . . would claim that the product of perception was either literally a picture in the head or literally a sentence in the head. Both ways of talking are reckoned as metaphors," he remarks (*SB*, p. 342). "We should be leery of metaphor," he goes on, "but is there any alternative at this point?" (*SB*, p. 349). In the end, Dennett argues, "the idea that we can identify *perceptual*—as opposed to conceptual—states by an evaluation of their contents turns out to be an illusion" (*SB*, p. 352). Who is to know what seeing is?

In illustrating this point, Dennett calls upon the classical celebration of hypotyposis as a presentation modeled on vision: "After all"—he mimes an interlocutor—"perceptions are like pictures, beliefs are like sentences, and a picture's worth a thousand words." "But," he goes on, "these are spurious connotations. *There is no upper bound on the richness of content of a proposition*" (*SB*, p. 341). The allusion to the rhetorical tradition is not casual: much of Dennett's discussion constitutes a commentary on metaphoric transfer from the perspective of empirical studies of perception. For the eliminativist Dennett, who believes that only technological obstacles prevent consciousness from being analyzed into directly or indirectly observable material elements, analogies between perception and cognition are not effectively aesthetic. Rather, it is the concept "cognition" that makes it sound as though there were magical substances or forces immune in principle even to the most powerful and indirect observation. For Dennett, cognitions are in principle observable, while under the current scientific understanding, perception is scarcely less enigmatic than cognition. A cognition is like a perception not because it is as plain as day but because it is as clear as mud. Thus it is neither illuminating nor mystifying to compare cognition to perception. Because there is no nonmetaphorical way of talking about even what a *perception* is, *seeing*—in all its sense-conflating ambiguity—after all better represents the state of knowledge regarding perception and cognition than a distinction between "perception" and "cognition" that can be made logically but cannot be evidenced by any difference in content.

Perceptions are like pictures, beliefs are like sentences—and perceptions are like sentences, and beliefs are like pictures. Until we know more, a thousand words on the topic are not yet worth a dime. As a deconstructive materialist writing in the wake of Paul de Man, I would rather end there, prosaically, than "burden the system with extra machinery," as Dennett puts it—"scene-painting machinery *or* script-writing machinery" (*SB*, p. 344). Either kind of machinery resubscribes to systems of mind that understate the complexity, not only of reading, but of the very idea of sensory perception, which nonetheless remains the only channel epistemology gets.

APPENDIX I

Courses Taught by Paul de Man during the Yale Era

Marc Redfield

Unlike that of most thinkers—even professional academic thinkers—Paul de Man's legacy remains inseparable from his role as a teacher. Since this pedagogical persona figures largely in the phantasmatics of the de Man legend as well as in more prosaic forms of his reception, it has seemed worth documenting here the courses he taught, both at Yale and elsewhere, after accepting a Yale professorship in 1970. I have been able to assemble a substantially complete list of courses for those years, though one or two seminars may be missing (the semesters of Fall '72 and Spring '81 look as though they should record another course), and in one or two cases I was unable to find course numbers to go with the titles. I would have been glad to have been able to provide a more extensive record of de Man's teaching career from 1960 (the year he took his Ph.D. from Harvard University and joined the Cornell University faculty) onward, but concrete information about de Man's teaching at Cornell or Johns Hopkins has thus far eluded me. Many thanks to Tom Keenan, Kevin Newmark, and Andrzej Warminski for their help with what follows.

All the Yale courses are graduate courses except for "Literature Z," as it was called when de Man and Geoffrey Hartman introduced it in 1977; after that first year it was renamed "Literature 130." The graduate seminars are more or less self-explanatory (though they raise interesting questions: I know of no study, for instance, that addresses itself to de Man's abiding interest in Gide). The story behind Lit. Z, however, is worth telling. Most senior faculty at Yale have regular undergraduate teaching duties, but de Man, who had administrative responsibilities during most of these years as well as a couple of external teaching grants, taught relatively few undergraduates during his decade at Yale. (He chaired the French Department from 1974 to 1977, then Comparative Literature from 1978 until his death in 1983; furthermore, as detailed below, he led NEH-funded seminars in 1976–78.) Lit. Z came into being as part of the Literature Major, which had been founded in 1972 by Peter Brooks, Alvin Kernan, and Michael Holquist as an undergraduate version of comparative literature. During its first few years—until course-numbering was regularized in the late 1970s—the Literature Major had core courses bearing letter names: Lit. X ("Man and His Fictions," a course with structuralist and narratological leanings that was later retitled for gender neutrality), and Lit. Y (an overview of twentieth-century literary theory, usually taught as a lecture course by Peter Demetz). De Man seems to have been the main force behind the idea of a third Lit course. In appendix 2, below, we have reproduced an internal position paper proposing the course; it is unsigned and undated, but written in de Man's distinctive style, presumably around 1975. It proposes Lit. Z as "an introductory course in the reading and the interpretation of primary and secondary texts" to be team-taught by de Man and Hartman. The new course is to be

> quite different from Literature X which deals with the relationship between literary fictions and society, and from Literature Y, which deals with the history of contemporary critical theory rather than with exegesis, or the practical application of critical theories. In Literature Z, students will read a series of increasingly difficult texts (poetic, narrative, dramatic, as well as historical, philosophical, and critical) and are initiated at the same time into the bewildering variety of ways in which such texts can be read. Through this emphasis on exegesis and interpretation they are also introduced to the linguistic and rhetorical models that may explain this semantic complexity. The purpose of the course is practical: it sets out to refine the process of reading and writing by drawing attention to some of its intrinsic complications. It can also help students to decide how gifted they in fact are for literary study. It should therefore be taken early in the student's career, preferably in the sophomore or junior year. Though the course has no language requirement, it makes use of some foreign language material, and one of its functions is to demonstrate the necessity of the knowledge of a second language for competent literary interpretation.

(I thank Peter Brooks for his help in making this document available to me; for further acknowledgments, see the headnote to appendix 2, below.) The course was approved, and de Man and Hartman team-directed it in the spring of 1977 and in several subsequent springs, as detailed below.

Lit. 130 occasioned some anecdotes that have circulated ever since among theory buffs (de Man coming to the podium after a Hartman lecture on Keats, saying, "We've had beauty, now we'll have the truth"; de Man lecturing on Shelley's *Triumph of Life*, joking about his inability to pronounce the difference between "tread" and "thread," on which his interpretation was hanging). But the course also played a more serious role in the institutional production and transmission of de Manian rhetorical reading. Andrzej Warminski has pointed out to me that, in addition to its two lecturer-directors, Lit. 130 also employed TAs (usually two, though in the first years de Man and Hartman each taught a section); these TAs, whose main job was to lead sections, were also expected to give a lecture apiece, and out of these lectures came many of the first "de Manian" readings to achieve publication (e.g., Barbara Johnson on Melville; Timothy Bahti on Benjamin; Andrzej Warminski on Hegel; other critics whose early publications include essays that began as Lit. 130 lectures include Claudia Brodsky, Cathy Caruth, Tom Cohen, Deborah Esch, David Ferris, Tom Keenan, and Kevin Newmark).

Lit. 130 no longer exists at Yale, though it survived de Man's death by a few years. It was taught by Barbara Johnson in 1985, team-taught by Andrzej Warminski and Kevin Newmark in 1986 and 1987, by Cathy Caruth and David Ferris in 1988, and by Caruth and Newmark in 1989. This course remains an intriguing and, to date, unexamined example of de Man's interest in and approach to literary-critical pedagogy—providing an important complement to, and concretization of, his remarks in "The Return to Philology" on Reuben Brower's Hum. 6 undergraduate course at Harvard (for which de Man had been a TA in the 1950s). Furthermore, as these brief notes have tried to suggest, like the special issue of *Studies in Romanticism* that Sara Guyer discusses in the present collection, above, Lit. 130 merits study as a significant institutional medium of de Man's legacy within professional criticism.

[Appointed to Yale, but on leave with Guggenheim Fellowship, 1970–71]

1971–72:
    F '71: Comp. Lit. 130a: "Nietzsche's Theory of Rhetoric"
            French 142a: "Jean-Jacques Rousseau"

S '72: Comp. Lit. 131b: "The Image of Rousseau in European Romanticism"
French 163b: "Proust et la théorie du roman"

1972–73:
F '72: French 142a: "Jean-Jacques Rousseau (2ème partie)"
S '73: Comp. Lit. 138b: "Romantic Autobiography"
French 167b: "Mallarmé"

[On leave 1973–74: teaches "Methodology" and "Nietzsche" and "Rousseau" at the University of Zurich; "Rousseau" at the Free University of Berlin]

1974–75:
F '74: French 149a: "Théorie du roman au XVIII siècle (Marivaux, Prévost et Diderot)"
S '75: Comp. Lit. 140b: "Theories of Language in the 18th and Early 19th Centuries"
French 165b: "André Gide"

1975–76:
F '75: French 174a: "Lecture de textes théoriques"
S '76: Comp. Lit. 142b: "Theory of Irony"
French 162b: "La poésie de Paul Valéry"

[Teaches a NEH seminar, summer 1976]

1976–77:
F '76: [continuation of NEH seminar]
S '77: Lit. Zb: "Reading and Rhetorical Structures" (with Geoffrey Hartman)
"Epistemology of Metaphor"

1977–78:
F '77: [NEH seminar 1977–78: a full-year seminar (led to *Studies in Romanticism* issue)]
S '78: Lit. 130b (formerly Lit. Zb) (with Geoffrey Hartman)
Comp. Lit. 910b: "Baudelaire, Yeats, Rilke"

[Teaches "Rhetoric of Romanticism" and "Lyric: Baudelaire, Yeats, Rilke" at the University of Constanz, and "Baudelaire and Rimbaud" at the University of Zurich during the summer of 1978]

1978–79:
F '78: Comp. Lit. 800a: "Autobiography"

S '79: Lit. 130b (with J. Hillis Miller)
French 850b: "Descartes and Pascal"

[Teaches Comp. Lit. 377: "Baudelaire/Rilke/Yeats," and Comp. Lit. 388: "Theory of Rhetoric," at the University of Chicago, spring–summer 1979]

1979–80:
F '79: "Rhetorical Readings"
S '80: Lit. 130b (with Geoffrey Hartman)
Comp. Lit. 815b: "Hegel's *Aesthetik*"

1980–81:
F '80: Comp. Lit. 816a: "Hegel and English Romanticism" (with Hartman)
S '81: Lit. 130b (with Geoffrey Hartman)

[Teaches NEH summer seminar: "Rhetorical Readings," summer 1981]

[On leave with Guggenheim Fellowship 1981–82; Lit. 130b is taught by Hartman and Warminski]

[Teaches "Rhetoric, Aesthetics, and Ideology" at the School of Criticism and Theory, Northwestern University, summer 1982]

1982–83:
F '82: Comp. Lit. 817a: "Aesthetic Theory from Kant to Hegel"
S '83: Comp. Lit. 790b: "Théories esthétiques de Diderot à Baudelaire"
Lit. 130b (with Andrzej Warminski)

1983–84:
F '83: "Theory of Rhetoric in the 18th and 20th Centuries"

APPENDIX 2

Paul de Man, "Course Proposal: Literature Z"

[This document—untitled, undated, and unsigned—is almost certainly by Paul de Man, and dates from around 1975. It proposes a new undergraduate course for the Literature Major at Yale University for "the Fall or latest the Spring semester of 1976"; a handwritten correction to this phrase changes "1976" to "1977," and inserts "of 1976" after "Fall." The course actually debuted in the spring of 1977, team-taught by Paul de Man and Geoffrey Hartman. For more on the Literature Major at Yale and the importance of "Literature Z" as an institutional support for rhetorical reading, see the headnote to appendix 1, above.

I have not edited this document, except to flag one small peculiarity or error with "sic": the reference to "Literature I" is probably intended as a reference to Lit. Y (see the headnote to appendix 1). The footnote is original to the document. This text is published with the kind permission of the Yale Comparative Literature Department. Many thanks to Peter Brooks for making the document available to me, and to David Quint, Chair of the Department of Comparative Literature, for approving its publication. A copy of this document has been donated to the Paul de Man archive at the University of California, Irvine.]

* * *

This document is for internal use only. It is not written for presentation to a foundation but as a preliminary position paper for discussion towards such a presentation.

I

The curriculum for the teaching of literature, at Yale and elsewhere, has undergone very little change over the last two or three decades. The main organization of the program remains the same: a sharp distinction, without overlap, into national literatures and, within each national literature, a tripartite division into (1) introductory survey courses (English 25 and 29, French 41, Literature I, etc.), (2) a sequence of period courses diachronically ordered, and (3) more advanced courses reflecting the particular interests of available instructors. The underlying conception is genetic, seeing literature as a succession of periods and movements that can be articulated as an historical narrative. With regard to individual works, the conception is essentially paraphrastic and thematic, the assumption being that literature can be reduced to a set of statements which, taken together, lead to a better understanding of human existence. Literary studies then become, on the one hand, a branch of the history of culture and, on the other hand, a branch of existential and anthropological philosophy in its individual as well as its more collective aspects.

While remaining highly useful and entirely legitimate, this program does not sufficiently reflect the concerns of literary studies as they have developed, here and abroad, over the last fifty years. The emphasis has increasingly moved towards literature as a language about language, or a metalinguistic discipline best understood as a response to the specific complexities and resources of language. From this perspective, the anthropological function of literature cannot be examined with any rigor before its epistemological and verbal status has been understood. This emphasis on the metalinguistic aspects of literature is a characteristic of all the major theoretical trends in literary studies of the twentieth century, regardless of whether they are historical (as in Curtius, Auerbach, or Gadamer, for example) or synchronic (as in Russian formalism, American New Criticism, structuralism, or semiology).* This fact is widely acknowledged, but

---

*This orientation of literary studies towards language, far from being something new-fangled, represents in fact a return to an age-long tradition which rooted the study of literature in philology, poetics, rhetoric, and grammar.

it has had little effect on the actual teaching curriculum despite its considerable impact on the research of teachers themselves, as well as on an expanding canon of literary texts.

The result is a widening gap between literary instruction and literary research, detrimental to the professional training of the prospective student of literature as well as to the formal influence that the study of literature can have on students whose main interests are elsewhere. The growing discontinuity between undergraduate and graduate curricula in literature is also symptomatic of this evolution, as is the decline in foreign language study. One reason, certainly, for the decline of foreign language study is that the cultural knowledge of *national* literature is no longer sufficient incentive for the demanding task of learning a foreign tongue: as long as a truly literary and intellectual motivation is missing, the important link with other nations and mentalities which foreign study helps to promote will continue to atrophy.

At Yale, the relative one-sidedness of the present literary curriculum has been acknowledged and it has been corrected by the proliferation of alternative programs (H.A.L., Directed Studies, The Combined Major and, most recently, the Literature Major). It has also led to methodological tensions within new introductory courses and occasionally to a wasteful redundancy of courses. The present proposal attempts to give a firmer direction to these corrective efforts by bringing them closely in touch with recent critical and methodological trends and, correlatively, by stressing the increased importance for literary education of such auxiliary fields as linguistics, psychology, philosophy of language, and others.

Next to the existing track, as exemplified in the course program of the major departments, the option of a consistently organized second track should be made available to students. And the obvious place for the organization of such a course sequence is the literature major, which has already come into being as a result of very similar considerations.

II

We propose the creation of a new introductory course in Literature (Literature Z) and of a series of follow-up courses to be integrated, if possible, within the Literature Major. All these courses, however, should be available to students of any major, in the Humanities or the Sciences.

1. *Literature Z*

Literature Z is an introductory course in the reading and the interpretation of primary and secondary texts. It is quite different from Literature X, which deals with the relationship between literary fictions and society, and from Literature Y, which deals with the history of contemporary critical theory rather than with exegesis, or the practical application of critical theories. In Literature Z, students will read a series of increasingly difficult texts (poetic, narrative, dramatic, as well as historical, philosophical, and critical) and are initiated at the same time into the bewildering variety of ways in which such texts can be read. Through this emphasis on exegesis and interpretation they are also introduced to the linguistic and rhetorical models that may explain this semantic complexity. The purpose of the course is practical: it sets out to refine the process of reading and writing by drawing attention to some of its intrinsic complication. It can also help students to decide how gifted they in fact are for literary study. It should therefore be taken early in the student's career, preferably in the sophomore or junior year. Though the course has no language requirement, it makes use of some foreign language material, and one its functions is to demonstrate the necessity of knowledge of a second language for competent literary interpretation.

The course should be taught to a group of approximately sixty students, divided into sections of about twelve each. One weekly lecture for the entire group is envisaged, given by the directors and some of the staff members, and one two-hour session per week. Directed written exercises are frequently assigned (at least one every two weeks) and one of the main functions of the staff is the elaboration and correction of these exercises; the sections also deal at least half of the time with the critical discussion of the written work. The course should start out as a one-semester course. Its relationship to such courses as English 15, Literature X, Literature I [sic], and possibly others is a subject for later discussions.

The course would be started under the joint direction of Professors Hartman and de Man for the Fall (^ "of 1976") or latest the Spring semester of ~~1976~~ 1977. It would be staffed by three Teaching Fellows or Assistant Professors (for an enrollment of sixty students) with each of the Directors taking on a section. It is assumed that, after a period of two or three years, other directors will become available.

2. *Follow-up Courses or Seminars*

We suggest the creation of a series of courses in which the various problems of interpretation empirically revealed in Literature X and theoretically surveyed in Literature Y would be taken up systematically. These courses should be open to juniors and seniors as well as graduate students. The listing of some tentative topics makes clear the function and the orientation of these courses:

(a) History and Taxonomy of Rhetoric
(b) Psychoanalysis and Literary Criticism
(c) Theories of Grammar and their Application to Literary Studies
(d) Introduction to Literary Semiology
(e) Prosody and Narratology
(f) Problems of Literary Historiography; History and Literature
(g) History of the Study of Literature
(h) Sociology of Literary Scholarship

III

The cost of such an extension and reinforcement of literary study at Yale consists primarily of instructional time to be purchased from the various departments. These could—and perhaps should—include History, Philosophy, and Linguistics as well as English, Classics, and the Foreign Languages. A nucleus of people competent to teach the courses proposed here exists at Yale, but this nucleus would have to be expanded over the two or so years following on the inception of the program. It would be best, therefore, to plan now for two incremental appointments: one at the level, perhaps, of a Humanities Divisional Professorship (to help or replace the Directors once the program has been launched), the other at the level of an Associate Professorship. On the junior level, there is no need to foresee appointments specifically within the Literature Major, although joint appointments between it and another department should not be ruled out. The main concern should be, however, that staff members qualified to teach courses of this kind are given significant consideration for their work in this enterprise in the appointment policy of the cooperating department.

CONTRIBUTORS

IAN BALFOUR teaches in English and in Social and Political Thought at York University. He is the author of *The Rhetoric of Romantic Prophecy* (2002) and is coeditor, with Atom Egoyan, of *Subtitles: On the Foreignness of Film* (2004), and, with Eduardo Cadava, of *And Justice for All? The Claims of Human Rights*, a special double issue of *South Atlantic Quarterly*. He is currently completing a book on the sublime.

CYNTHIA CHASE is Professor of English and Comparative Literature at Cornell University. She is the author of *Decomposing Figures: Rhetorical Readings in the Romantic Tradition* (1986), and editor of *Romanticism* (1993).

SARA GUYER is Assistant Professor of English at the University of Wisconsin, Madison. Her book *Romanticism after Auschwitz* is forthcoming from Stanford University Press. She is currently at work on a book about John Clare, Friedrich Hölderlin, and the poetics of homelessness.

JAN MIESZKOWSKI is Associate Professor of German and Humanities at Reed College. His first book, *Labors of Imagination: Aesthetics and Political Economy from Kant to Althusser* (2006), explores the intersections between romanticism and classical political economy. He is currently at work on a project about the aesthetics of war spectatorship.

ARKADY PLOTNITSKY is Professor of English and a University Faculty Scholar at Purdue University, where he also directs the Theory and Cultural Studies program. He has written several books and many articles on English and European romanticism, critical theory, Continental philosophy, philosophy of quantum theory, and the relationships among literature, philosophy, and science. His most recent books are *The Knowable and the Unknowable: Modern Science, Nonclassical Theory, and the "Two Cultures"* (2002) and *Idealism without Absolutes: Philosophy and Romantic Culture* (2004), a volume he coedited with Tilottama Rajan. He is currently completing two books, *Reading Niels Bohr: Physics and Philosophy* and *Minute Particulars: Romanticism, Sciences, and the Nature of Modern Knowledge*.

MARC REDFIELD is Professor of English and John D. and Lillian Maguire Distinguished Chair in the Humanities at Claremont Graduate University. He is the author of *Phantom Formations: Aesthetic Ideology and the Bildungsroman* (1996) and *The Politics of Aesthetics: Nationalism, Gender, Romanticism* (2003). He has edited two special issues of *Diacritics*, "Addictions" (1997) and "Theory, Cultural Studies, Globalization, and the Remains of the University" (2001), and, with Janet Brodie, has coedited *High Anxieties: Cultural Studies in Addiction* (2002). Most recently he has edited a special issue of *The Wordsworth Circle* on the work of Geoffrey Hartman (2006).

REI TERADA is Professor of Comparative Literature and English at the University of California, Irvine. She is the author of *Feeling in Theory: Emotion after the "Death of the Subject"* (2001) and is currently at work on *Phenomenality and Dissatisfaction: Kant to Adorno*.

ANDRZEJ WARMINSKI is Professor of English and Comparative Literature at the University of California, Irvine. He studied and worked with Paul de Man at Yale, where he spent fifteen years (1972–87) as a graduate student, assistant professor, and associate professor of comparative literature. He is the author of *Readings in Interpretation: Hölderlin, Hegel, Heidegger* (1987) and of *Material Inscriptions* (two volumes, forthcoming). He is the editor of de Man's *Aesthetic Ideology* (1996) and coedited, with E. S. Burt and Kevin Newmark, *Romanticism and Contemporary Criticism* (1992), and, with Tom Cohen, Barbara Cohen, and J. Hillis Miller, *Material Events: Paul de Man and the Aftermath of Theory* (2000).

NOTES

INTRODUCTION: LEGACIES OF PAUL DE MAN
Marc Redfield

1. Bill Readings, *The University in Ruins* (Cambridge: Cambridge University Press, 1996).

2. I refer here to "The Lesson of Paul de Man," *Yale French Studies* 69 (1985), and to the public debates in 1988–89 about de Man's collaborationist journalism: for these last, see above all Jacques Derrida, "Like the Sound of the Sea Deep Within a Shell: Paul de Man's War," *Critical Inquiry* 14:3 (1988): 530–652, and subsequent debate, *Critical Inquiry*, 15:4 (1989): 765–73; see also Werner Hamacher, Neil Hertz, and Tom Keenan, eds., *Responses: On Paul de Man's Wartime Journalism* (Lincoln: University of Nebraska Press, 1989). For the texts under dispute, see Paul de Man, *Wartime Journalism, 1939–1943* (Lincoln: University of Nebraska Press, 1988).

3. Avital Ronell, *Stupidity* (Urbana and Chicago: University of Illinois Press. 2002), esp. pp. 97–161.

4. Ibid., p. 105.

5. I refer here to Christopher Norris, *Paul de Man: Deconstruction and the Critique of Aesthetic Ideology* (New York and London: Routledge, 1988); Luc Herman, Kris Humbeeck, and Geert Lernout, eds., *(Dis)continuities: Essays on Paul de Man*, Postmodern Studies, 2 (Amsterdam: Rodopi, 1989); Lindsay Waters and Wlad Godzich, eds., *Reading de Man Reading* (Minneapolis: University of Minnesota Press, 1989); *Diacritics* 20:3 (1990); Ortwin de Graef, *Serenity in Crisis: A Preface to Paul de Man, 1939–1960* (Lincoln: University of Nebraska Press, 1993), and idem, *Titanic Light: Paul de Man's Post-Romanticism, 1960–1969* (Lincoln: University of Nebraska Press, 1995); Tom Cohen, Barbara Cohen, J. Hillis Miller, and Andrzej Warminski, eds., *Material Events: Paul de Man and the Afterlife of Theory* (Minneapolis: University of Minnesota Press, 2000); Martin McQuillan, *Paul de Man*, Critical Thinkers Series (London and New York: Routledge, 2001). I know of two European essay collections devoted to de Man (in addition to *(Dis)continuities*, which I included above because all of its essays are in English): a special issue of *Colloquium Helveticum* 11–12 (1990) (the essays, stemming from a colloquium at the University of

Zurich, are in German and English); and Karl Heinz Bohrer, ed. *Ästhetik und Rhetorik: Lektüren zu Paul de Man* (Frankfurt: Suhrkamp, 1993) (these essays are of course in German). An impressive if not utterly complete bibliography of de Man is available electronically: see Eddie Yeghiayan's magnificent "Paul de Man bibliography" online at http://sun3.lib.uci.edu/~scctr/Wellek/deman/.

6. Rodolphe Gasché, *The Wild Card of Reading: On Paul de Man* (Cambridge, Mass.: Harvard University Press, 1998), p. 269.

7. Cathy Caruth edited special issues of the psychoanalytic journal *American Imago* on trauma in 1991; these were republished as a book, *Trauma: Explorations in Memory* (Baltimore: Johns Hopkins University Press, 1995). Caruth has offered her own extended reflections on this topic in *Unclaimed Experience: Trauma, Narrative, and History* (Baltimore: Johns Hopkins University Press, 1996). For Felman's important work on trauma and the Holocaust, see Shoshana Felman and Dori Laub, *Testimony: Crises of Witnessing in Literature, Psychoanalysis, and History* (New York: Routledge, 1992).

8. For my discussions of de Man, see my *Phantom Formations: Aesthetic Ideology and the Bildungsroman* (Ithaca: Cornell University Press, 1996), pp. 1–40, and *The Politics of Aesthetics: Nationalism, Gender, Romanticism* (Stanford: Stanford University Press, 2003), pp. 5–9, 95–124. John Guillory deserves credit for making this point forcefully in the opening pages of his chapter on de Man in *Cultural Capital*: see John Guillory, *Cultural Capital: The Problem of Literary Canon Formation* (Chicago: University of Chicago Press, 1993), pp. 178–79. I discuss Guillory's book in my contribution to this volume.

9. For an example of the habit (which goes back to the late 1970s) of pairing Derrida with de Man and abjecting the latter, see Jeffrey T. Nealon, "The Discipline of Deconstruction." *PMLA* 107:5 (1992): 266–79.

10. Walter Benn Michaels, *The Shape of the Signifier* (Princeton: Princeton University Press, 2004). Michaels's mishearing and misrepresentation of deconstruction is so severe that Derridean and de Manian theses are turned into their opposite: what de Man calls "materiality" is treated as what de Man called "phenomenality." The misreading of Derrida is particularly stark, given the relatively systematic character of Derrida's thought in comparison with de Man's, and the relative accessibility of the arguments about iterability and difference in much-discussed and much-taught texts such as "Signature Event Context." Michaels imagines that Derrida's notion of a mark reduces to the "physical features" of a text (13): "the appeal to the 'purely formal' is an appeal to the physical, to the shape of the signifier" (57); "the mark is and must be nothing other than its shape" (125), etc. The Derridean trace is thus erased and transformed into sensuous presence and the logocentric promise of form: it becomes the sensory object one *sees*, rather than the differential mark one

reads. It is hard to imagine a more fundamental misreading of Derrida's notion of *difference* or of the trace or mark. For a focused corrective, see Jacques Derrida, *Limited Inc*, ed. Gerald Graff (Evanston, Ill.: Northwestern University Press, 1988), esp. pp. 50–54. And yet, crucial though this distortion of Derrida is to Michaels's argument, it is Paul de Man whom Michaels names as "the central figure" of his narrative (15). De Man's thematization of "materiality" remains, for reasons I am trying to clarify here, the irritant around which the book circles.

11. Paul de Man, *The Resistance to Theory* (Minneapolis: University of Minnesota Press, 1986), p. 19.

12. Paul de Man, *The Rhetoric of Romanticism* (New York: Columbia University Press, 1984), p. 241.

13. Jacques Derrida, *Margins of Philosophy*, trans. Alan Bass (Chicago: University of Chicago Press, 1982), p. 243, Derrida's italics.

14. See Paul de Man's massive critique of Riffaterre in "Hypogram and Inscription," available in *The Resistance to Theory*, pp. 27–53. For Riffaterre's notion of the hypogram, see Michael Riffaterre, *Semiotics of Poetry* (Bloomington: Indiana University Press, 1984).

15. Paul de Man, *Blindness and Insight: Essays in the Rhetoric of Contemporary Criticism*, rev. ed. (Minneapolis: University of Minnesota Press, 1983), p. 165.

16. Guillory, *Cultural Capital*, p. 179.

17. Ibid., pp. 237, 245.

DOUBLE-TAKE: READING DE MAN AND DERRIDA WRITING ON TROPES
Cynthia Chase

1. The Messenger Lectures. De Man's lectures were, in order, "Anthropomorphism and Trope in the Lyric," published in Paul de Man, *The Rhetoric of Romanticism* (New York: Columbia University Press, 1984); "Aesthetic Formalization: Kleist's 'Über das Marionnettentheater'"; "Hegel on the Sublime"; "Phenomenality and Materiality in Kant"; and "Kant and Schiller," all published in Paul de Man, *Aesthetic Ideology*, ed. Andrzej Warminski (Minneapolis: University of Minnesota Press, 1996); and "Conclusions: Walter Benjamin's 'The Task of the Translator,'" published in Paul de Man, *The Resistance to Theory* (Minneapolis: University of Minnesota Press, 1986).

2. De Man also carries out a reading of the passage in "Rhetoric of Tropes (Nietzsche)," in *Allegories of Reading* (New Haven: Yale University Press, 1981), pp. 110–13. These pages address a subject that is also addressed in the opening of "White Mythology." "Granted that the misinterpretation of reality that Nietzsche finds systematically repeated throughout the tradition is indeed rooted in the rhetorical structure of language, can we then not hope to escape from it by an equally systematic cleansing of this language from its

dangerously seductive figural properties? Is it not possible to progress from the rhetorical language of literature to a language that, like the language of science or mathematics, would be epistemologically more reliable?" (110). De Man's answer will be no.

3. De Man, *Rhetoric*, p. 239.

4. Jacques Derrida, "The Supplement of Copula: Philosophy before Linguistics," in *Margins of Philosophy*, trans. Alan Bass (Chicago: University of Chicago Press, 1982), p. 178.

5. De Man, *Rhetoric*, p. 241.

6. Derrida, "Supplement of Copula," p. 179.

7. De Man, *Rhetoric*, p. 241.

8. Ibid.

9. Ibid, pp. 241–42.

10. Jacques Derrida. "White Mythology," in *Margins of Philosophy*, p. 243. In De Man's terms in another essay: "Semantic determinants [are textually inscribed] within a non-determinable system of figuration" (*Resistance to Theory*, p. 411).

11. Derrida, "White Mythology," p. 243.

12. Ibid., pp. 242–43.

13. De Man, *Rhetoric*, p. 241.

14. De Man, *Allegories*, pp. 120–24.

15. Derrida, "White Mythology," p. 243.

16. De Man, *Rhetoric*, p. 241.

17. Derrida, "White Mythology," p. 243.

18. De Man, *Rhetoric*, p. 241.

19. Derrida, "Supplement of Copula," p. 179.

20. Ibid., p. 177.

21. Ibid., p. 178.

22. De Man, *Allegories*, p. 120.

23. Ibid., p. 123.

24. De Man, *Rhetoric*, p. 117.

25. Ibid., p. 239.

26. Ibid., p. 240.

27. Ibid.

28. Ibid., pp. 241–42.

29. Ibid., p. 241.

30. Ibid., p. 130.

31. Ibid., pp. 251–52.

32. De Man, *Resistance to Theory*, p. 37.

33. Derrida, "White Mythology," p. 243.

READING, BEGGING, PAUL DE MAN
Jan Mieszkowski

1. Edgar Allan Poe, *The Fall of the House of Usher and Other Writings*, ed. David Galloway (New York: Penguin, 1986), pp. 179, 188 (further references to this work will be cited in the body of the text). Only in the last sentence of the story is it (at least apparently) revealed that this "certain German book" refers to the *Hortulus Animæ*, a prayer manual that was popular in both its Latin and German editions in the sixteenth century. This clarification is offered indirectly, when the narrator says of the text that the "worst heart of the world is a grosser book" than it (188). Walter Benjamin famously discusses Poe's story in "On Some Motifs in Baudelaire," in *Selected Writings*, vol. 4, ed. Howard Eiland and Michael W. Jennings (Cambridge, Mass.: Harvard University Press, 2003), pp. 324–30.

2. Paul de Man, *Allegories of Reading* (New Haven: Yale University Press, 1981), p. 245.

3. Ibid., p. 209.

4. From this perspective, we have to question Rodolphe Gasché's claim that in de Man "literariness, writing, and the text are understood according to the model of a conscious subjectivity, that is, of a self-reflexive presence." *Inventions of Difference: On Jacques Derrida* (Cambridge, Mass.: Harvard University Press, 1994), p. 55. Werner Hamacher has challenged the preeminence of self-reflexive presence in de Man. Hamacher writes: "The language of allegory relates itself to language not reflexively but rather as an epistemologically uncertain praxis: language relates to itself in the mode of possible unrelatedness. If allegory thematizes the unreadability of texts, it can do so only because, in an epistemological paradox, it becomes the praxis of reading, of an other reading, of allegorical reading. It can make clear their intransparency only to the degree that it increases their readability." "LECTIO: de Man's Imperative," in *Reading de Man Reading*, ed. Lindsay Waters and Wlad Godzich (Minneapolis: University of Minnesota Press, 1989), p. 187.

5. The translation presented here is based on the German original: Heinrich von Kleist, *Sämtliche Werke und Briefe*, ed. Helmut Sembdner (Munich: DTV, 1987), vol. 2, pp. 196–98. I relied extensively on two existing English translations: one in *Selected Writings*, ed. and trans. David Constantine (London: J. M. Dent, 1997), pp. 351–53; and the other in *The Marquise of O– and other stories*, trans. David Luke and Nigel Reeves (New York: Penguin, 1978), pp. 214–16.

6. Jacob and Wilhelm Grimm, *Deutsches Wörterbuch* (Leipzig: Hirzel, 1965–).

7. Thomas Dutoit links the rising and falling rhythms of the story to Kant's description of the sublime in "Ghost Stories, the Sublime and Fantastic

Thirds in Kant and Kleist," *Colloquia Germanica* 27:2 (1994): 225–54. The role of sublimity in the tale is also explored by Grant Profant McAllister in *Kleist's Female Leading Characters and the Subversion of Idealist Discourse* (New York: Peter Lang, 2005).

8. Although the OED states that the etymology of "glitch" is unknown, it probably comes from the Yiddish *glitsh* ("a slip, lapse"), which derives from the Middle High German *glitschen* ("to glide"). *The Oxford English Dictionary*, 2d ed. (Oxford: Clarendon Press, 1989).

9. See Jurgen Schroder, "'Das Bettelweib von Locarno': Zum Gespenstischen in den Novellen Heinrich von Kleists," *Germanisch-Romanische Monatsschrift* 17 (1967): 195.

10. See Emil Staiger, "Kleists 'Bettelweib von Locarno': Zum Problem des dramatischen Stils," *Deutsche Vierteljahrsschrift für Literaturwissenschaft und Geistesgeschichte* 20 (1942): 5.

11. For a detailed analysis of the grammar and syntax of Kleist's story that comes to somewhat different conclusions than that of the present essay, see Katherine Arens, "Kleist's 'Bettelweib von Locarno': A Propositional Analysis," *Deutsche Vierteljahrsschrift für Literaturwissenschaft und Geistesgeschichte* 57:3 (September 1983): 450–68.

12. On *Hund, und,* and the role of the dog as a mediating term, see Dutoit, "Ghost Stories," esp. 243–46.

13. Paul de Man, *The Rhetoric of Romanticism* (New York: Columbia University Press, 1984), p. 122.

14. In his reading of Shelley, de Man argues something similar: "The undoing of the representational and iconic function of figuration by the play of the signifier does *not* suffice to bring about the disfiguration which *The Triumph of Life* acts out or represents." *The Rhetoric of Romanticism*, p. 114; emphasis added.

HISTORY AGAINST HISTORICISM, FORMAL MATTERS, AND THE EVENT OF THE TEXT: DE MAN WITH BENJAMIN
Ian Balfour

1. On the original French "quarrel" and its aftermath in German letters, see Hans Robert Jauss, "Schlegels und Schillers Replik auf die 'Querelle des Anciens et des Modernes,'" in *Literaturgeschichte als Provokation* (Frankfurt am Main: Suhrkamp, 1974), pp. 67–106. On the same topic, primarily in the British context, with an account of the French original as well, see Joseph M. Levine, *The Battle of the Books: History and Literature in the Augustan Age* (Ithaca and London: Cornell University Press, 1991), esp. chaps. 4, 7, 10, 11, and 12.

2. Paul de Man, *Blindness and Insight*, 2d ed. (Minneapolis: University of Minnesota Press, 1983), p. 165.

3. Edward W. Said, "Reflections on American 'Left' Literary Criticism," in *The World, the Text, and the Critic* (Cambridge, Mass.: Harvard University Press, 1983), p. 161ff.

4. De Man, *Blindness and Insight*, p. 165.

5. Paul de Man, *The Resistance to Theory* (Minneapolis: University of Minnesota Press, 1986), p. 23.

6. Reuben A. Brower, "Reading in Slow Motion," in *In Defense of Reading: A Reader's Approach to Literary Criticism*, ed. Reuben A. Brower and Richard Poirier (New York: E. P. Dutton, 1963), pp. 3–21. The volume edited by Brower and Poirier (and prefaced only by Brower) is interesting as a historical document of the work of a number of major critics early in their careers: Neil Hertz, Stephen Orgel, Paul de Man, Paul Alpers, and others.

7. Cleanth Brooks, *Modern Poetry and the Tradition* (Chapel Hill: University of North Carolina Press), pp. 215 and 236ff.

8. Paul de Man, *The Rhetoric of Romanticism* (New York: Columbia University Press, 1984), p. 188. Further citations from this work will appear in the text.

9. It nonetheless seems clear, in the later essay, which of the two readings is "preferable," for de Man, namely, the one not modeled on the organic images of the poem and the putative organicism of the final question of "Among School Children."

10. De Man, *The Rhetoric of Romanticism*, p. 189.

11. De Man, *Blindness and Insight*, p. 20.

12. Theodor Adorno, *Aesthetic Theory*, trans. Robert Hullot-Kentor (Minneapolis: University of Minnesota Press, 1997), p. 194.

13. On these matters, see de Man, *The Resistance to Theory*, p. 82ff.

14. De Man, *The Rhetoric of Romanticism*, p. 123.

15. De Man, *The Resistance to Theory*, pp. 103–4.

16. Jacques Derrida, "Typewriter Ribbon: Limited Ink (2)," in *Material Events: Paul de Man and the Afterlife of Theory*, ed. Tom Cohen, Barbara Cohen, J. Hillis Miller, and Andrzej Warminski (Minneapolis: University of Minnesota Press, 2000), pp. 277–360.

17. Paul de Man, *Allegories of Reading* (New Haven and London: Yale University Press, 1979), p. 270.

18. De Man, *The Rhetoric of Romanticism*, p. 262.

DISCONTINUOUS SHIFTS: HISTORY READING HISTORY
Andrzej Warminski

1. Paul de Man, *The Rhetoric of Romanticism* (New York: Columbia University Press, 1984), p. viii.

2. Ibid.

3. Paul de Man, *Allegories of Reading* (New Haven: Yale University Press, 1979), p. ix.

4. Paul de Man, *Romanticism and Contemporary Criticism*, ed. E. S. Burt, Kevin Newmark, and Andrzej Warminski (Baltimore: Johns Hopkins University Press, 1993), p. 56. Further citations of this work will appear in the text.

5. See de Man's "Form and Intent in the American New Criticism" and "The Literary Self as Origin: The Work of Georges Poulet," both in *Blindness and Insight* (New York: Oxford University Press, 1971).

6. See de Man's "Phenomenality and Materiality in Kant" in idem, *Aesthetic Ideology*, ed. Andrzej Warminski (Minneapolis: University of Minnesota Press, 1996), p. 79. On de Man's reading of Kant's sublimes, see my "'As the poets do it': On the Material Sublime" in *Material Events: Paul de Man and the Afterlife of Theory*, ed. Tom Cohen, Barbara Cohen, J. Hillis Miller, and Andrzej Warminski (Minneapolis: University of Minnesota Press, 2001), pp. 3–31.

7. De Man, *Aesthetic Ideology*, p. 133.

8. It is worth noting that the alleged shift from "history" to "reading" was, in fact, always already a shift *from* "reading" *to* "reading," since the itinerary goes *from* de Man's having begun "to *read* [my emphasis] Rousseau," *through* his being "unable to progress beyond local difficulties of interpretation," *to* end up with "the problematics of *reading* [my emphasis]" (*Allegories of Reading*, p. ix). That this "shift" from reading to reading is in fact—also always already—a shift from history to history is . . . the point!

9. De Man, *Aesthetic Ideology*, p. 89.

"AT THE FAR END OF THIS ONGOING ENTERPRISE . . ."
Sara Guyer

Thanks to the Special Collections librarians at the University of California, Irvine, and to Mrs. Patricia de Man for allowing me to reprint archival materials. Thanks also to David Wagenknecht for sharing with me his experiences of editing the issue, to Jack Dudley for assistance with preparing the manuscript, to Steven Miller for conversations about parricide, and to Tres Pyle for thinking with me about distant inheritances.

1. More than the other essays collected in the issue, these two seem to have direct bearing upon the introduction—both to the extent that they are explicit applications of de Man's readings (Ray's is undertaken in advance of, and referred to in, a footnote to de Man's own Kleist essay) and to the extent that they give a frame for the topics addressed in the introduction, even as they break that frame, because they are not the work of de Man's students in quite the same manner as the others. The other essays by members of the NEH seminar were not included.

2. For another version of this figure, one more explicitly linked to the question of legacy and initiating from Freud, rather than Kleist, see Jacques Derrida, "Freud's Legacy." Derrida reads Freud's legend of "fils" (strings/sons): "The legacy and jealousy of a repetition (already jealous of itself) are not accidents which overtake the *fort: da*, rather they more or less strictly pull its strings. And assign it to an auto-bio-thanato-hetero-graphic scene of writing. This scene of writing does not recount something, the content of an event which would be called the *fort: da*. This remains unrepresentable, but produces, there producing itself, the scene of writing." Jacques Derrida, "Freud's Legacy," in *The Post Card: From Socrates to Freud and Beyond*, trans. Alan Bass (Chicago: University of Chicago Press, 1987), p. 336. De Man's introduction concerns the question of the relation between legacy and the production of the scene of instruction.

3. See for example de Man's description of the dancing marionettes who have in them a potential for grace in excess of any human dancer as one model for this inheritance. This model acknowledges the puppeteer's charge over the graceful text: "The puppets have no motion by themselves but only in relation to the motions of the puppeteer, to whom they are connected by a system of lines and threads. All their aesthetic charm stems from the transformations undergone by the linear motion of the puppeteer as it becomes a dazzling display of curves and arabesques. By itself, the motion is devoid of any aesthetic interest or effect. The aesthetic power is located neither in the puppet nor in the puppeteer but in the text that spins itself between them." Paul de Man, *The Rhetoric of Romanticism* (New York: Columbia University Press, 1984), p. 285.

4. Paul de Man Papers, MS-C 4, Special Collections and Archives, the UCI Libraries, Irvine, California, Box 8, Folder 31.

5. See Wordsworth, preface to *Lyrical Ballads*, in William Wordsworth and Samuel Taylor Coleridge, *Lyrical Ballads*, ed. R. L. Brett and A. R. Jones, 2d ed. (London: Routledge, 1991), p. 250. That Bahti's essay might be understood to be "romantic" for precisely the reasons that Wagenknecht understands it to sacrifice Wordsworth and the Wordsworthians is a topic that will have to be taken up on another occasion.

6. Bahti, "Figures of Interpretation, The Interpretation of Figures: A Reading of Wordsworth's 'Dream of the Arab,'" in "The Rhetoric of Romanticism," ed. Paul de Man, special issue, *Studies in Romanticism* 18, no. 4 (1979): 601–28. The quote from Bloom appears on page 607 of Bahti's essay. Also key—but undiscussed in Wagenknecht's letter—is Bahti's "engagement" with J. Hillis Miller's essay on Wordsworth's "Dream of the Arab," which, at the time Bahti was writing, had appeared only in French. Bahti's discussion of Miller—largely in the mode of accolade and quotation—is relegated almost entirely to footnotes.

7. Wagenknecht's emphasis. Bahti explains: "This [the structure whereby the figural always turns into the literal and vice versa] is a rhetorical understanding of a Wordsworthian (and more than Wordsworthian) rhetorical structure, but thus far we have approached it less through a reading of Wordsworth than through a reading of the reading offered by the man Harold Bloom has called 'the most defiantly Wordsworthian of modern critics'" (Bahti, "Figures of Interpretation," p. 607). Wagenknecht of course refers to the draft version of the essay.

8. Perhaps it is no wonder, then, that what is at stake in de Man's introduction could be understood as the uncomfortable relation between obsequiousness and obsequy, that is, between the awkward coincidence of following one's teachers and issuing their burial rites.

9. At the end of this paragraph Wagenknecht tells de Man that Bahti's concluding claim (that the rhetorical reading of the "Dream of the Arab" episode could be extended to other key passages, above all, those in Books 6 and 14, in which "imagination would find itself in and of nature" [Bahti, "Figures of Interpretation," p. 626]) "rang very hollow in my ears."

10. De Man, MS-C 4.

11. De Man to Wagenknecht, October 5, 1978. Paul de Man Papers, ibid. Wagenknecht finally tracks down de Man in Kruzlingen, Switzerland, and justifiably admits in a letter of June 28, 1978: "I think you've treated me cavalierly, and I'm mad as hell."

12. De Man, ed. "The Rhetoric of Romanticism," special issue, *Studies in Romanticism* 18, no. 4 (1979): 495. Hereafter cited as *SR*.

13. For a description of the model *Arbeitsgruppe*—to which de Man suggests his seminars do not match up—see the introduction to Timothy Bahti's 1982 translation of H. R. Jauss's *Toward an Aesthetic of Reception*, also included under the title "Reading and History" in *The Resistance to Theory*. De Man explains: "By his own volition the work of the German literary historian and theorist Hans Robert Jauss has been associated with a study group for which he is a spokesman and which practices a specific way of investigating and teaching literature. In the field of literary theory, the existence of such groups is not an unusual occurrence. They are, at times, centered on a single, dominating personality and take on all the exacted exclusiveness of a secret society, with its rituals of initiation, exclusion, and hero-worship. Nothing could be more remote from the spirit of the group of which Jauss is a prominent member. The Konstanz school of literary studies, so named because several of its members taught or are teaching at the newly founded University of Konstanz in Southern Germany, is a liberal association of scholars, informally united by methodological concerns that allow for considerable diversity. It has the character of a continuing research seminar that includes some constant members

(of which H. R. Jauss is one) next to more casual participants; a somewhat comparable instance of such a group, in structure, if not in content, would have been, in this country, the Chicago critics of the forties and fifties, who shared an interest in Aristotelian poetics." Paul de Man, *The Resistance to Theory* (Minneapolis: University of Minnesota Press, 1986), p. 54. That de Man, three years after the introduction to *Studies in Romanticism* points to Chicago in the 50s rather than New Haven in the 70s in order to show "a comparable instance" of an *Arbeitsgruppe* indicates all the more the ambivalence of the introduction's opening, but in comparison with Jauss, this gesture also is self-implicating, and suggests perhaps that it is "by his own volition" that de Man was associated with a study group centered around the authority of a dominating personality.

14. It has always struck me that the genitive structure of "The Rhetoric of Romanticism" requires some interrogation: romanticism is the trope under analysis and the tropes and figures of romanticism provide the terms of that analysis. It is in this sense that all of the works that appear under this ambivalent heading are not only studies of romanticism or of romantic-period writers, but are also studies of the critics of romanticism, a point made most evident in the posthumously published Gauss Lectures, which deal with not only Wordsworth, Hölderlin, and Rousseau, but also Heidegger, Starobinski, Girard, and Hartman.

15. This leads de Man to remark: "of all the coercions exercised by graduate instruction none is more tyrannical than the predetermination of the textual canon" (*SR*, p. 495).

16. An earlier, manuscript version of the introduction reveals that in the final sentence, de Man initially incorporated a pun on Derrida's essay on Blanchot, "The Law of Genre," and plays on the relevance of romanticism to this discussion of generation: "It is a matter of chance ~~that generations are not to be mixed in this collection and~~ that the ~~authors can be said~~ authors turn out to belong by and large to the same generation. ~~As a result, the temptation to comment on the ongoing interpretation of romanticism as a generational process is hard to resist.~~" The phrase, as it appears in the opening sentence of Derrida's essay is "Ne pas mêler les genres." Jacques Derrida, *Parages* (Paris: Galilée, 1986), p. 251.

17. The unstable language of the event belongs to Jean-François Lyotard; see in particular his "The Sublime and the Avant-Garde," in *The Inhuman: Reflections on Time*, trans. Geoffrey Bennington and Rachel Bowlby (Stanford: Stanford University Press, 1991), pp. 89–107. In that essay, Lyotard recalls that, for Barnett Newman, the now "is what dismantles consciousness, and what deposes consciousness, it is what consciousness cannot formulate, even what consciousness forgets in order to constitute itself" (ibid., 90). Lyotard

translates this nonconsciousness—which we also could understand as the condition of generation or happening in de Man's essay—as a question mark, and states: "The event happens as a question mark 'before' happening as a question. *It happens* is rather 'in the first place' *is it happening, is this it, is it possible?* Only 'then' is any mark determined by the questioning: is this or that happening, is it this or something else, is it possible that this or that?" (ibid., 90).

18. The figure of birth without birth, a birth into death, or a birth without life—which de Man will take from Nietzsche's *Birth of Tragedy* and Carol Jacobs's reading of it—also appears in the final sentences of his foreword to Jacobs's book: "But whereas the apparent fluidity of Nietzsche's text turns out to be a stammer, the high quality of Carol Jacobs's readings threaten her with a worse danger. She cannot prevent her stammering text from being impeccably fluid. Parable turns into paraphrase after all, even and especially when one is as fully aware as she is of this inconsistency. The result is no longer the birth of something purely tragic, though it is certainly not benign. It may well be the birth of criticism as truly critical reading, a birth that is forever aborted and forever repeated but that, in the meantime, makes for indispensable reading." Paul de Man, *Critical Writings 1953–1978*, edited by Lindsay Waters (Minneapolis: University of Minnesota Press, 1989), p. 223. One way of figuring this entire predicament would be in terms of "liquidation."

19. William Flesch considers the "disdainful" aspect of de Man's praise here, and understands it to contribute to a transferential structure in de Man's pedagogical relations. He explains: "One way that I think de Man encouraged the transference was by taking a disdainful view of his disciples (see, for example, his introduction to the issue of *Studies in Romanticism* that he edited) but always making you feel that you were exempt from this otherwise general, though subtle, contempt, precisely because you could see the contempt he had for others (never your friends, though)—because you got the irony of his never quite believable praise of others. But of course you always believed it when he praised you." William Flesch, "De Man and Idolatry," in *Tainted Greatness: Antisemitism and Cultural Heroes*, ed. Nancy A. Harrowitz (Philadelphia: Temple University Press, 1994), p. 240. Flesch's account of transference is most interesting to me in the context of an analysis of legacy. For example, in "Freud's Legacy," Derrida links transference to legacy in the formula: "no legacy without transference" (*Post Card*, p. 339). This is not simply a statement of transference as the condition of legacy's possibility, but, as he elaborates, it "also gives us to understand that if every legacy is propagated in transference, it can get underway only in the form of an inheritance of transference" ["pas de legs sans transfert. Cela donne aussi à entendre que, si tout legs se propage en trasfert, il n'est en train que dans la forme d'un héritage de trasfert"] (*Postcard*, p. 339; *Carte Postale*, p. 360). In some sense, this ambivalence may come down to the ambivalence of radicality (and rootedness) itself.

20. De Man, *SR*, pp. 495.

21. "Freud's Legacy" opens with a discussion of the difference in Freud between fear and anxiety, and Freud's account of anxiety as "more a protection against trauma, linked to repression" (Derrida, *Postcard*, p. 297). While I leave a comprehensive reading of Derrida's essay for another occasion, I do wish to point out that the recurring figure of the dance in his reading of Freud (the various "pas") raises the specter of Kleist's dancing marionettes and amputees. Indeed it is tempting and possible here to link the question of "legacy" (legs) to the marionette's dancing legs, to the grace whereby the seemingly proper or faithful inheritance (in this case of reading and of romanticism, of the rhetoric of romanticism—in advance) is also parricidal thanks to the unconsciousness of elegance and nonanxiety. In other words, anxiety is a prophylactic device not wholly dissimilar from grace, and both emerge as responses to the nonconsciousness of a trauma.

22. De Man, *SR*, pp. 495–96.

23. See, for example, the preface to *The Rhetoric of Romanticism*: "This collection of essays on the general topic of European romantic and post-romantic literature was established at the initiative of William P. Germano, Editor-in-Chief at the Columbia University Press. . . . With the possible addition of the essay entitled 'The Rhetoric of Temporality' (now reprinted in a new edition of *Blindness and Insight*), the collection presents the main bulk of what I have written on romanticism. Except for some passing allusions, *Allegories of Reading* is in no way a book about romanticism or its heritage." Paul de Man, *The Rhetoric of Romanticism* (New York: Columbia University Press, 1984), p. vii. Hereafter cited as *RR*.

24. De Man, *RR*, p. viii. As de Man says of *The Rhetoric of Romanticism*: "The principle of selection for this volume is clearly historical: all the essays deal with romantic poetry and its aftermath. The historical topology makes sense to the extent that the original papers were part of a project that was itself historically oriented. The choice of authors is banal enough to require no further justification" (p. vii). For a description of this project, see E. S. Burt, Kevin Newmark, and Andrzej Warminski's preface to de Man's *Romanticism and Contemporary Criticism: The Gauss Seminar and Other Papers* (Baltimore: Johns Hopkins University Press, 1993) (a text that might be read as the inversion of the introduction to *Studies in Romanticism*): "[S]ince this romantic historical consciousness is, according to de Man, a powerful 'source' for our own consciousness, a historical study of romanticism would also necessarily be a reflection on our own historical predicament, our history. De Man had in fact projected such a historical study of romanticism, and, around 1968, had collected the Gauss lectures and his other essays on romantic texts in a manuscript volume entitled *The Unimaginable Touch of Time*" (p. viii).

25. De Man, *SR*, p. 496. For de Man's account of his own response to this predicament, see the preface to "his" *The Rhetoric of Romanticism*: "Such massive evidence of the failure to make the various individual readings coalesce is a somewhat melancholy spectacle. The fragmentary aspect of the whole is made more obvious still by the hypotactic manner that prevails in each of the essays taken in isolation, by the continued attempt, however ironized, to present a closed and linear argument. This apparent coherence *within* each essay is not matched by a corresponding coherence *between* them. Laid out diachronically in a roughly chronological sequence, they do not evolve in a manner that easily allows for dialectical progression or, ultimately, for historical totalization. Rather, it seems that they always start again from scratch and that their conclusions fail to add up to anything. If some secret principle of summation is at work here, I do not feel qualified to articulate it and, as far as the general question of romanticism is concerned, I must leave the task of its historical definition to others" (*RR*, p. viii). Here de Man positions his "fragmentary" and suspended work in relation to the failed *summae* he describes in the introduction to the special issue of *Studies in Romanticism*.

26. My emphasis. Paul de Man, *Allegories of Reading: Figural Language in Rousseau, Nietzsche, Rilke, and Proust* (New Haven: Yale University Press, 1979), p. ix. Hereafter cited as *AR*.

27. De Man, *RR*, p. viii.

28. He writes: "What emerges is a process of reading in which rhetoric is a disruptive intertwining of trope and persuasion or—which is not quite the same thing—of cognitive and performative language" (*AR*, p. ix).

29. See, for example, the foreword to the second edition of *Blindness and Insight*: "I am not given to retrospective self-examination and mercifully forget what I have written with the same alacrity that I forget bad movies—although, as with bad movies, certain scenes or phrases return at times to embarrass and haunt me like a guilty conscience. When one imagines to have felt the exhilaration of renewal, one is certainly the last to know whether such a change actually took place or whether one is just restating, in a slightly different mode, earlier and unresolved obsessions." Paul de Man, *Blindness and Insight: Essays in the Rhetoric of Contemporary Culture*, 2d rev. ed. (Minneapolis: University of Minnesota Press, 1983), p. xii.

30. De Man, *SR*, pp. 497–98.

31. Ibid., p. 498.

32. E. S. Burt, Kevin Newmark, and Andrzej Warminski, preface to *Romanticism and Contemporary Criticism*, p. vii. The authors explain that "romantic historical consciousness is, according to de Man, a powerful 'source' for our own consciousness." For other versions of this claim, see Cynthia Chase's

introduction to *Romanticism* (London: Longman, 1993) and Philippe Lacoue-Labarthe and Jean-Luc Nancy, *The Literary Absolute: The Theory of Literature in German Romanticism*, trans. Philip Barnard and Cheryl Lester (Albany: State University of New York Press, 1988).

33. Compare "For the other is not the possible. So it would be necessary to say that the only possible invention would be the invention of the impossible. But an invention of the impossible is impossible, the other would say. Indeed. But it is the only possible invention: an invention has to declare itself to be the invention of that which did not appear to be possible; otherwise it only makes explicit a program of possibilities within the economy of the same." Jacques Derrida, "Psyche: Inventions of the Other," trans. Carolyn Porter, in *Reading de Man Reading*, ed. Lindsay Waters and Wlad Godzich (Minneapolis: University of Minnesota Press, 1989), pp. 25–65, quotation on p. 60.

34. On the fable, see Thomas Keenan's brilliant *Fables of Responsibility: Aberrations and Predicaments in Ethics and Politics* (Stanford: Stanford University Press, 1997). Keenan's work is helpful not only for thinking about "the rhetorical mechanism of the fable" and its relation to ethics and politics, but also for thinking further about the meaning and possibility of de Man's legacy.

35. *Tension* evokes the entire specular metaphorics and the predicament of self-reflection as the impossibility of invention at work here, specifically the metaphorics of *Psyche* (as mirror and woman) rendered in terms of an inextricable temporality ("tense"). Minimally, *Tension*, the act or action of stretching, recalls *Psyche*, outstretched, as we find her in Freud and in Nancy. Jean-Luc Nancy, "Psyche," trans. Emily McVarish, in *The Birth to Presence* (Stanford: Stanford University Press, 1995), p. 393; Jacques Derrida, *On Touching, Jean-Luc Nancy* (Stanford: Stanford University Press, 2005); Jacques Derrida, "Psyche: Inventions of the Other," trans. Carolyn Porter, in *Reading de Man Reading*, ed. Lindsay Waters and Wlad Godzich (Minneapolis: University of Minnesota Press, 1989), pp. 25–65.

36. This recalls the trap (*Fälle*) that de Man discusses in the final paragraph of "Aesthetic Formalization in Kleist" and that Cynthia Chase will come to consider the in "Trappings of an Education," her contribution to *Responses*. De Man writes: "But *Fälle* also means 'trap,' the trap which is the ultimate textual model of this and of all texts, the trap of an aesthetic education which inevitably confuses dismemberment of language by the power of the letter with the gracefulness of a dance. This dance, regardless of whether it occurs as a mirror, as imitation, as history, as the fencing match of interpretation, or as the anamorphic transformations of tropes, is the ultimate trap, as unavoidable as it is deadly" (*RR*, p. 290). I find it curious that the mention of a "trap" in the introduction to a volume in which her own essay on Wordsworth appears goes unmentioned in Chase's later essay.

37. For a particularly compelling account of an unconscious legacy articulated in terms of "haunting" and ventriloquism, see Nicolas Abraham's and Maria Torok's various accounts of the "Transgenerational Phantom," in particular Abraham's 1975 "Notes on the Phantom: A Complement to Freud's Metapsychology" in Nicolas Abraham and Maria Torok, *The Shell and the Kernel*, ed. and trans. Nicholas T. Rand (Chicago: University of Chicago Press, 1994), 165–76.

38. De Man, *SR*, p. 499.

39. Ibid., p. 498.

40. De Man's description of the scope ("certainly not wider, far from it") and serenity ("far from causing anxiety . . .") of these papers resonates with his description of the work of his predecessors, for whom "no general works on Romanticism were produced comparable is scope and serenity to those of the previous decades" (*SR*, p. 496). It seems as if de Man's complaint is that these papers—as well as Jacobs's *Dissimulating Harmony*, against which he offers more or less the same criticism—are both limited in scope and untroubled by the difficulties they would seem to encounter. Granted, the criticism, if taken seriously, seems devastating—suggesting that this text not only describes a guiltless parricide, but also enacts a violent infanticide in the recovery of absent guilt, that is, in the accusation of parricide.

41. De Man, *SR*, p. 498.

42. De Man, *Critical Writings*, p. 223.

43. De Man, *SR*, p. 498.

44. Compare Heinrich von Kleist, "On the Marionette Theater," trans. Roman Paska, in *Fragments for a History of the Human Body*, Part 1, ed. Michel Feher with Ramona Nadaff and Nadia Tazi (New York: Zone, 1989), pp. 415–20: "'Have you,' he asked, as I cast my eyes silently to the ground, 'have you heard of those mechanical legs that English artists fabricate for the unfortunates who have lost their limbs?' I said no, I had never set eyes on such things. 'That's too bad,' he replied, 'for if I tell you that those unfortunates dance with them, I'm almost afraid you won't believe me. What am I saying! Dance? Certainly the range of their movements is limited; but those at their disposal are accomplished with an ease, lightness and grace that astonish every sensitive mind'" (pp. 416–17). De Man turns to these "dancing invalids" in the final paragraphs of his essay on Kleist's parable: "The dancing invalid in Kleist's story is one more victim in a long series of mutilated bodies that attend on the progress of enlightened self-knowledge, a series that includes Wordsworth's mute country-dwellers and blind city-beggars. The point is not that the dance fails and that Schiller's idyllic description of a graceful but confined freedom is aberrant. Aesthetic education by no means fails; it succeeds all too well, to the point of hiding the violence that makes it possible" (*RR*, p. 289).

In de Man's translation of Kleist, the phrase reads: "The circle of his motions may be restricted, but as for those available to him, he accomplishes them with an ease, elegance, and gracefulness which fills any thinking mind with amazement" (*RR*, pp. 288–89).

45. De Man, *SR*, p. 498.
46. Ibid., p. 498.
47. Ibid., pp. 498–99.
48. Timothy Bahti, *Allegories of History: Literary Historiography after Hegel* (Baltimore: Johns Hopkins University Press, 1992), p. 293.

PROFESSING LITERATURE:
JOHN GUILLORY'S MISREADING OF PAUL DE MAN
Marc Redfield

1. John Guillory, *Cultural Capital: The Problem of Literary Canon-formation* (Chicago: University of Chicago Press, 1993), p. 203.

2. As I note a little later in this essay, Peggy Kamuf's fine review of *Cultural Capital* in *Diacritics* has almost nothing to say about the book's chapter on de Man: see Peggy Kamuf, "The Division of Literature," *Diacritics* 25:3 (1995): 53–72. I have found Guillory's work a helpful irritant over the years, and the present essay represents something of an effort to make payments on an overdue account by decompressing the brief critiques of *Cultural Capital* (and especially of its de Man chapter) that I offer in *Phantom Formations: Aesthetic Ideology and the Bildungsroman* (Ithaca: Cornell University Press, 1996), pp. 28–29, 35–36, 211–13, and *The Politics of Aesthetics: Nationalism, Gender, Romanticism* (Stanford: Stanford University Press, 2003), pp. 5–8, 187–88.

3. Guillory, *Cultural Capital*, p. vii. Subsequent references to this book will be given parenthetically in the body of the text.

4. Guillory borrows the notion of cultural capital from Pierre Bourdieu: of Bourdieu's many writings in this area, see especially *Distinction: A Social Critique of the Judgment of Taste*, trans. Richard Nice (Cambridge, Mass.: Harvard University Press, 1984). The idea of cultural capital goes back to Mannheim (at least): "the modern bourgeoisie had from the beginning a twofold social root—on the one hand the owners of capital, on the other those individuals whose only capital consisted in their education." Karl Mannheim, *Ideology and Utopia: An Introduction to the Sociology of Knowledge*, trans. Louis Wirth and Edward Shils (New York: Harcourt, Brace, 1936 [1929]).

5. Pierre Machery and Etienne Balibar, "Literature as an Ideological Form: Some Marxist Propositions," trans. James Kavanaugh, *Praxis* 5 (1981): 57, cited in Guillory, *Cultural Capital*, p. 80.

6. Friedrich Schiller, *On the Aesthetic Education of Man, in a Series of Letters*, trans. Elizabeth M. Wilkinson and L. A. Willoughby (Oxford: Clarendon

Press, 1967), p. 219. I discuss Schiller's notion of the Aesthetic State in *Phantom Formations* (via a reading of Goethe's *Wilhelm Meisters Wanderjahre*), pp. 95–133; see also pp. 211–13 for a critique of these closing remarks of Guillory's.

7. The writing staff of *The Simpsons* is famous for being dominated by *Harvard Lampoon* alumni—a factoid of significance to the extent that it can remind us that the graduates of elite schools continue to play a substantial role in the culture industry. This is not to dispute the "decline of the humanities," or, for that matter, the retreat of print culture itself. According to a National Endowment for the Arts report released as I completed this essay, only about 50 percent of Americans read any sort of novel (or play or story, etc.) at all over the past year (see "Fewer Noses Stuck in Books in America, Survey Finds," *New York Times*, July 8, 2004). The point is only that the difference between "high" and "mass" culture is far more fluid than writers such as Guillory tend to imply. Furthermore, as I shall remark later in this essay, the discourse of aesthetics is not simply a "high-cultural" phenomenon; quite the contrary.

8. Kamuf, "Division of Literature," p. 62. Subsequent citations of this work will appear in the body of the text.

9. Ernesto Laclau and Chantal Mouffe, *Hegemony and Socialist Strategy: Towards a Radical Democratic Politics* (London: Verso, 1985), p. 129.

10. Once again, I permit myself to refer to *Phantom Formations*, pp. 1–37, and *The Politics of Aesthetics*, pp. 1–4, passim. The persistence of aesthetics beyond differences between "elite" and "mass" culture is what Guillory misses—for the sake of the aesthetic. On this point I would grant precedence to David Lloyd and Paul Thomas's analysis: "The differential position of culture . . . so deeply saturates the structure of bourgeois society that even the so-called aestheticization of daily life in the postmodern era has not fundamentally altered its significance. The structure of 'recreationary space,' whether defined as Arnoldian culture or the mass media, is, in relation to the specialization of the workplace or the interests of politics, fundamentally little changed and continues to provide the mechanisms by which the formal subject of the state is produced as *in this domain* undivided. Without a radical critique, not only of the terms but also of the conditions of possibility of such differentiation of spheres, the function of culture in the reproduction of the state and material social relations cannot adequately be addressed." David Lloyd and Paul Thomas, *Culture and the State* (London and New York: Routledge, 1998), p. 15.

11. Kamuf dismisses Guillory's explanation of his focus on de Man with little more than an exclamation of incredulity: " 'The equation theory-deconstruction-de Man' is, he claims, 'already present in the professional imaginary' (Guillory, *Cultural Capital*, p. 178). Oh, really? Reading that, one may be re-

lieved, alarmed, or merely amused at the idea that there is someone out there who believes he has his finger on the pulse of the 'professional imaginary.' Or even at the idea that someone would so confidently invoke such a concept, which illustrates too well the violence of conceptual totalization. To escape this violence many, if not most, of Guillory's readers (I include myself) will probably choose to ignore the claim. Which is not to say that this framing device is easy to ignore: on the contrary, it intrudes and insists on almost every page of the [fourth] chapter" (Kamuf, "Division of Literature," pp. 62–63).

12. Continuing what is no doubt, on the one hand, shameless self-promotion and, on the other hand, the exhibitionistic airing of an obsession, I take the liberty of noting that reflections on de Man's charisma are to be found in my essay "De Man, Schiller, and the Politics of Reception," *Diacritics* 20:3 (1990): 50–70 (esp. 50–51, 64–65), which predates Guillory's book by a couple of years. (A revised and expanded version of this essay now makes up chapter 3 of *The Politics of Aesthetics*.) Many critics have commented in passing on de Man's peculiar antitheatrical charisma; Samuel Weber, for instance, has this interesting remark in an interview: "I have long felt that de Man, in his practice as teacher and as writer, was the most Lacanian, or Freudian, or psychoanalytic of literary critics. Not explicitly, of course, but in his use of authority, in his tendency to multiply apodictic statements in a way that undermined the absoluteness of the claims they seemed to be making." Samuel Weber, *Mass Mediauras: Form, Technics, Media* (Stanford: Stanford University Press, 1996), p. 185.

13. Thomas Pepper, *Singularities: Extremes of Theory in the Twentieth Century* (Cambridge: Cambridge University Press, 1997), p. 96n9.

14. See the introduction to this volume for some reflections on the breadth and complexity of de Man's influence in the Anglo-American academy.

15. Jacques Derrida, *La carte postale: de Socrate à Freud et au-delà* (Paris: Flammarion, 1980), p. 360.

16. A revised version of "Semiology and Rhetoric," originally published in *Diacritics* 3:3 (1973): 27–33, became the first chapter of *Allegories of Reading*. In the citations of works by de Man that will appear in the text below, I shall be using conventional acronyms: *Aesthetic Ideology*, ed. Andrzej Warminski (Minneapolis: University of Minnesota Press, 1996) [*AI*]; *Allegories of Reading: Figural Language in Rousseau, Nietzsche, Rilke, and Proust* (New Haven: Yale University Press, 1979) [*AR*]; *The Resistance to Theory* (Minneapolis: University of Minnesota Press, 1986) [*RT*]; *The Rhetoric of Romanticism* (New York: Columbia University Press, 1984) [*RR*]; *Romanticism and Contemporary Criticism: The Gauss Seminar and Other Papers*, ed. E. S. Burt, Kevin Newmark, and Andrzej Warminski (Baltimore: Johns Hopkins University Press, 1993) [*RCC*]. References to these works will be indicated by acronym and page number in the body of the text.

17. On de Man's introduction to *Studies in Romanticism* 18:4 (1979): 495–99, see Sara Guyer's contribution to this volume.

18. "Theory of Metaphor" was originally published as an article in *Studies in Romanticism* 12:2 (1973): 475–98. The Proust essay first appeared as "Proust et l'allégorie de la lecture," in a *Festschrift* for Georges Poulet, *Movements premiers* (Paris: Jose Corti, 1972), pp. 231–50; versions of *Allegories of Reading*'s Rilke chapter and one of its Nietzsche chapters also appeared in 1972: see introduction to Rainer Maria Rilke, *Poesie*, vol. 2 of *Oeuvres* (Paris: Seuil, 1972), pp. 7–42; and "Genesis and Genealogy in Nietzsche's *Birth of Tragedy*," *Diacritics* 2:4 (1972): 44–53. The order of composition of these texts is, so far as I know, a moot question.

19. Jacques Derrida, *The Politics of Friendship*, trans. George Collins (London: Verso, 1997), pp. 26–47, 67, passim.

20. I believe one can bring de Man's thought into useful proximity with Derrida's here: the imperative-to-theme (which is also to say the imperative-to-language) in de Man may be thought in Derridean terms as the promise and affirmation—the "yes yes"—that opens language as an infinite relation to the other. Derrida's powerful reading of de Man in *Memoires* runs in this direction, as he glosses de Man's pun on Heidegger, "Die Sprache verspricht (sich)" (*AR*, p. 277; the play is on Heidegger's dictum *Die Sprache spricht*—"Die Sprache verspricht" means "language promises"; "die Sprache verspricht sich" means "language mis-speaks"). "Everything begins," Derrida suggests, "with this apparently post-originary and performative modalization of Sprache. . . . This is not to say that all of this performativity is of the type of the promise, in the narrow and everyday sense of the term. But this performative thereby reveals a structure or destination of the Sprache. . . . What is essential here is that a pure promise cannot properly take place, even though promising is inevitable as soon as we open our mouths—or rather as soon as there is a text." Jacques Derrida, *Memoires: For Paul de Man*, rev. ed. (New York: Columbia University Press, 1988), pp. 97–98. This "yes yes" of language broaches what Derrida, particularly in *The Politics of Friendship*, calls the "perhaps." The fundamental problematic of the "perhaps," which for Derrida makes responsibility and the decision (impossibly) possible, may be called "undecidability" in Derrida's idiom as well as in de Man's: "Undecidability . . . is not a sentence that a decision can leave behind. The crucial experience of the *perhaps* imposed by the undecidable—that is to say, the condition of decision—is not a moment to be exceeded, forgotten, or suppressed" (*Politics*, 219).

21. One need look no further than this volume to find an interesting debate over de Manian materialism: see especially Rei Terada's contribution, "Seeing Is Reading." For a collection of essays more or less dedicated to this

question, see Tom Cohen, Barbara Cohen, J. Hillis Miller, and Andrzej Warminski, eds. *Material Events: Paul de Man and the Afterlife of Theory* (Minneapolis: University of Minnesota Press, 2000).

22. Jacques Derrida, "Typewriter Ribbon: Limited Ink (2) ("within such limits")," in Cohen, Cohen, Miller, and Warminski, *Material Events*, p. 281.

23. There is one apparent counterexample to my claim here: a sentence in "Hegel on the Sublime" wherein de Man speaks of a moment in Hegel in which "the idea leaves a material trace, accessible to the senses, upon the world" (*AI*, p. 108). But as even this fragment of a sentence, let alone the rest of the discussion, makes clear, the point is that, although the material trace, like any sign, is accessible to the senses, its status *as* sign causes the phenomenal "presence" of a sensation to be contaminated by the differential structure of the trace.

24. I have elsewhere tried to sketch out an interplay among aesthetics, technics, and theory: see *Politics of Aesthetics*, pp. 14–29. For an extremely helpful reading of Heidegger that clarifies how technics may be understood both as a power to fix and control, and as a "movement of unsecuring," see Weber, *Mass Mediauras*, pp. 55–75.

25. Derrida, *Memoires*, pp. 108, 110.

26. Guillory engages in a hard-working and generally respectful argument with Neil Hertz's essay "Lurid Figures" (see Guillory, *Cultural Capital*, pp. 233–35). I leave aside here the extremely interesting topic of pathos in de Man; on this subject, see Hertz's extraordinary "Lurid Figures," in Lindsay Waters and Wlad Godzich, eds., *Reading de Man Reading* (Minneapolis: University of Minnesota Press, 1989), and his follow-up essay "More Lurid Figures," *Diacritics* 20:3 (1990): 2–49; see also my *Politics of Aesthetics*, pp. 95–124; and, most recently, Rei Terada, *Feeling in Theory: Emotion after the "Death of the Subject"* (Cambridge, Mass.: Harvard University Press, 2001), pp. 48–89 and passim.

27. Once again, see the introduction to this volume for a discussion of the diverse sorts of work that de Manian theory has inspired.

28. Derrida, *Memoires*, p. 16.

29. Avital Ronell, *Stupidity* (Urbana and Chicago: University of Illinois Press, 2002), p. 97.

30. For a meditation on the political dimension of de Man's thought that is particularly attentive to the violence of formalization, see Cynthia Chase, "Trappings of an Education: Toward That Which We Do Not Yet Have," in Werner Hamacher, Neil Hertz, and Thomas Keenan, eds., *Responses: On Paul de Man's Wartime Journalism* (Lincoln: University of Nebraska Press, 1989), pp. 44–79. The de Manian project may only be accused of performing an "imaginary reduction of the social to an instance of the linguistic" if one has

reduced language to a communicational and social phenomenon. When de Man tells us that historical and political systems are the "correlate" of textual models (*RR*, p. 289), his claim does not amount to a *reduction* of epistemological or ontological complexity. Language provides no ontological ground to which one could reduce.

THINKING SINGULARITY WITH IMMANUEL KANT AND PAUL DE MAN: AESTHETICS, EPISTEMOLOGY, HISTORY, AND POLITICS
Arkady Plotnitsky

1. Rodolphe Gasché invokes the idea of the "pre-cognitive" in context: see *The Idea of Form: Reading Kant's Aesthetics* (Stanford: Stanford University Press, 2002).

2. Paul de Man, *Aesthetic Ideology* (Minneapolis: University of Minnesota Press, 1996), p. 104.

3. Ibid., p. 90.

4. Immanuel Kant, *Critique of Judgment*, trans. Werner S. Pluhar (Indianapolis: Hackett, 1990), p. 52.

5. Ibid., p. 43n1.

6. Ibid., p. 53.

7. De Man, *Aesthetic Ideology*, p. 82.

8. Kant, *Critique of Judgment*, p. 52. I translate *Wohlgefallen* as "feeling of liking," imperfectly but, I would argue, less inaccurately than Werner Pluhar does by rendering it as "liking."

9. Jacques Derrida's "Parergon" and "Economimesis" come to mind as possible exceptions, but they do not strictly offer readings of the beautiful either. See Jacques Derrida, "Economimesis," *Diacritics* 11:3 (1981): 3–25; and "Parergon," in *The Truth in Painting*, trans. Geoffrey Bennington and Ian MacLeod (Chicago: University of Chicago Press, 1987).

10. Kant, *Critique of Judgment*, pp. 98–100.

11. One could also speak of the protocognitive or, along the lines of Gasché's discussion in *The Idea of Form*, precognitive processes involved in this model. The epistemological model to be developed in this article and a reading of Kant it implies are, however, different from the one that emerges in Gasché's reading of Kant. Gasché does not bring de Man's work to bear on his reading of Kant in *The Idea of Form*, which is peculiar given that he discusses de Man at length in his excellent *The Wild Card of Reading: On Paul de Man* (Cambridge, Mass.: Harvard University Press, 1996). But then, Gasché's reading of de Man, too, significantly differs from the one to be offered here. Gasché, however, rightly relates all three of Kant's *Critiques* through the epistemological problematic of the third *Critique*, which de Man does as well, along the lines of his allegorical epistemology, as discussed here.

12. Kant, *Critique of Judgment*, p. 59.
13. Ibid., p. 59.
14. One can formulate a parallel proposition for the sublime, although in the case of the sublime, according to Kant, there would be no corresponding object.
15. Martin Heidegger, *Nietzsche: Volumes One and Two*, trans. David Farrell Krell (New York: HarperCollins, 1991), pp. 1:107–14.
16. I refer, in particular, to Jean-Francois Lyotard's discussions in *The Postmodern Condition: A Report on Knowledge*, trans. Brian Massumi (Minneapolis: University of Minnesota Press, 1985), and *The Differend: Phrases in Dispute*, trans. Georges Van Den Abbeele (Minneapolis: University of Minnesota Press, 1988), although the problematic persists throughout his work on postmodernity. Lyotard juxtaposes Kant and Hegel in this context, in my view, not altogether justifiably. By contrast, de Man cogently relates Kant and Hegel along these lines.
17. Immanuel Kant, *Critique of Pure Reason*, trans. Paul Geyer and Allen D. Wood (Cambridge: Cambridge University Press, 1999), p. 115.
18. A possibly nonclassical view of the ultimate constitution of nature, such as that found in quantum theory, would not change this status of the body, since it is still *thinkable*, even if not knowable, in these nonclassical terms— unless we consider the body as a quantum system, which may well make it nonclassically unthinkable at the ultimate level. Short of the latter case, Kant's requirements are still fulfilled with respect to the logical structure of our arguments or our practical justifications for such arguments, including specifically those for the possibility or necessity of nonclassicality. As will be seen, in a different (allegorical or, de Man calls it, "linguistic") register, de Man, via his reading of Kant, approaches the nonclassical epistemology of the body and, interactively, language itself, by dismembering or disfiguring both. For the discussion of the nonclassical epistemology of quantum theory, I permit myself to refer to previously published works: Arkady Plotnitsky, *The Knowable and the Unknowable: Nonclassical Theory, Modern Science, and the "Two Cultures"* (Ann Arbor: University of Michigan Press, 2002), and, in the context of de Man, "Algebra and Allegory: Nonclassical Epistemology, Quantum Theory and the Work of Paul de Man," in Tom Cohen, Barbara Cohen, J. Hillis Miller, and Andrzej Warminski, eds., *Material Events: Paul de Man and the Afterlife of Theory* (Minneapolis: University of Minnesota Press, 2000).
19. See, for example, Sigmund Freud, "The Unconscious," in *General Psychological Theory: Papers on Metapsychology* (New York: Collier, 1963), and Jacques Lacan, *The Four Fundamental Concepts of Psychoanalysis*, trans. Alan Sheridan (New York: Norton, 1981).
20. The epistemology becomes classical once such exclusion takes place. This difficulty is one of Derrida's concerns in "Economimesis."

21. Georges Bataille, *Oeuvres Completes*, 12 vols. (Paris: Gallimard, 1970–88), p. 8:219. This edition omits the first passage just cited, which is found in Georges Bataille, "Conférences sur le Non-Savoir," *Tel Quel* 10 (1962): 5.

22. On the relationships between this type of (nonclassical) argument and Heidegger's concept of Being [*Sein*], on the one hand, and Derrida's epistemology, on the other, see Derrida's discussions of Heidegger in *Of Grammatology*, trans. Gayatri Chakravorty Spivak (Baltimore: Johns Hopkins University Press, 1976); *Margins of Philosophy*, trans. Alan Bass (Chicago: University of Chicago Press, 1982); and other early works.

23. This concept of singularity has affinities (although is not equivalent) to that of Gilles Deleuze, introduced by him at the outset of *Difference and Repetition*, trans. Paul Patton (New York: Columbia University Press, 1993), and pursued throughout his work. He contrasts the "singular," as that which is outside the law (physical, moral, or other) and, thus, outside the general, and is subject to "repetition" in his special sense of the term, to the "particular," which is part of the general and subject to law. This scheme, including Deleuze's concept of repetition, could be related to de Man's argument to be discussed below (also via Hegel and, on repetition, Kierkegaard). Deleuze comes closest to the present concept of singularity in his analysis of Leibniz's monads in *The Fold: Leibniz and the Baroque*, trans. Tom Conley (Minneapolis: University of Minnesota Press, 1993).

24. As I have indicated, one can also encounter situations that are mixed, that is, organized partly classically and partly nonclassically, and the present analysis could be easily adjusted to accommodate such mixed cases.

25. Under these conditions, the very category of consensus becomes problematic. Although differently from the way in which Lyotard argues the case in his debate with Jürgen Habermas, from this perspective, too, the post-Enlightenment ideas and ideals of democracy or justice and consensus may be in conflict rather than, as Habermas wants to argue, in accord with each other.

26. De Man, *Aesthetic Ideology*, p. 51.

27. Ibid., p. 120.

28. Ibid., p. 132.

29. Ibid., p. 69.

30. Paul de Man, *The Rhetoric of Romanticism* (New York: Columbia University Press, 1984), p. 122.

31. De Man, *Aesthetic Ideology*, p. 132.

32. Ibid., pp. 133–34. De Man's reading of Hegel proceeds along similar lines rather than, as is more common, strictly along the lines of a continuous model of history.

33. Ibid., p. 132.

34. Ibid., pp. 132–33.

35. Ibid., pp. 133–34.
36. Ibid.
37. For this type of reason, "event" becomes a crucial concept in recent theoretical discussion in and following de Man, Deleuze, and Derrida.
38. De Man, *Rhetoric of Romanticism*, p. 122.
39. Ibid., pp. 122–23.
40. Both de Man's and Derrida's readings of, and exchanges on, Rousseau involve these problematics as well.
41. De Man, *Rhetoric of Romanticism*, p. 93.
42. Ibid., p. 121.
43. De Man, *Aesthetic Ideology*, pp. 88–89.
44. The question of allegorical or, again, *linguistic* aspects of mathematical and scientific theories or *texts* (the *textuality* of mathematics and science is itself part of this question) is of major interest in this context, but it can only be registered rather than discussed here. I, again, permit myself to refer to my "Algebra and Allegory," which moves in this direction.
45. Friedrich Schiller, *On the Aesthetic Education of Man, in a Series of Letters*, trans. Elizabeth M. Wilkinson and L. A. Willoughby (Oxford: Clarendon, 1967), p. 300; de Man, *Rhetoric of Romanticism*, p. 263.
46. Gasché, *The Wild Card of Reading*, p. 113.
47. De Man, *Rhetoric of Romanticism*, p. 288.
48. Compare also de Man's reading of Keats's *The Fall of Hyperion* in "The Resistance to Theory," in *The Resistance to Theory* (Minneapolis: University of Minnesota Press, 1986).
49. De Man, *Rhetoric of Romanticism*, pp. 288–89.
50. De Man, *Aesthetic Ideology*, p. 88.
51. Ibid., pp. 88–89.
52. Ibid., p. 89.
53. It is difficult to be certain given the complexities of the concept and the very signifier of "correspondence" in de Man. Compare Andrzej Warminski's analysis of de Man's reading of Baudelaire's "Correspondances" in "As Poets Do It," in Cohen, Cohen, Miller, and Warminski, *Material Events: Paul de Man and the Afterlife of Theory*. It would also be instructive to follow de Man's earlier approach to "correspondences" of that type in "The Rhetoric of Temporality," in *Blindness and Insight: Essays in the Rhetoric of Contemporary Criticism*, rev. ed. (Minneapolis: University of Minnesota Press, 1983).
54. Compare also de Man's analysis of Nietzsche and Rousseau in *Allegories of Reading: Figural Language in Rousseau, Nietzsche, Rilke, and Proust* (New Haven: Yale University Press, 1979), and in "The Epistemology of Metaphor," *Aesthetic Ideology*, pp. 34–50.
55. De Man, *Rhetoric of Romanticism*, pp. 289–90.

56. De Man, *Aesthetic Ideology*, p. 88.

57. Derrida closes with this passage his analysis of the third *Critique* in "Parergon," p. 147.

58. Kant, *Critique of Judgment*, p. 113.

59. The sublime, however, is not infinite either, only "almost infinite," as Derrida notes in the same section, "The Colossal," in "Parergon," pp. 119–47.

60. Maurice Blanchot, *The Infinite Conversation*, trans. Susan Hanson (Minneapolis: University of Minnesota Press, 1993), p. 350.

61. De Man, *Aesthetic Ideology*, p. 82.

SEEING IS READING
Rei Terada

1. Paul de Man, *Aesthetic Ideology*, ed. Andrzej Warminski (Minneapolis: University of Minnesota Press, 1996), p. 73; hereafter *AI*. Subsequent citations from this work will appear in the body of the text.

2. Paul de Man, "The Resistance to Theory," in *The Resistance to Theory* (Minneapolis: University of Minnesota Press, 1986), p. 8; hereafter *RT*. Subsequent citations from this work will appear in the body of the text.

3. Complementarily, there is no warrant to treat thematics of materiality as particularly material instances of language. For a similar caution about the thematics of "form," see Eyal Amiran, "After Dynamic Narratology," *Style* 34 (2000): 212–26.

4. For other considerations of "seeing" as a figure of something beyond transparency, see David L. Clark, "How to Do Things with Shakespeare: Illustrative Theory and Practice in Blake's Pity," in *The Mind in Creation: Essays on English Romantic Literature in Honour of Ross G. Woodman*, ed. J. Douglas Kneale (Montreal: McGill-Queen's University Press, 1962), pp. 106–33, and Cynthia Chase, *Decomposing Figures: Rhetorical Readings in the Romantic Tradition* (Baltimore: Johns Hopkins University Press, 1986).

5. Frances Ferguson, *Solitude and the Sublime: Romanticism and the Aesthetics of Individuation* (New York: Routledge, 1992), p. 21.

6. The classic discussion is Minae Mizumura's "Renunciation," *Yale French Studies* 69 (1985): 81–97; see also Ortwin de Graef, *Serenity in Crisis: A Preface to Paul de Man, 1930–1960* (Lincoln: University of Nebraska Press, 1995), pp. 90, 93, 171–72. My attempt to think about this was "De Man and Mallarmé 'Between the Two Deaths,'" in *Meetings with Mallarmé in Contemporary French Culture*, ed. Michael Temple (Exeter: University of Exeter Press, 1998), pp. 107–25, 247–50. It is tempting to say that the "necessary degradation of melody into harmony . . . [,] of metaphor into literal meaning" in *Blindness and*

Insight hardens in the late texts from "literal meaning" into material letters (Paul de Man, *Blindness and Insight* [New York: Oxford University Press, 1971], p. 136).

7. Tom Cohen, Barbara Cohen, J. Hillis Miller, "A 'Materiality Without Matter'?" in Tom Cohen, Barbara Cohen, J. Hillis Miller, and Andrzej Warminski, eds., *Material Events: Paul de Man and the Afterlife of Theory* (Minneapolis: University of Minnesota Press, 2001), p. viii; hereafter *CCM*. Subsequent citations from this work will appear in the body of the text. Many arguments of "A 'Materiality without Matter'?" also occur in Tom Cohen's *Anti-Mimesis from Plato to Hitchcock* (Cambridge: Cambridge University Press, 1994) and *Ideology and Inscription: "Cultural Studies" after Benjamin, de Man, and Bakhtin* (Cambridge: Cambridge University Press, 1998). For a different perspective on de Man's materiality, see Cathy Caruth and Deborah Esch, eds., *Critical Encounters: Reference and Responsibility in Deconstructive Writing* (New Brunswick, N.J.: Rutgers University Press, 1995).

8. Jacques Derrida's *Archive Fever: A Freudian Impression*, trans. Eric Prenowitz (Chicago: University of Chicago Press, 1996), would seem to be a more substantial inspiration.

9. See Arthur Lovejoy, "The Chain of Being and Some Internal Conflicts in Medieval Thought," in *The Great Chain of Being: A Study of the History of An Idea* (New York: Harper and Row, 1936), pp. 67–98.

10. Lovejoy, *Great Chain of Being*, pp. 331–32, quoted in Paul de Man, *Critical Writings 1953–1978*, ed. Lindsay Waters (Minneapolis: University of Minnesota Press, 1989), pp. 81–82.

11. See de Man, *AI*, p. 147. E. S. Burt deals with a similar problem, de Man's emphasis on the one-way arrow of history as inscription, by identifying that history with a revolutionary will to the future, that is, revolution as something other than intervention (E. S. Burt, *Poetry's Appeal: Nineteenth-Century French Lyric and the Political Space* [Stanford: Stanford University Press, 1999], pp. 185–86). For other thoughts on the irreversibility of inscription, see Jacques Derrida, "Typewriter Ribbon: Limited Ink (2)," in *Material Events: Paul de Man and the Afterlife of Theory*, ed. Tom Cohen, Barbara Cohen, J. Hillis Miller, and Andrzej Warminski (Minneapolis: University of Minnesota Press, 2001), p. 320; and Andrzej Warminski, "'As the Poets Do It': On the Material Sublime," in *Material Events*, esp. pp. 10–11.

12. Elaine Scarry, *Dreaming by the Book: Imagining Under Authorial Instruction* (Boston: Farrar, Straus, Giroux, 2001), p. 5; hereafter *DBB*. Subsequent citations from this work will appear in the body of the text.

13. Natural symmetry forms the basis for Scarry's equally ideological idea of justice in *On Beauty and Being Just* (Princeton: Princeton University Press, 1999).

14. In poet-critic Sarah Riggs's *Word Sightings: Visual Apparatus and Verbal Reality in Stevens, Bishop, and O'Hara* (New York: Routledge, 2002), it is the sensory experience of our failing struggle to produce any mental image that is credited to the idea of the mental image and thus helps to substantiate its absence—a phantom-limb model.

15. Rodolphe Gasché, *The Idea of Form: Rethinking Kant's Aesthetics* (Stanford: Stanford University Press, 2002), p. 207.

16. Quoted in ibid.

17. Immanuel Kant, *Critique of Judgment*, trans. Werner S. Pluhar (Indianapolis: Hackett, 1987).

18. Alternatively, my not knowing what a hand-mill is demonstrates Kant's point over again. The hand-mill is a Riffaterrean object, a generic object that does not contribute anything beyond its illustrative function, yet functions even though we might not know what is doing the illustrating, because we understand enough of the terms in the mutually implicated network of references of which it is part. The hand-mill, like any other single term, can be an example whose content is bracketed: there is nothing in this hand-mill.

19. Claudia Brodsky brilliantly analyzes the discourse-method interdependence in Descartes in *Lines of Thought: Discourse, Architectonics, and the Origin of Modern Philosophy* (Durham, N.C.: Duke University Press, 1996).

20. Thus Ian Hacking remarks that Thomas Kuhn's emphasis on "anomalies" in *The Structure of Scientific Revolutions* "cannot lead us to a *very* strict nominalism, for the anomalies '*really*' *do have to seem* to be resolved in order for a revolutionary achievement to be recognized" (*Historical Ontology* [Cambridge, Mass.: Harvard University Press, 2002], p. 40; my emphasis). The corresponding moment of real seeming in Schiller is when (in de Man's translation of Schiller's essay "On the Sublime") "'even the imaginary representation of danger, if it is at all vivid, suffices to awaken our sense of self-preservation, and it produces something analogous to what the real experience would produce'" (*Werke* [Weimar: Hermann Bohlaus Nachfolger, 1963], vol. 20, p. 181; quoted in de Man's translation in *AI*, p. 143). "'Analogous' is an important word," de Man comments there.

21. Derrida, "Typewriter Ribbon," pp. 336, 350, 353, 352–53 (in order of appearance).

22. Thanks to Benjamin Bishop for thought-provoking ideas on indexicals.

23. Judith Butler's discussion of the two possible senses of "transcendental" is helpful: "In the Kantian vein, 'transcendental' can mean: the condition without which nothing can appear. But it can also mean: the regulatory and constitutive conditions of the appearance of any given object. The latter sense is the one in which the condition is not external to the object it occasions, but

is its constitutive condition and the principle of its development and appearance" ("Competing Universalities," in *Contingency, Hegemony, Universality: Contemporary Dialogues on the Left*, ed. Judith Butler, Ernesto Laclau, and Slavoj Žižek [London: Verso, 2000], p. 147). Inscription for Cohen, Cohen, and Miller is transcendental in the second sense; as Butler notes, such a transcendental condition can be "considered to have a historicity—that is . . . considered to be a shifting episteme which might be altered and revised over time" (ibid., 147). Like post-Lacanian political philosophy, Cohen, Cohen, and Miller's use of inscription, and perhaps also Derrida's in "Typewriter Ribbon," employs the second model of transcendental condition to fold historical contingency into a priori form and power. But since such a folding is the goal of Kantian aesthetics in the first place, and *non*transcendental ways of conceiving the relation between contingency and form are available, second-tier transcendentalism often looks as though it were motivated by the desire to preserve first-tier transcendentalism. A similar question may be rasied about the notion of the "quasi-transcendental" in late Derrida; for a consideration of quasi-transcendentality in relation to the crises of the Kantian system, see Geoffrey Bennington, "X," in his *Interrupting Derrida* (London: Routledge, 2000), pp. 76–92.

24. Gasché gives an eloquent, comprehensive, and rather shocked account of de Man's project as aiming to break the text into a "radically irreducible empiricalness of . . . agencies and instances" ("In-Difference to Philosophy: de Man on Kant, Hegel, and Nietzsche," in *Reading de Man Reading*, ed. Wlad Godzich and Lindsay Waters [Minneapolis: University of Minnesota Press, 1989], p. 282). Gasché himself is so deeply formalistic that he cannot take an empirical philosophy seriously: "It is a longstanding philosophical truth that empiricism is capable of explaining everything except explication itself, that is, the difference that explication makes. . . . If they ["the nonphenomenal material and formal properties" of language] are empirical qualities, pragmatic properties, they will never be able to elevate themselves to the thought of difference. If they are universal and general properties, then they are properties that make *the* difference, and all that has been achieved is a, perhaps, more sophisticated philosophical questioning of philosophical difference" (ibid., p. 292). But there are answers from radical empiricism that, from its (perhaps incommensurable) perspective, deal with these complaints. For a recent version, see Bas C. Van Fraassen, *The Empirical Stance* (New Haven: Yale University Press, 2002).

25. Paul de Man, *Allegories of Reading: Figural Language in Rousseau, Nietzsche, Rilke, and Proust* (New Haven: Yale University Press, 1979), p. 262; hereafter *AR*. Subsequent citations from this work will appear in the body of the text.

26. De Man notes that this passage "is crossed out in the manuscript... for reasons on which one can speculate" (*AR*, p. 259n11). Many thanks to Cynthia Chase for providing me with this reference and some of my phrasing in the text above.

27. Timothy Bahti, *Ends of Lyric: Direction and Consequence in Western Poetry* (Baltimore: Johns Hopkins University Press, 1997); hereafter *EL*. Subsequent citations from this work will appear in the body of the text.

28. Daniel Dennett, "Seeing Is Believing—or Is it?," in *Perception*, ed. Robert Schwartz (London: Blackwell, 2004), pp. 340, 337; hereafter *SB*. Subsequent citations from this work will appear in the body of the text.

Index

Adorno, Theodor, 9, 57–58, 68–69, 164
aesthetics, 12–14, 129–35, 156–57, 161; as ideology, 94, 96–97, 126, 150, 152, 155, 159, 162–77 passim
allegory, 4, 32, 54, 141, 146–53 passim, 158
anthropomorphism, 6, 17, 22, 24–28
Aristotle, 6, 18, 20–27
Arnold, Matthew, 99
Auerbach, Erich, 68–69, 186

Bahti, Timothy, 77–80, 174–76, 181
Barthes, Roland, 49
Bataille, Georges, 140
Baudelaire, Charles, 22, 27, 182–83
Benjamin, Walter, 9, 53, 57–59, 174
Benveniste, Emil, 18, 23, 28
Blanchot, Maurice, 85, 120, 160–61
Bloom, Harold, 79
Borges, Jorge Luis, 59
Bourdieu, Pierre, 96
Brodsky, Claudia, 181
Brooks, Cleanth, 51–55, 60
Brooks, Peter, 180–81, 185
Brower, Reuben, 51–52, 181
Burt, E. S., 77, 80

Caruth, Cathy, 4, 61, 181
catachresis, 7, 21–22, 71
Celan, Paul, 58
Chase, Cynthia, 77, 80
Chomsky, Noam, 172
Cicero, 170
Cohen, Barbara, 13, 165–66, 169, 173–74
Cohen, Tom, 13, 165–66, 169, 173–74, 181
criticism, *see* reading; theory
Curtius, Ernst Robert, 186

deconstruction, 1–2, 5, 56, 71, 99–100, 121–22; as the epitome of "theory," 100. *See also* reading; theory
de Graef, Ortwin, 4
de Man, Paul, as charismatic figure, 2, 4, 11–12, 101–106, 121, 125; as embodiment of "theory," 2, 5, 100–1, 108, 117, 125; courses taught at Yale, 179–83; question of legacy, 1–6, 10–14, 33–34, 43, 61, 77–126 passim, 179–81; wartime journalism, 2, 50, 91–92, 100, 117. Texts (given by essay title except for the texts making up *Allegories of Reading*, which are assimilated to the entry for *Allegories*): "Aesthetic Formalization in Kleist," 106, 123, 154–57, 159; *Allegories of Reading*, 23–25, 33–34, 63, 71, 83–84, 106–7, 109–14, 123, 174; "Anthropomorphism and Trope," 6, 17–28, 60–61; *Blindness and Insight*, 165; "Criticism and the Theme of Faust," 166; "The Dead-End of Formalist Criticism," 53; "Dialogue and Dialogism," 107; "Foreword" to Jacobs, *Dissimulating Harmony*, 106; "Form and Intent in the American New Criticism," 55–56, 64; "Hegel and the Sublime," 115; "Hypogram and Inscription," 115–16; "Image and Emblem in Yeats," 53–55; "Introduction" to special issue of *Studies in Romanticism*, 10, 77–92 passim; "Kant and Schiller," 72, 148–49, 166, 168–69, 172; "Kant's Materialism," 115, 156; "Literary History and Literary Modernity," 8, 50; "The Literary Self as Origin," 64; "Pascal's Allegory of Persuasion," 146–47, 151; "Patterns of

223

Temporality in Hölderlin," 8, 63–69, 72; "Phenomenality and Materiality in Kant," 115, 136, 153, 156–59, 162–63, 166, 172–73; "The Resistance to Theory," 105, 120, 122, 163, 166–67; "The Return to Philology," 51–52, 124; *The Rhetoric of Romanticism*, 62, 83; "The Rhetoric of Temporality," 146, 150; *Romanticism and Contemporary Criticism*, 63; "Semiology and Rhetoric," 8, 54, 104; "Shelley Disfigured," 22, 24, 40, 59, 114–15, 119, 150–53; "Sign and Symbol in Hegel's *Aesthetics*," 115, 130; "Theory of Metaphor in Rousseau's Second Discourse," 113; "Time and History in Wordsworth," 10, 69–72, 113
Demetz, Peter, 180
Dennett, Daniel, 176–77
Derrida, Jacques, 5, 49, 55, 58, 89, 104, 117, 120, 122, 124, 133, 164; *Mémoires of Paul de Man*, 119; "Psyche: Inventions of the Other," 86, 92; "The Supplement of Copula," 18–19, 22–24; "Typewriter Ribbon," 60, 116, 172; "White Mythology," 6–7, 17–28
Descartes, René, 172
Diderot, Denis, 156, 183
Donne, John, 51

Edelman, Lee, 61
Einstein, Albert, 155, 160
Eliot, T. S., 51, 98
Empson, William, 52, 56
Esch, Deborah, 61, 181

Felman, Shoshana, 4, 61
Ferguson, Frances, 164
Ferris, David, 181
figure, figuration: *see* rhetoric; trope
Fish, Stanley, 124
Foucault, Michel, 117
Freud, Sigmund, 136

Gadamer, Hans-Georg, 186
Gasché, Rodolphe, 4, 155, 170
Gide, André, 180
Goethe, Johann Wolfgang von, 58, 111
Gray, Thomas, 96

Greimas, Algirdas, 167
Guillory, John, 11–12, 93–126

Hardy, Thomas, 153
Hartman, Geoffrey, 6, 63, 79–80, 179–83, 185, 188
Hegel, Georg Wilhelm Friedrich, 12, 50, 68, 130, 151, 183
Heidegger, Martin, 9, 13, 53, 63–69
Herrnstein Smith, Barbara, 96
history, 8–10, 49–73, 83–92 passim, 126, 129, 140, 147–53, 174. *See also* materiality
Hölderlin, Friedrich, 9–10, 63–69, 72
Holquist, Michael, 180
Hugo, Victor, 116

irony, 141, 146–47

Jacobs, Carol, 80, 88
Jameson, Fredric, 50
Johnson, Barbara, 77, 80, 181

Kamuf, Peggy, 98–100, 118
Kant, Immanuel, 12, 14, 24, 60, 72, 115, 129–73 passim, 183
Keats, John, 151, 181
Keenan, Tom, 61, 179, 181
Kermode, Frank, 53–54
Kernan, Alvin, 180
Kleist, Heinrich von, 7–8, 34–45, 78, 88–89, 106, 123, 135, 147, 150–52, 155–60 passim

Lacan, Jacques, 136, 173
Laclau, Ernesto, 99
language, 5, 9, 18–28, 31–34, 42, 56, 63–65, 68, 72, 95–98, 105, 112–14, 118–21, 154, 157–58, 162–63, 169, 172, 186–87. *See also* materiality; performative; rhetoric; trope
legacy: *see* de Man, Paul
Leibnitz, Gottfried Wilhelm, 144
Lévi-Strauss, Claude, 49
Levinas, Emmanuel, 133
literary criticism: *see* literature; reading; theory
literary history: *see* history; literature; romanticism
literariness: *see* literature.
literature, 8–9, 11, 51–61, 120, 186–87; as cultural capital, 95–98, 101; as literariness, 109, 120, 126

Index

"Literature Z" (a.k.a. "Literature 130"), 6, 179–89
Lovejoy, A. O., 166
Lyotard, Jean-François, 135

Mallarmé, Stéphane, 182
materiality, 5, 10, 12–14, 59, 62–73 passim, 115–16, 119, 140, 148–49, 153–54, 157–77
Marx, Karl, 59
McQuillan, Michael, 4
metaphor, 6–7, 17–28, 70–71, 110–14, 176–77
metonymy, 6, 17, 70–71, 110–13
Michaels, Walter Benn, 5
Miller, J. Hillis, 13, 165–66, 169, 173–74, 183
Milton, John, 160
Mouffe, Chantal, 99

New Criticism, 8, 51–56, 64, 96, 98, 123, 186
Newmark, Kevin, 179, 181
Newton, Sir Isaac, 155, 160
Nietzsche, Friedrich, 6, 17–19, 22–28, 52, 181–82
Norris, Christopher, 3

Paglia, Camille, 117
pedagogy, 10–12, 51, 77–92, 102–7, 179–89
Pepper, Thomas, 103
performative, 26, 33, 72, 114–15, 149
personification: *see* anthropomorphism; de Man, Paul as embodiment of "theory"
Poe, Edgar Allan, 7, 29–33, 41–42
Proust, Marcel, 109–13, 182

Quint, David, 185

reading, 4, 6–8, 10, 13–14, 51–52, 81–88, 147–51, 162–69, 174–77; as rhetorical reading, 7, 11–12, 17–28, 53–55, 58, 62–73, 87, 90–91, 101–2, 109–16, 120, 122, 126, 132, 162, 167; in relation to unreadability, 7–8, 29–43 passim, 73. *See also* rhetoric; theory
Ray, William, 77
Readings, Bill, 1

Redfield, Marc, 61
rhetoric, 5–7, 10, 17–28, 63, 65, 68–73, 108–14, 118–20, 146–61, 169–73, 186–87. *See also* allegory; anthropomorphism; catachresis; irony; metaphor; metonymy; performative; trope
rhetorical reading: *see* deconstruction; reading; theory
Richards, I. A., 51
Riffaterre, Michael, 8, 116
Rilke, Rainer Maria, 182
romanticism, 8, 13, 54, 62–63, 83–91 passim, 150, 152–53, 160
Ronell, Avital, 3, 123
Rossi, Stefano, 123
Rousseau, Jean-Jacques, 33–34, 60, 63, 103, 113–14, 150, 152, 174, 181–82
Russell, Bertrand, 172

Said, Edward, 50
Saussure, Ferdinand de, 18, 27, 49, 115
Scarry, Elaine, 13–14, 167–69, 176
Schelling, Friedrich, 68
Schiller, Friedrich, 12, 97, 99, 135, 147, 150, 154–55, 169
Schlegel, Friedrich, 9, 58
Shakespeare, William, 174–75
Shelley, Percy, 22, 40, 119, 135, 147, 150–53, 158
Spector, Stephen J., 77
Spivak, Gayatri Chakravorty, 2, 3, 61
Staiger, Emil, 39
Starobinski, Jean, 27
Stein, Gertrude, 133
Stevens, Wallace, 98

teaching: *see* pedagogy
technics, technicity, 99, 118–20
temporality, 64–73 passim, 150
theme, thematization, 108–15
theory, 1–5, 12–14, 49–50, 60, 100–4, 120, 125, 132, 135–45, 163; as epitomized by deconstruction, 2, 100; as resistance to itself, 5, 102–3, 114, 117–18. *See also* deconstruction; reading; rhetoric
trope, tropological, 6–7, 17–28, 68–72, 109–14, 118–19, 149, 154, 158. *See also* allegory; anthropomorphism; catachresis; irony; metaphor; metonymy; rhetoric

Valéry, Paul, 182
Vico, Giambattista, 50

Wagenknecht, David, 10, 78–80
Warminski, Andrzej, 165, 179, 181, 183
Weber, Samuel, 61
Wimsatt, William, 51–52

Wittgenstein, Ludwig, 172
Wordsworth, William, 10, 69–72, 79–80, 89, 103

Yeats, William Butler, 53–55, 182

Žižek, Slavoj, 173

www.ingramcontent.com/pod-product-compliance
Lightning Source LLC
Chambersburg PA
CBHW031242290426
44109CB00012B/405